T0197917

"Roxane Gay is so great at weaving the intimate and personal with what is most bewildering and upsetting at this moment in culture. She is always looking, always thinking, always passionate, always careful, always right there."

—Sheila Heti

"Trailblazing."

—*Salon*

"What makes *Bad Feminist* such a good read isn't only Gay's ability to deftly weave razor-sharp pop cultural analysis and criticism with a voice that is both intimate and relatable. It's that she's incapable of blindly accepting any kind of orthodoxy. . . . Gay isn't a bad feminist at all. In fact, she's one of the best."

—*San Francisco Chronicle*

"*Bad Feminist* places pop culture under her sharp, often hilarious, always insightful microscope."

—GQ.com

"A collection of sharp, Sontag-ianly searing pieces on everything from *Orange Is the New Black* to likability in fiction to abortion legislation. . . . Her pieces manage to be at once conversational and full of pithy aphorisms."

—*L Magazine*

"The bold, charming, and ever-brilliant Roxane Gay presents an explosive set of essays. . . . Gay is nothing short of a critical genius."

—*Bustle*

"As a feminist who has been around awhile I have a message for these girls: it's okay—you can skip the rigors of Betty Friedan and Andrea Dworkin and go straight to Roxane Gay, where feminism is not just friendly, but more relevant than ever."

—*Los Angeles Review of Books*

"With trenchant thoughts on *Sweet Valley High*, *The Help*, abortion, and Chris Brown, Gay isn't really a bad feminist, just an uncommonly entertaining one."

—*Vulture*

"Gay's writing is thoughtful and funny, compassionate and bold, and she's just as likely to discuss *Sweet Valley High* as *Django Unchained* or Judith Butler."

—*Refinery29*

"A prolific and exceptionally insightful writer. . . . *Bad Feminist* doesn't show us how Gay should be, but something much better: how Roxane Gay actually is. . . . Gay unquestionably succeeds at leading us in her way."

—*Globe and Mail* (Toronto)

"As a culture critic, Gay has X-ray eyes. Her writing is smart and trenchant, but she has something else as well: a hard-to-define quality that makes her readers root for her. She's disarming and one of us, only smarter. She has a tumblr and she writes about Internet dating. We love her, you know?"

—*Philadelphia Inquirer*

"A thoughtful and often hilarious new collection of essays."

—*Chicago Tribune*

"Gay's energetic and thought-provoking first essay collection will become as widely read as other generation-defining works, like Nora Ephron's *Crazy Salad* and Joan Morgan's *When Chickenheads Come Home to Roost*."

—*Essence*

"Roxane Gay delivers sermons that read like easy conversations. *Bad Feminist* is an important collection of prose—prose that matters to those still trying to find their voice."

—*Ebony*

"*Bad Feminist* is often LOL funny but continuously ruthless. Its forty-one essays range from book and movie reviews to political issues and, in some of the most charming pieces, Gay's accounts of a few of her personal passions, like tournament Scrabble, the color pink, and *The Hunger Games*."

—*San Antonio Express-News*

"One of the liveliest, most joy-inducing books of the year. . . . Gay writes in a manner that's inviting and incredibly generous. There is no 'bad feminism' at play here—just plain ole badassery with lashings of common sense and humanity. . . . *Bad Feminist* is a tour de force and Roxane Gay is a writer of considerable power, intelligence, and moral acuity."

—*Huffington Post*

"*Bad Feminist* surveys culture and politics from the perspective of one of the most astute critics writing today."

—*Boston Review*

"Roxane Gay's *Bad Feminist* hardly needs more praise, but no other book speaks more eloquently, or more directly, about today's most crucial issues: race, gender, power. Gay's essays are intimate and accessible, but broad in scope and deep in insight. . . . I'm so grateful for her voice."

—Celeste Ng, "Writers' favorite books," *SFGATE* (San Francisco)

"Entertaining and enlightening. . . . *Bad Feminist* is an outtake of her wisdom, and we would all do well to take heed."

—*Bitch* magazine

Bad Feminist

Also by Roxane Gay

NONFICTION
Hunger
Not That Bad (editor)
Opinions

FICTION
Difficult Women
An Untamed State
Ayiti

Bad Feminist

TENTH ANNIVERSARY EDITION

Essays

Roxane Gay

HARPER ⬤ PERENNIAL

NEW YORK • LONDON • TORONTO • SYDNEY • NEW DELHI • AUCKLAND

HARPER PERENNIAL

HarperCollins books may be purchased for educational, business, or sales promotional use. For information please e-mail the Special Markets Department at SPsales@harpercollins.com.

First Harper Perennial edition published 2014.
Tenth anniversary edition published 2024.

Designed by Sunil Manchikanti

Library of Congress Cataloging-in-Publication Data is available upon request.

ISBN 978-0-06-338480-4 (pbk.)
978-0-06-338829-1 (simultaneous hardcover)

24 25 26 27 28 LBC 6 5 4 3 2

Contents

[INTRODUCTION]

Feminism (n.): Plural   *ix*

[ME]

Feel Me. See Me. Hear Me. Reach Me.   *3*

Peculiar Benefits   *15*

Typical First Year Professor   *20*

To Scratch, Claw, or Grope Clumsily or Frantically   *29*

[GENDER & SEXUALITY]

How to Be Friends with Another Woman   *47*

Girls, Girls, Girls   *51*

I Once Was Miss America   *61*

Garish, Glorious Spectacles   *71*

Not Here to Make Friends   *83*

How We All Lose   *96*

Reaching for Catharsis: Getting Fat Right
(or Wrong) and Diana Spechler's *Skinny*   *109*

The Smooth Surfaces of Idyll   *121*

The Careless Language of Sexual Violence   *128*

What We Hunger For   *137*

The Illusion of Safety/The Safety of Illusion   *147*
The Spectacle of Broken Men   *154*
A Tale of Three Coming Out Stories   *160*
Beyond the Measure of Men   *170*
Some Jokes Are Funnier Than Others   *177*
Dear Young Ladies Who Love Chris Brown
So Much They Would Let Him Beat Them   *183*
Blurred Lines, Indeed   *187*
The Trouble with Prince Charming,
or He Who Trespassed Against Us   *192*

[RACE & ENTERTAINMENT]

The Solace of Preparing Fried Foods and
Other Quaint Remembrances from
1960s Mississippi: Thoughts on *The Help*   *207*
Surviving *Django*   *218*
Beyond the Struggle Narrative   *227*
The Morality of Tyler Perry   *233*
The Last Day of a Young Black Man   *243*
When Less Is More   *250*

[POLITICS, GENDER & RACE]

The Politics of Respectability   *257*
When Twitter Does What Journalism Cannot   *261*
The Alienable Rights of Women   *267*
Holding Out for a Hero   *280*
A Tale of Two Profiles   *285*
The Racism We All Carry   *290*
Tragedy. Call. Compassion. Response.   *294*

[BACK TO ME]

Bad Feminist: Take One　*303*
Bad Feminist: Take Two　*314*

Acknowledgments　*319*

Introduction

Feminism (n.): Plural

The world changes faster than we can fathom in ways that are complicated. These bewildering changes often leave us raw. The cultural climate is shifting, particularly for women as we contend with the retrenchment of reproductive freedom, the persistence of rape culture, and the flawed if not damaging representations of women we're consuming in music, movies, and literature.

We have a comedian asking his fans to touch women lightly on their stomachs because ignoring personal boundaries is oh so funny. We have all manner of music glorifying the degradation of women, and damnit, that music is catchy so I often find myself singing along as my very being is diminished. Singers like Robin Thicke know "we want it." Rappers like Jay-Z use the word "bitch" like punctuation. Movies, more often than not, tell the stories of men as if men's stories are the only stories that matter. When women are involved, they are sidekicks, the romantic interests, the afterthoughts. Rarely do women get to be the center of attention. Rarely do our stories get to matter.

How do we bring attention to these issues? How do we do so

in ways that will actually be heard? How do we find the necessary language for talking about the inequalities and injustices women face, both great and small? As I've gotten older, feminism has answered these questions, at least in part.

Feminism is flawed, but it offers, at its best, a way to navigate this shifting cultural climate. Feminism has certainly helped me find my voice. Feminism has helped me believe my voice matters, even in this world where there are so many voices demanding to be heard.

How do we reconcile the imperfections of feminism with all the good it can do? In truth, feminism is flawed because it is a movement powered by people and people are inherently flawed. For whatever reason, we hold feminism to an unreasonable standard where the movement must be everything we want and must always make the best choices. When feminism falls short of our expectations, we decide the problem is with feminism rather than with the flawed people who act in the name of the movement.

The problem with movements is that, all too often, they are associated only with the most visible figures, the people with the biggest platforms and the loudest, most provocative voices. But feminism is not whatever philosophy is being spouted by the popular media feminist flavor of the week, at least not entirely.

Feminism, as of late, has suffered from a certain guilt by association because we conflate feminism with women who advocate feminism as part of their personal brand. When these figureheads say what we want to hear, we put them up on the Feminist Pedestal, and when they do something we don't like, we knock them right off and then say there's something wrong with feminism because our feminist leaders have failed us. We forget the difference between feminism and Professional Feminists.

I openly embrace the label of bad feminist. I do so because I am flawed and human. I am not terribly well versed in feminist history. I am not as well read in key feminist texts as I would like to be. I have certain . . . interests and personality traits and opinions that may not fall in line with mainstream feminism, but I am still a feminist. I cannot tell you how freeing it has been to accept this about myself.

I embrace the label of bad feminist because I am human. I am messy. I'm not trying to be an example. I am not trying to be perfect. I am not trying to say I have all the answers. I am not trying to say I'm right. I am just trying—trying to support what I believe in, trying to do some good in this world, trying to make some noise with my writing while also being myself: a woman who loves pink and likes to get freaky and sometimes dances her ass off to music she knows, she *knows*, is terrible for women and who sometimes plays dumb with repairmen because it's just easier to let them feel macho than it is to stand on the moral high ground.

I am a bad feminist because I never want to be placed on a Feminist Pedestal. People who are placed on pedestals are expected to pose, perfectly. Then they get knocked off when they fuck it up. I regularly fuck it up. Consider me already knocked off.

When I was younger, I disavowed feminism with alarming frequency. I understand why women still fall over themselves to disavow feminism, to distance themselves. I disavowed feminism because when I was called a feminist, the label felt like an insult. In fact, it was generally intended as such. When I was called a feminist, during those days, my first thought was, *But I willingly give blow jobs.* I had it in my head that I could not both be a feminist and be sexually open. I had lots of strange things in my head during my teens and twenties.

I disavowed feminism because I had no rational understanding of the movement. I was called a feminist, and what I heard was, "You are an angry, sex-hating, man-hating victim lady person."

This caricature is how feminists have been warped by the people who fear feminism most, the same people who have the most to lose when feminism succeeds. Anytime I remember how I once disavowed feminism, I am ashamed of my ignorance. I am ashamed of my fear because mostly the disavowal was grounded in the fear that I would be ostracized, that I would be seen as a troublemaker, that I would never be accepted by the mainstream.

I get angry when women disavow feminism and shun the feminist label but say they support all the advances born of feminism because I see a disconnect that does not need to be there. I get angry but I understand and hope someday we will live in a culture where we don't need to distance ourselves from the feminist label, where the label doesn't make us afraid of being alone, of being too different, of wanting too much.

I try to keep my feminism simple. I know feminism is complex and evolving and flawed. I know feminism will not and cannot fix everything. I believe in equal opportunities for women and men. I believe in women having reproductive freedom and affordable and unfettered access to the health care they need. I believe women should be paid as much as men for doing the same work. Feminism is a choice, and if a woman does not want to be a feminist, that is her right, but it is still my responsibility to fight for her rights. I believe feminism is grounded in supporting the choices of women even if we wouldn't make certain choices for ourselves. I believe women not just in the United States but throughout the world deserve equality and freedom but know I am in no position to tell women of other cultures what that equality and freedom should look like.

I resisted feminism in my late teens and my twenties because I worried that feminism wouldn't allow me to be the mess of a woman I knew myself to be. But then I began to learn more about feminism. I learned to separate feminism from Feminism or Feminists or the idea of an Essential Feminism—one true feminism to dominate all of womankind. It was easy to embrace feminism when I realized it was advocating for gender equality in all realms, while also making the effort to be intersectional, to consider all the other factors that influence who we are and how we move through the world. Feminism has given me peace. Feminism has given me guiding principles for how I write, how I read, how I live. I do stray from these principles, but I also know it's okay when I do not live up to my best feminist self.

Women of color, queer women, and transgender women need to be better included in the feminist project. Women from these groups have been shamefully abandoned by Capital-F Feminism, time and again. This is a hard, painful truth. This is where a lot of people run into resisting feminism, trying to create distance between the movement and where they stand. Believe me, I understand. For years, I decided feminism wasn't for me as a black woman, as a woman who has been queer identified at varying points in her life, because feminism has, historically, been far more invested in improving the lives of heterosexual white women to the detriment of all others.

But two wrongs do not make a right. Feminism's failings do not mean we should eschew feminism entirely. People do terrible things all the time, but we don't regularly disown our humanity. We disavow the terrible things. We should disavow the failures of feminism without disavowing its many successes and how far we have come.

We don't all have to believe in the same feminism. Feminism can be pluralistic so long as we respect the different feminisms we carry with us, so long as we give enough of a damn to try to minimize the fractures among us.

Feminism will better succeed with collective effort, but feminist success can also rise out of personal conduct. I hear many young women say they can't find well-known feminists with whom they identify. That can be disheartening, but I say, let us (try to) become the feminists we would like to see moving through the world.

When you can't find someone to follow, you have to find a way to lead by example. In this collection of essays, I'm trying to lead, in a small, imperfect way. I am raising my voice as a bad feminist. I am taking a stand as a bad feminist. I offer insights on our culture and how we consume it. The essays in this collection also examine race in contemporary film, the limits of "diversity," and how innovation is rarely satisfying; it is rarely enough. I call for creating new, more inclusive measures for literary excellence and take a closer look at HBO's *Girls* and the phenomenon of the Fifty Shades trilogy. These essays are political and they are personal. They are, like feminism, flawed, but they come from a genuine place. I am just one woman trying to make sense of this world we live in. I'm raising my voice to show all the ways we have room to want more, to do better.

Bad Feminist

[ME]

Feel Me. See Me.
Hear Me. Reach Me.

Niche dating sites are interesting. You can go to JDate or Christian Mingle or Black People Meet or any number of dating websites expressly designed for birds of a feather to flock together. If you have certain criteria, you can find people who look like you or who share your faith or who enjoy having sex in furry costumes. In the world of the Internet, no one is alone in his or her interests. When you go to these niche dating sites, you can hope you are working with a known quantity. You can hope that in love online, a lingua franca will make all things possible.

I think constantly about connection and loneliness and community and belonging, and a great deal, perhaps too much, of how my writing evidences me working through the intersections of these things. So many of us are reaching out, hoping someone out there will grab our hands and remind us we are not as alone as we fear.

I tell some of the same stories over and over because certain experiences have affected me profoundly. Sometimes, I hope that by telling these stories again and again, I will have a better understanding of how the world works.

In addition to not having done much online dating, I have never really dated anyone I have a lot in common with. I blame my astrological sign. Over time, I definitely find common ground in my relationships, but the people I tend to date are often quite different from me. A friend recently told me I only date white boys and accused me of being . . . I'm not sure what. She lives in a city and takes for granted the diversity around her. In retaliation, I told her I dated a Chinese boy in college. I told her I date the boys who ask me out. If a brotha asked me out and I was into him, I'd go out with him, happily. Brothas don't step to me unless they're in their seventies, and I'm not trying to date a geriatric. I also seem to have a penchant for libertarians. I seriously cannot get enough of them and their radical need for freedom from tyranny and taxation. I cannot imagine what it would be like to have a lot in common with someone I'm dating from the first encounter forward. I do not mean to suggest that I would have a lot in common with someone simply because we're both black or both Democrats or both writers. I don't know that there is someone in the world with whom I have a lot in common, especially not in the ways that would make sense on the kinds of websites where you enter some key characteristics and preferences and might somehow meet your match. I haven't even tried, which I do not see as a bad thing. I love being with someone who is endlessly interesting because we are so different. Wanting to belong to people or a person is not about finding a mirror image of myself.

BET is not a network I watch regularly because I am very committed to Lifetime Movie Network and lesser cable network reality programming. Also, the shoddy programming on BET is a travesty, and considering that I have watched two episodes of WE tv's *Amsale Girls*, my tolerance for shoddy programming is exceptional. It's a shame how black people consistently have to settle for less when it comes to quality programming. It's a shame so few options exist beyond BET. The networks offer a numbing sea of whiteness save for shows produced by Shonda Rhimes (*Grey's Anatomy, Private Practice, Scandal*), who makes a deliberate effort to address race, gender, and, to a lesser extent, sexuality when she casts. Beyond that, black people—all people of color, really—only get to see themselves as lawyers and sassy friends and, of course, as The Help. Even when a new show promises to break new ground, like Lena Dunham's *Girls*, an HBO show set in Brooklyn, New York, that follows the lives of four friends in their twenties, we are forced to swallow more of the same—a general erasure or ignorance of race.

Where BET is concerned, we settle for nothing at all unless it is airing reruns of *Girlfriends*, which is criminally underrated. It took me a long time to appreciate *Girlfriends*, but that show was onto something and never got the support it deserved. Sometimes, though, I feel like looking at people who look like me. Brown skin is beautiful; I like seeing different kinds of stories. The problem is that I see people on BET who look like me, but that's where the similarities end. This is partly because I'm in my late thirties. In BET years, I am ancient. As much as I am plugged in to pop culture, there are things I don't know about. Geography and my profession don't help. As I began writing this essay, there was a show airing on BET called *Toya*. I've seen the name when I've browsed TV listings, but I've never really watched it. I eventually saw a couple of episodes and don't even understand why this show is a show. What is the premise? I consulted Dr. Google and learned Toya is the ex-wife of Lil Wayne, but that's it. She's not even a backup singer or video ho, I don't think. The threshold for fame weakens ever so rapidly.

I watched the *Toya* show, and there was nothing about any of it I could relate to other than caring about my family. I vaguely got the sense that Toya cares for her family and is trying to help them get on the right track, but it was fairly unclear because mostly the show involved people talking about boring things. During the show she dated someone named Memphitz (they are now married), who was looking at gorgeous diamond rings. Is he a rapper? What do these people do for a living? Lil Wayne's child support can't be that good. I wish BET did more to represent the full spectrum of black experiences in a balanced manner. If you watch BET, you get the sense that the only way black people succeed is through professional sports, music, or marrying/fucking/being a baby mama of someone who is involved with professional sports or music.

Once in a while, I would love to see an example of black success that involves other professional venues. On most television shows, white characters provide viewers with a veritable panoply of options for "What I Want to Be When I Grow Up." There are exceptions, certainly. Laurence Fishburne played the lead on *CSI* for a season or two. Back in the day, Blair Underwood played a lawyer on *L.A. Law*. There are the aforementioned Shonda Rhimes–helmed shows. I suppose the thinking is that a person of color as a lawyer or doctor or writer or, hell, a jazz musician or school teacher or professor or postal worker or waitress wouldn't be as interesting for the *kids* because the allure of current offerings is undeniable. And yet. At some point, we have to stop selling every black child in this country the idea that he or she only needs to hold a ball or a microphone to achieve something. Bill Cosby is kind of crazy these days, but he knows what he's talking about, and he's kind of crazy because he's been fighting this fight for his whole damn life. BET frustrates me because it is a painful reminder that you can have something and nothing in common with people at the same time. I enjoy difference, but once in a while, I do want to catch a glimpse of myself in others.

In graduate school I was the adviser of the black student association. There was a negligible black faculty presence on campus (you could count them on one hand), and those folks were either too busy or burnt out or completely uninterested in the job. After four years, I understood. The older I get, the more I understand lots of things. Advising a black student association is exhausting and thankless and heartbreaking. It kind of destroys your faith after a while. A new black faculty member came to campus a couple years in, and I asked why she didn't work with the black students. She said, "That's not my job." That person said, "They're unreachable." I hate when people say something is not their job or that something isn't possible. We all say these things, sure, but some people actually believe they don't have to work beyond what is written in their job description or that they don't have to try to reach those who seemingly cannot be reached.

I get my work ethic from my tireless father. When it comes to showing young black students there are teachers who look like them, when it comes to mentoring and being there to support students, I feel it's everyone's job (regardless of ethnicity), and if you don't believe that as a black academic, you need to check yourself, immediately, and then check yourself again and keep checking yourself until you get your head on right.

When I was an adviser, the black students respected me, probably, but they didn't really like me a lot of the time. I get it. I am an acquired taste. Mostly, they thought I was "bougie." Many of them called me redbone and laughed when I got irritated. They thought the way I use slang is hilarious because I round my vowels. They'd tell me, "Say 'holla' again," and I would because that's one of my favorite words even if I maybe say it wrong according to the kids. I kind of singsong the word. They especially loved how I said "gangsta." I didn't mind the teasing. I minded how they thought I expected too much from them where the definition of "too much" was to have any expectations at all.

Yes, I was a demanding bitch, and at times I was probably unreasonable. I insisted on excellence. I get that from my mother.

My expectations were things like requiring the officers to show up to the executive meetings, insisting officers and members show up to general meetings at least five minutes early because to be early is to be on time, insisting that if students agreed to perform a given task they follow through, insisting they do their homework, insisting they ask for help and get tutoring when they needed that kind of support, insisting they stop thinking a C or D is a good grade, insisting they take college seriously, insisting they stop seeing conspiracy theories everywhere, insisting that not every teacher who did something they didn't like was being racist.

Many of those kids, I quickly realized, did not know how to read or be a student. When talking about social issues in academia and even in intellectual circles, we talk about privilege a lot and how we all have privilege and need to be aware of it. I have always known the ways in which I am privileged, but working with these students, most of them from inner-city Detroit, made me realize the extent of my privilege. Whenever someone tells me I don't acknowledge my privilege, I really want him or her to shut the fuck up. You think I don't know? I'm crystal clear on privilege. The notion that I should be fine with the status quo even if I am not wholly affected by the status quo is repulsive.

These kids didn't know how to read so I got them dictionaries, and because they were too shy to discuss literacy in meetings, they would catch me walking across campus or in my office and whisper, "I need help reading." It had never crossed my mind before that it was possible for a child to be educated in this country and make it to college unable to read at a college level. Shame on me, certainly, for being so ignorant about the galling disparities in how children are educated. Shame on me. I learned so much more in grad school out of the classroom than I ever did sitting around a table talking about theoretical concepts. I learned about how ignorant I am. I am still working to correct this.

One-on-one, the students and I got along much better. They were far more open. I had no idea what I was doing. How do you teach someone to read? I consulted Dr. Google regularly. I bought a book with some basic grammar exercises. Sometimes, we just read their homework word for word, and when they didn't know a word, I made them write it down and look it up and write the definition down too because that's how my mother taught me. I had a mother who was home every day after school and who sat with me day after day and year after year until I went away for high school, helping me with my homework, encouraging me, and certainly pushing me toward excellence. There were things in my life my mother was unable to see, but when it came to my education and making sure I was a good, well-mannered person, she was on point in every way.

At times, I resented the amount of schoolwork I had to do at home. My American classmates didn't have to do any of the stuff I had to do. I didn't understand why my mom, both of my parents really, was so hell-bent on making us use our minds. There was a lot of pressure in our household. A lot. I was a pretty stressed-out kid, and some of that pressure was self-induced and some of it wasn't. I enjoyed being the best and making my parents proud. I enjoyed the sense of control I felt by being good at school when there were other parts of my life that were desperately out of control. I was expected to get straight As. Bringing home a grade less than an A was not an option so I didn't. This is a typical child-of-immigrants story, not at all interesting. When I worked with those kids in graduate school, I understood why my parents showed us how we had to work three times harder than white kids to get half the consideration. They did not impart this reality with bitterness. They were protecting us.

At the end of our sessions, the students I worked with would generally say, "Don't tell anyone I came to see you." It wasn't that they were embarrassed to get help, most of the time. They were embarrassed to be seen putting effort into their education, to be seen caring. Sometimes, they'd open up about their lives. Many of the kids I worked with did not have parents who would or could prepare their children for the world the way mine did. Many of them were eldest children, the first in their families to go to college. One boy was the eldest of nine. One girl was the eldest of seven. Another girl was the eldest of six. There were many absent fathers, incarcerated mothers and fathers and cousins and aunties and siblings. There was alcoholism and drug addiction and abuse. There were parents who resented that their children were in college and tried to sabotage them. There were students who were sending their student loan refund checks back home to support their families and spending the semester without textbooks, without enough money to eat, because the mouths back at home needed to be fed. There were certainly students with a great parent or parents, with families who were supportive, who knew nothing of poverty, who were well prepared for the college experience or well prepared to do what it took to get up to speed. Those students were the exception. I often think about the danger of a single story, as discussed by Chimamanda Adichie in her TED Talk, but sometimes, there actually is a single story and it tears my heart open.

By the end of my last year of school, with all the other things I was dealing with in my personal life, I was completely burnt out. I had nothing left to give. All too often, the students just did not give a damn and neither did I. I'm not proud of this, but I really was dealing with a lot. That's what I tell myself. The students didn't show up to the BSA meetings. They half-assed their participation in club events and didn't promote events and dropped the ball, and I no longer had the energy to glare and yell and push and prod and make them want to do better. If after four years they had learned nothing, I had failed, and there was little I could do to rectify that. They were just being college students, of course, but it was frustrating. When the last semester ended, I was relieved. I would miss the students because they were, to be clear, a great joy—bright, funny, charming, kind of crazy, but good kids. I still needed a break, a very, very long break.

The woman who recruited me to grad school had worked with the black students for about twenty years. When she retired, she was so burnt out she couldn't even talk about them without being overwhelmed by her frustration with their unwillingness to change, the ways they had been wronged, their lack of faith that there was a different, better way, the administration's piss-poor efforts to create change, all of it. I understood her burnout too. It took me a mere four years, but I got there. And yet. There was an end-of-the-year banquet where the students surprised me. They gave me a plaque and read a beautiful speech where they said I was the epitome of integrity and grace. They thanked me for recognizing they were talented and powerful beyond measure. They said I stood up for them even when they were wrong and that I was family, which did nicely explain our relationship—unconditional but complicated. They said lots of other gorgeously flattering things. They didn't have to say any of it. I left grad school feeling like I had reached them. They certainly reached me, made me feel like I was a part of something even though it was my job to make them feel like part of something.

As a faculty member, I haven't sought out the black student association yet because I've been trying to summon the energy. I feel guilty about how I'm dragging my feet. I feel this sense of responsibility. I feel weak and stupid.

I had a black student in my class during my first year who felt I was picking on him because he was black. I'm told this comes up often for black faculty. I wasn't picking on this kid. For one, I don't have that kind of time. Also, I expect excellence from all my students, without exception. He had a perfect GPA before and simply couldn't believe he was not earning an A in my class.

He was incredulous that I did not think he deserved a proverbial cookie for having been a good student before coming to my class. I was incredulous at his arrogance. I got the sense he wanted me to be impressed that he was "different," that he was a good student, like I should just grade him on past performance instead of how he did in my class. He once told me, "I'm not like the other [N-words] on campus." I told him he'd better check his attitude and his language. We had some very tense conversations, one of which was so tense my boss, unbeknownst to me, stood in the hallway just out of sight the entire time because he felt this kid might get rowdy. I thought the kid was going to get rowdy. It took me a whole semester to get a handle on this kid's issue. I eventually realized he didn't want to be seen as one of those students who come in and don't know enough to get through or don't care enough to get through. His way of doing that, of proving he was different, was to maintain his perfect GPA by any means necessary. That student graduated and I don't know where he is now, but I hope he won't spend his life negotiating respectability politics.

I work hard. I volunteer for things. I try to deliver when I say I will do something. I try to do my job well. I extend myself, then overextend myself. I work at work and I work at home. I study my teaching evaluations, trying to make sense of my imperfections so that next time, I might get it right. I sit with my colleagues and think, *Please like me. Please like me. Please like me. Please respect me. At the very least, don't hate me.* People often misunderstand me, misunderstand my motivations. The pressure is constant and suffocating. I say I'm a workaholic and maybe I am, but maybe I'm just trying, like my student, to show how I'm different.

In graduate school, early on, I once overheard a classmate talking in her office as I walked by. She didn't know I was there.

She was gossiping about me to a group of our classmates and said I was the affirmative-action student. I went to my office, trying to hold it together until I was alone. I was not going to be the girl who cried in the hallway. As soon as I crossed the threshold, I started sobbing because that was my greatest fear, that I wasn't good enough and that everyone knew it. Rationally, I know it was absurd, but hearing how she and maybe others saw me hurt real bad. There was no one I could really talk to about what I had heard because I was the only student of color in the program. There was no one else who would understand. Sure, I had friends, good friends who would commiserate, but they wouldn't *get* it and I would never be able to trust that they didn't feel the same way.

I stopped joking about being a slacker. I tripled the number of projects I was involved with. I was excellent most of the time. I fell short some of the time. I made sure I got good grades. I made sure my comprehensive exams were solid. I wrote conference proposals and had them accepted. I published. I designed an overly ambitious research project for my dissertation that kind of made me want to die. No matter what I did, I heard that girl, that girl who had accomplished a fraction of a fraction of what I had, telling a group of our peers I was the one who did not deserve to be in our program. Those peers, by the way, did not defend me. They did not disagree. That hurt too. Her words kept me up at night. I can still hear her, the clarity of her voice, the confidence of her conviction. At work, I constantly worry, *Do they think I'm the affirmative-action hire?* I worry, *Do I deserve to be here?* I worry, *Am I doing enough?* I have a PhD I damn well earned, and I worry I am not good enough. It's insane, irrational, and exhausting. Frankly, it's depressing.

I know none of this might make sense, but for me, it is all connected.

I am still writing my way toward a place where I fit, but I am also finding my people in unexpected places—California, Chicago, upper Michigan, other places, some not on any kind of map. Writing bridges many differences. Kindness bridges many differences too, and so does a love of *One Tree Hill* or *Lost* or beautiful books or terrible movies. There are times when I wish finding community was as simple as entering some personal information and letting an algorithm show me where I belong. And then I realize that in many ways, this is what the Internet and social networking has done for me—offered community.

Or perhaps I am not looking for an algorithm at all.

An algorithm is a procedure for solving a problem in a finite number of steps. An algorithm leads to a neat way of understanding a problem too complex for the human mind to solve.

That's not what I am looking for. John Louis von Neumann said, "If people do not believe that mathematics is simple, it is only because they do not realize how complicated life is." Mathematics may well be simple, but the complexities of race and culture are often irreducible. They cannot be wholly addressed in a single essay or book or television show or movie.

I will keep writing about these intersections as a writer and a teacher, as a black woman, as a bad feminist, until I no longer feel like what I want is impossible. I no longer want to believe these problems are too complex for us to make sense of them.

Peculiar Benefits

When I was young, my parents took our family to Haiti during the summers. For them, it was a homecoming. For my brothers and me it was an adventure, sometimes a chore, and always a necessary education on privilege and the grace of an American passport. Until visiting Haiti, I had no idea what poverty really was or the difference between relative and absolute poverty. To see poverty so plainly and pervasively left a profound mark on me.

To this day, I remember my first visit, and how at every intersection, men and women, shiny with sweat, would mob our car, their skinny arms stretched out, hoping for a few gourdes or American dollars. I saw the sprawling slums, the shanties housing entire families, the trash piled in the streets, and also the gorgeous beach and the young men in uniforms who brought us Coca-Cola in glass bottles and made us hats and boats out of palm fronds. It was hard for a child to begin to grasp the contrast of such inescapable poverty alongside almost repulsive luxury, and then the United States, a mere eight hundred miles away, with its gleaming cities rising out of the landscape and the well-maintained interstates stretching across the country, the running water and the electricity. It wasn't until many, many years later that I realized my education on privilege began long before I could appreciate it in any meaningful way.

Privilege is a right or immunity granted as a peculiar benefit, advantage, or favor. There is racial privilege, gender (and identity) privilege, heterosexual privilege, economic privilege, able-bodied privilege, educational privilege, religious privilege, and the list goes on and on. At some point, you have to surrender to the kinds of privilege you hold. Nearly everyone, particularly in the developed world, has something someone else doesn't, something someone else yearns for.

The problem is, cultural critics talk about privilege with such alarming frequency and in such empty ways, we have diluted the word's meaning. When people wield the word "privilege," it tends to fall on deaf ears because we hear that word so damn much it has become white noise.

One of the hardest things I've ever had to do is accept and acknowledge my privilege. It's an ongoing project. I'm a woman, a person of color, and the child of immigrants, but I also grew up middle class and then upper middle class. My parents raised my siblings and me in a strict but loving environment. They were and are happily married, so I didn't have to deal with divorce or crappy intramarital dynamics. I attended elite schools. My master's and doctoral degrees were funded. I got a tenure-track position my first time out. My bills are paid. I have the time and resources for frivolity. I am reasonably well published. I have an agent and books to my name. My life has been far from perfect, but it's somewhat embarrassing for me to accept just how much privilege I have.

It's also really difficult for me to consider the ways in which I lack privilege or the ways in which my privilege hasn't magically rescued me from a world of hurt. On my more difficult days, I'm not sure what's more of a pain in my ass—being black or being a woman. I'm happy to be both of these things, but the world keeps intervening. There are all kinds of infuriating reminders of my place in the world—random people questioning me in the parking lot at work as if it is unfathomable that I'm a faculty member, the persistence of lawmakers trying to legislate the female body, street harassment, strangers wanting to touch my hair.

We tend to believe that accusations of privilege imply we have it easy, which we resent because life is hard for nearly everyone. Of course we resent these accusations. Look at white men when they are accused of having privilege. They tend to be immediately defensive (and, at times, understandably so). They say, "It's not my fault I am a white man," or "I'm [insert other condition that discounts their privilege]," instead of simply accepting that, in this regard, yes, they benefit from certain privileges others do not. To have privilege in one or more areas does not mean you are wholly privileged. Surrendering to the acceptance of privilege is difficult, but it is really all that is expected. What I remind myself, regularly, is this: the acknowledgment of my privilege is not a denial of the ways I have been and am marginalized, the ways I have suffered.

You don't necessarily *have* to do anything once you acknowledge your privilege. You don't have to apologize for it. You need to understand the extent of your privilege, the consequences of your privilege, and remain aware that people who are different from you move through and experience the world in ways you might never know anything about. They might endure situations you can never know anything about. You could, however, use that privilege for the greater good—to try to level the playing field for everyone, to work for social justice, to bring attention to how those without certain privileges are disenfranchised. We've seen what the hoarding of privilege has done, and the results are shameful.

When we talk about privilege, some people start to play a very pointless and dangerous game where they try to mix and match various demographic characteristics to determine who wins at the Game of Privilege. Who would win in a privilege battle between a wealthy black woman and a wealthy white man? Who would win a privilege battle between a queer white man and a queer Asian woman? Who would win in a privilege battle between a working-class white man and a wealthy, differently abled Mexican woman? We could play this game all day and never find a winner. Playing the Game of Privilege is mental masturbation—it only feels good to those playing the game.

Too many people have become self-appointed privilege police, patrolling the halls of discourse, ready to remind people of their privilege whether those people have denied that privilege or not. In online discourse, in particular, the specter of privilege is always looming darkly. When someone writes from experience, there is often someone else, at the ready, pointing a trembling finger, accusing that writer of having various kinds of privilege. How dare someone speak to a personal experience without accounting for every possible configuration of privilege or the lack thereof? We would live in a world of silence if the only people who were allowed to write or speak from experience or about difference were those absolutely without privilege.

When people wield accusations of privilege, more often than not, they want to be heard and seen. Their need is acute, if not desperate, and that need rises out of the many historical and ongoing attempts to silence and render invisible marginalized groups. Must we satisfy our need to be heard and seen by preventing anyone else from being heard and seen? Does privilege automatically negate any merits of what a privilege holder has to say? Do we ignore everything, for example, that white men have to say?

We need to get to a place where we discuss privilege by way

of observation and acknowledgment rather than accusation. We need to be able to argue beyond the threat of privilege. We need to stop playing Privilege or Oppression Olympics because we'll never get anywhere until we find more effective ways of talking through difference. We should be able to say, "This is my truth," and have that truth stand without a hundred clamoring voices shouting, giving the impression that multiple truths cannot co-exist. Because at some point, doesn't privilege become beside the point?

Privilege is relative and contextual. Few people in the developed world, and particularly in the United States, have no privilege at all. Among those of us who participate in intellectual communities, privilege runs rampant. We have disposable time and the ability to access the Internet regularly. We have the freedom to express our opinions without the threat of retaliation. We have smartphones and iProducts and desktops and laptops. If you are reading this essay, you have some kind of privilege. It may be hard to hear that, I know, but if you cannot recognize your privilege, you have a lot of work to do; get started.

Typical First Year
Professor

I go to school for a very long time and get some degrees and finally move to a very small town in the middle of a cornfield. I leave someone behind. I tell myself I have worked so hard I can't choose a man over a career. I want to choose the man over the career. I rent an apartment, the nicest place I've ever lived as an adult. I have a guest bathroom. I don't save lives, but I try not to ruin them.

This is the dream, everyone says—a good job, tenure track. I have an office I don't have to share with two or four people. My name is on the engraved panel just outside my door. My name is spelled correctly. I have my own printer. The luxury of this cannot be overstated. I randomly print out a document; I sigh happily as the printer spits it out, warm. I have a phone with an extension, and when people call the number they are often looking for me. There are a lot of shelves, but I like my books at home. In every movie I've ever seen about professors, there are books. I quickly unpack three boxes, detritus I accumulated in graduate school—sad drawer trash, books I'll rarely open again—but I'm a professor now. I must have books on display in my office. It is an unspoken rule.

I put a dry-erase board on my door. Old habits die hard. Every few weeks I pose a new question. What's your favorite movie? (*Pretty Woman.*) What's your favorite musical? (*West Side Story.*) What do you want for Christmas? (Peace of mind.) Currently: What is your favorite cocktail? Best answer: "Free."

The department's administrative assistant gives me the rundown on important things—mailbox, office supplies, photocopy code. I forget the code weekly. She is friendly, patient, kind, but if you cross her, there will be trouble. I vow to never cross her.

There is a mind-numbing orientation that begins with a student playing acoustic guitar. A threatening sing-along vibe fills the room. The student is not a chanteur. Most of the audience cringes visibly. I hide in the very last row. For the next two days I accumulate knowledge I will never use—math all over again.

I'll be teaching three classes, two of which I've not quite taught before. Turns out when you say you can do something, people believe you.

Ten minutes before my first class, I run to the bathroom and vomit. I'm afraid of public speaking, which makes teaching complicated.

When I walk into the classroom, the students stare at me like I'm in charge. They wait for me to say something. I stare back and wait for them to do something. It's a silent power struggle. Finally, I tell them to do things and they do those things. I realize I am, in fact, in charge. We'll be playing with Legos. For a few minutes I am awesome because I have brought toys.

Teaching three classes requires serious memorization when it comes to student names. The students tend to blur. It will take nearly three weeks for me to remember Ashley A. and Ashley M.

and Matt and Matt and Mark and Mark and so on. I rely heavily on pointing. I color-code the students. *You in the green shirt. You in the orange hat.*

I get my first paycheck. We are paid once a month, which requires the kind of budgeting I am incapable of. Life is unpleasant after the twenty-third or so. I've been a graduate student for so long it's hard to fathom that one check can have four numbers and change. Then I see how much The Man takes. Damn The Man.

Students don't know what to make of me. I wear jeans and Converse. I have tattoos up and down my arms. I'm tall. I am not petite. I am the child of immigrants. Many of my students have never had a black teacher before. I can't help them with that. I'm the only black professor in my department. This will probably never change for the whole of my career, no matter where I teach. I'm used to it. I wish I weren't. There seems to be some unspoken rule about the number of academic spaces people of color can occupy at the same time. I have grown weary of being the only one.

When I was a student listening to a boring professor drone endlessly, I usually thought, *I will never be that teacher.* One day, I am delivering a lecture and realize, in that moment, I am *that* teacher. I stare out at the students, most of them not taking notes, giving me that soul-crushing dead-eye stare that tells me, *I wish I were anywhere but here.* I think, *I wish I were anywhere but here.* I talk faster and faster to put us all out of our misery. I become incoherent. Their dead-eye stares haunt me for the rest of the day, then longer.

I keep in touch with my closest friend from graduate school. We both really enjoy our new jobs, but the learning curve is steep. There is no shallow end. We dance around metaphors about drowning. During long conversations we question the choice to be proper, modern women. There is so much grading. There's a lot to be said for barefoot kitchen work when staring down a stack of research papers.

Walking down the hall, I hear a young woman saying "Dr. Gay" over and over and think, *That Dr. Gay is rather rude for ignoring that poor student.* I turn around to say something before I realize she is talking to me.

I worry some of my students don't own any clothes with zippers or buttons or other methods of closure and fastening. I see a lot of words faded and stretched across asses, bra straps, pajama pants, often ill-fitting. In the winter, when there is snow and ice outside, boys come to class in basketball shorts and flip-flops. I worry about their feet, their poor little toes.

Helicopter parents e-mail me for information about their children. *How is my son doing? Is my daughter attending class?* I encourage them to open lines of communication with their children. I politely tell them there are laws preventing such communication without their child's written consent. The child rarely consents.

There is nothing new in the new town, and I know no one. The town is a flat, scarred strip of land with half-abandoned strip malls. And then there is the corn, so much of it, everywhere, stretching in every direction for miles. Most of my colleagues live fifty miles away. Most of my colleagues have families. I go north to Chicago. I go east to Indianapolis. I go south to St. Louis. I take up competitive Scrabble and win the first tournament I enter. In the last round, I encounter a nemesis who gets so angry when I beat him he refuses to shake my hand and flounces out of the tournament in a huff. The sweetness of that victory lingers. The next time I see him, at another tournament, he'll point and say, "Best two out of three. Best. Two. Out. Of. Three." I best him in two out of three.

My own parents ask, *How is my daughter doing?* I offer them some version of the truth.

Sometimes, during class, I catch students staring at their cell phones beneath their desks like they're in a cone of invisibility. It's as funny as it is irritating. Sometimes, I cannot help but say, "I do see you." Other times, I confiscate their electronic devices.

Sometimes, when students are doing group work, I sneak a look at my own phone like I am in a cone of invisibility. I am part of the problem.

I try to make class fun, engaging, *experiential*. We hold a mock debate about social issues in composition. We use Twitter to learn about crafting microcontent in new media writing. We play *Jeopardy!* to learn about professional reports in professional writing. College and kindergarten aren't as different as you'd think. Every day, I wonder, *How do I keep these students meaningfully engaged, educated, and entertained for fifty minutes? How do I keep them from staring at me with dead eyes? How do I make them want to learn?* It's tiring. Sometimes, I think the answer to each of these questions is *I can't.*

There is a plague on grandmothers. The elder relations of my students begin passing away at an alarming rate one week. I want to warn the surviving grandmothers, somehow. I want them to live. The excuses students come up with for absences and homework amuse me in how ludicrous and improbable they are. They think I want to know. They think I need their explanations. They think I don't know they're lying. Sometimes I simply say, "I know you are lying. You say it best when you say nothing at all."

I try not to be old. I try not to think, *When I was your age . . .* , but often, I do remember when I was their age. I enjoyed school; I loved learning and worked hard. Most of the people I went to school with did too. We partied hard, but we still showed up to class and did what we had to do. An alarming number of my students don't seem to *want* to be in college. They are in school because they don't feel they have a choice or have nothing better to do; because their parents are making them attend college; because, like most of us, they've surrendered to the rhetoric that to succeed in this country you need a college degree. They are not necessarily incorrect. And yet, all too often, I find myself wishing I could teach more students who actually want to be in school, who don't resent the education being *foisted* upon them. I wish there were viable alternatives for students who would rather be anywhere but in a classroom. I wish, in all things, for a perfect world.

A number of students find my website. This is teaching in the digital age. They find my writing, much of which is, shall we say, explicit in nature. News travels fast. They want to talk to me about these things in the hall after class, in my office, out and about on campus. It's awkward and flattering but mostly awkward. They also know too much about my personal life. They know about the random guy who spent the night, who helped me kill a couple bottles of wine and made me breakfast. I have to start blogging differently.

I get along with the students. They are generally bright and charming even when they are frustrating. They make me love my job both in and out of the classroom. Students show up at my office to discuss their personal problems. I try to maintain boundaries. There are breakups with long-term boyfriends and bad dates and a lecherous professor in another department and a roommate who leaves her door open while she's getting nailed and this thing that happened at the bar on Friday and difficult decisions about whether to go to graduate school or go on the job market. Each of these situations is a crisis. I listen and try to dispense the proper advice. This is not the same advice my friends and I give to one another. What I really want to say to these students, most of them young women, is "GIRL!"

I am quite content to be in my thirties, and nothing affirms that more than being around people in their late teens and early twenties.

In grad school, we heard lurid tales of department meetings where heated words were exchanged and members of various factions almost came to blows. I was looking forward to the drama, only to learn my department meets once or twice a semester rather than every week. Instead, we meet in committees. The chairs of those committees report to the department chair. Committee meetings are not my favorite part of the job. There are politics and agendas and decades of history of which I know little and understand even less. Everyone means well, but there's a lot of bureaucracy. I prefer common sense.

The first semester ends and I receive my evaluations. Most of the students think I did a decent job, some think I did a great job, but then there are those who didn't. I assign too much work, they say. I expect too much. I don't consider these faults. A student writes, "Typical first year professor." I have no idea what that means.

Over winter break, my friend from graduate school and I have another long lamentation about choices and taking jobs in the middle of nowhere and the (relative) sacrifices academics must often make. It is tiring to constantly be told *how lucky we are.* Luck and loneliness, it would seem, are very compatible.

I go drinking with the guy I . . . go drinking with. To call it dating would be a stretch. We are a matter of convenience. I sip on a T&T and lament my evaluations. I want to be a good teacher, and most days, I think I am. I give a damn. I want students to *like* me. I am human. I am so full of want. He tells me not to worry with such authority I almost believe him. He orders me another drink and another. I hope we don't run into any of my students because I cannot pull off professorial in my current state. That's always my prayer when we go out. Because of this, we often end up in the city fifty miles up the road. At the end of the night, two very short men get into a fight. Clothing is torn. We stand in the parking lot and watch. The men's anger, the white heat of it, fascinates me. Later, after taking a cab home, I drunkenly call the man I left behind, the man who didn't follow me. "My students hate me," I say. He assures me they don't. He says that would not be possible. I say, "Everything is terrible. Everything is great." He says, "I know."

Another semester begins, three new classes. Winter settles, ice everywhere, barren plains. There are three new sets of students, different faces but similar names. *Hey you in the khaki hat. Hey you with the purple hair.*

The goal, we are told, is tenure. To that end all faculty, even first-year professors, have to compile an annual portfolio. I assemble a record of one semester's worth of work. I try to quantify my professional worth. My colleagues write letters to attest to my various accomplishments, verifying I am on such and such committee, that I participated in such and such event, that I am a valuable and contributing member of the department. I update my vita. I clip publications. I buy a neon-green three-ring binder. This is how I rage against the machine. I spend an afternoon collating and creating labels and writing about myself with equal parts humility and bravado. It's a fine balance. Later, I tell a friend, "It was like arts and crafts for adults. I went to graduate school for this."

I stop getting lost looking for the bathroom. The building is strange, with many hallways, some hidden, and an arcane numbering system that defies logic. When I leave my door open, students passing by will ask, "Where is Dr. So-and-So's office?" I say, "I have no idea."

Summer, we are told, is a time for rest, relaxation, and catching up. I teach two classes. I write a novel. I return to the place I moved from, spend weeks with the man I left behind. He says, *Don't go.* I say, *Please follow.* We remain at an impasse. I return to the cornfield. There are mere weeks of summer left. They are not enough.

A new semester begins. I have new responsibilities, including chairing a committee. Ten minutes before the first class on the first day, I run to the bathroom and puke. In my classroom, I stare at another group of students whose names I will have to remember. *You in the red shirt. You with the pink shorts.* I refuse to expect less. I try to learn better, do better. I have no idea how I got to be the one at the front of the classroom, the one who gets to be in charge of things. Most of the time, I feel like the kid who gets to sit at the adult table for the first time at Thanksgiving. I'm not sure which fork to use. My feet can't reach the floor.

To Scratch, Claw, or Grope Clumsily or Frantically[1]

My third tournament started with a brutal game where I lost by more than 200 points. I was the fifth seed, ranked like tennis with words, and feeling confident—too confident, really. "We Are the Champions" may have been on an infinite loop in my head. And yet. It was also early on a Saturday morning. I am not a morning person. Before the tournament started, people milled around the hotel meeting room, chatting idly about the heat, what we had done since the last time many of us had seen one another (the previous tournament in Illinois), and some of the more amazing plays we had made recently.

Scrabble[2] players love to talk, at length, with some repetition, about their vocabulary triumphs.

---

[1] This is the definition of the word "scrabble" according to *Merriam-Webster's Collegiate Dictionary*.

[2] In all seriousness, Scrabble was invented by a man named Alfred Mosher Butts.

There were twenty-one of us with various levels of ability, but really, if you're playing this game at the competitive level, you generally have some skill and can be a contender. The more experienced players, the Dragos to my Rocky, studied word lists and appeared intensely focused on something the rest of us couldn't see. Many wore fanny packs without irony—serious fanny packs bulging with mystery. As I waited for the tournament to begin, I studied the table of game-related accessories—books, a travel set, a towel, a deluxe board, and some milled French soaps clearly taken from someone's closet—all for drawings to be held later in the day.[3]

At nine o'clock, sharp, the tournament director,[4] Tom, began making announcements, one of which was that his wife had died just days earlier. The tournament was going to go on, he said. It was an awkward, touching moment because grief is so personal and this man was clearly grieving. The room was silent. It was difficult to know what to do. He announced that the first pairings would be posted in a few minutes, so we waited quietly until the pairings were posted around the room. We all hovered around the sheet of paper, quickly writing down the names of our first two opponents. I sat across from my first challenger. She was seeded nineteenth. My confidence swelled vulgarly. She stared at me, smug, almost imperious. I felt an uncomfortable chill. We determined she would go first. She drew her seven tiles. I started her time and fixed her with a hard stare as she began shuffling the seven plastic squares back and forth across

[3] Scrabble tournaments are a lot like soccer tournaments for four-year-olds in that, oftentimes, everyone goes home with a little something.

[4] Officially rated tournaments are run by NASPA-approved tournament directors. NASPA is the North American Scrabble Players Association. Tournament directors are generally encyclopedic in their knowledge of Scrabble and can easily clarify any confusion about the rules or negotiate disputes that arise during a tournament. Disputes, they arise.

her rack. I began drawing my tiles. Beneath the table, my legs were shaking.

This is competitive Scrabble.[5]

You have to understand. I was lonely in a new town where I knew no one. I wanted to be back home, with my boyfriend, in our apartment, complaining about how *SportsCenter* seems to air perpetually or listening to him nag me about my imaginary Internet friends. My apartment was empty, no furniture, because I left my sad graduate-student furniture behind. After work, I'd sit on my lone chair, a step above sad, purchased at Sofa Mart, wondering how my life had come to this.

When my new colleague invited me to her home to play with her Scrabble club,[6] I was so desperate I would have agreed to just about anything—cleaning her bathrooms, watching the grass grow in her backyard, something smarmy and vaguely illegal involving suburban prostitution, whatever.

I didn't quite know what a Scrabble club was, but I assumed it was a group of people enjoying friendly games of Scrabble on a

[5] This is how serious competitive Scrabble is: there is a national championship, held annually during the summer. The first national tournament was held in 1978. There are also world competitions (the first world championship was held in 1991), a cottage industry of Scrabble-related merchandise, game timers, boards, tiles, etc., plus books, documentaries, and academic articles on the nuances of competitive Scrabble. There are Scrabble-related apps for your iDevices (I use Zarf, CheckWord, the official Scrabble game, Lexulous, and Words With Friends). There are Scrabble games on Facebook (I play the official Hasbro game and Lexulous). Elsewhere online, there's the Internet Scrabble Club (ISC), where I also play. There is a website, cross-tables .com, dedicated to tracking all the official tournaments in the country with scores and rankings. I am ranked 1,336th in the country. I'm guessing that's out of 1,400 players, given my lowliness.

[6] There are more than two hundred Scrabble clubs in the United States. The club in my town meets monthly, while the club in Champaign, Illinois, meets weekly. In bigger cities, some clubs will even meet twice a week.

Saturday afternoon. I told my mother I was going to play Scrabble and she laughed, called me a geek, her accent wrapping around the word strangely. I was roundly mocked by my brothers, who were always the popular kids while I was the shunned nerd, a fact they gleefully reminded me of as they made a series of increasingly absurd Scrabble-related jokes, like, "You sure are going through a DRY SPELL." The man I left behind said, "Come home. You're freaking me out." I ignored them all.

My colleague Daiva and her husband, Marty, live in a large home in a wooded neighborhood on the very edge of our very small town. Everything is modern and unique and interesting to look at—slick leather chairs, pottery, African art. In their finished basement, there is enough space for ten to twenty people, sometimes more, to get together once a month to play Scrabble all day.

Marty[7] is a nationally ranked player, top fifteen. He knows every word ever invented as well as each word's meaning. If you give him a seven-letter combination, he'll tell you all the possible anagrams. I would not be surprised to learn he thinks in anagrams. There are thirty-nine possible Scrabble words in "anagram."[8]

When you are new to the club, Marty carefully explains the rules of competitive Scrabble, and rules, there are many. You have to keep score. When you have completed your turn, you have to press a button on a game timer. You have to monitor time because there are penalties if you exceed twenty-five total

[7] He is my Scrabble sensei. I almost beat him once, where "almost" is "not so much." Early in the match I played TRIPLEX for around 90 points. Then I played another bingo. I was way ahead and deluded myself into thinking I was on easy street. The sweetness of my imagined victory was nearly unbearable. Marty would go on to play ENTOZOAN across two Triple Word Score spaces for 203 points. He was Sub-Zero in *Mortal Kombat* tearing out my Scrabble spine with his bare hands—FATALITY. We have not played since. I have been properly humbled.

[8] I love anagrams. When I was a kid, my mom would write big words on lined paper and ask me to find all the possible words. Now, finding words is kind of my superpower.

minutes for your plays. There's a proper etiquette for drawing tiles (tile bag held above your eyes, head turned away).[9] There's a procedure if you draw too many tiles. There's a protocol for challenging if you believe your opponent has played a phony, a word that isn't in the Official Tournament and Club Word List.[10]

As Marty told me all these rules that first day, I laughed and rolled my eyes like an asshole and struggled to take any of it seriously. Until that day, my Scrabble playing had mostly involved drinking, friends, crazy made-up words, haphazard score keeping, and never ever any time constraints. It was an innocent time.

People slowly filed in with large round cases. One woman's case was wheeled, like a suitcase. They set their cases on tables and pulled out custom turntable Scrabble boards, timers, tile bags, and racks. They got out their scoring sheets and personal tokens. The games started, and the room hushed. I realized this was no time to crack jokes. I realized Scrabble is very serious business.

I have a Scrabble nemesis. His name is Henry.[11] He has the most gorgeous blue-gray eyes I have ever seen. The beauty of his perfect

[9] In the seventh round of the 2011 World Scrabble Championships, Edward Martin, while playing Chollapat Itthi-Aree, realized a tile was missing. The tournament director came up with a reasonable solution, but Itthi-Aree demanded Martin prove he wasn't hiding the missing tile on his person. Play resumed, and Martin eventually won by a single point. My friend/sensei Marty was totally sitting right next to these guys when this went down. He said, "It was a distraction."

[10] There are multiple official word lists. In North America, most Scrabble players use the Official Tournament and Club Word List (OWL). Outside of North America, players use the *Collins English Dictionary*. At some tournaments here in the United States, you will find smaller Collins divisions for those Scrabble players who want to test their skills using the Collins dictionary. The challenge is remembering which words are acceptable for Collins and then remembering which words are acceptable for OWL when returning to traditional play.

[11] Henry is not his name.

eyes only makes me hate him more. He has been known to wear a fanny pack and often scowls. Nemeses aren't born. They are made.

Shortly after I started playing with my local Scrabble club, Marty told me about a charity tournament he holds in Danville, said it would be a great experience for me to play. I had nothing to lose so I agreed. I had no idea what to expect as I walked into the main building of the community college in Danville. After I registered, I stood awkwardly, wondering what to do, until my club friends took mercy on me and showed me the lay of tournament land.

Serious Scrabble people study words and remember matches from eight years ago where they played a word for 173 points. They remember when they didn't challenge a phony and lost the match. They remember everything. Some serious Scrabble players are poor losers. I am a good loser. I love Scrabble so much I don't care if I lose. I also have to be a good loser because I lose a lot, so practicality plays a role. Unlike most serious Scrabble players, I don't have the patience to study all the possible three- and four-letter words, for example, but still, I am extremely competitive.[12] It's an awkward combination.

I began the tournament thinking, *I am going to win this tournament.* I approach most things in life with a dangerous level of confidence to balance my generally low self-esteem. This helps me as a writer. Each time I submit a story to fancy magazines like, say, *The New Yorker* or *The Paris Review*, I think, *This story is totally going to get published.*

My heart gets broken more than it should.

After getting all my paperwork and such, I looked around at the other word nerds. I felt like people were checking me out. I

---

[12] I have always enjoyed board games. I love rolling dice and moving small plastic or metal pieces around game boards. I collect Monopoly sets from around the world. I will play any game so long as there is a possibility I can win. I take games seriously. Sometimes I take them too seriously and conflate winning the Game of Life with winning at life.

was prepared to reenact the beginning of "Beat It" when everyone is silently stalking one another, trying to size up the competition. There were thirty-two players, four groups (based on ranking) with eight players in each. We would play seven rounds to determine the one Scrabble player to rule them all. The tournament director read off the name of each person in each group along with his or her seed. He read my name last, and I understood my place. I was the lowest-ranked (worst) player in the room.[13] I was the last kid who would be picked for dodge ball.

I sat down for my first round with the top seed in my division, and she was pretty cocky. I was too, or I was trying to project cockiness and calm. My hands were shaking under the table I was so nervous. My primary ambition was to not humiliate myself, make any missteps where Scrabble etiquette is concerned,[14] or

[13] Scrabble people are really quite friendly and gracious, but to be clear, they are also intense and serious as hell. I have an imagination. In my head, as we prepared to word rumble, I felt as if we were about to throw down like in the music video for Michael Jackson's "Bad." A lot of my life can be described in terms of Michael Jackson's music. I'd explain the significance of "Man in the Mirror," but then you'd think I was crazy.

[14] Players can be very . . . *particular* about how you comport yourself during a Scrabble game. Some players want complete silence during matches, so they won't appreciate your idle chatter. Some players think you're cheating if you play with your phone. Don't take a call should your phone ring, that's for sure. I once got a dirty look for tapping on my phone without muting it. Apparently, the gentle beeps were simply too much for that player. The longer you play, the more you finely hone these particularities. I, for example, have developed several Scrabble-related pet peeves and preferences. I have strong opinions on the type of scoring sheets I use and the kind of pens I use to keep score (Uni-ball .5mm roller ball). I now have a very low tolerance for players who draw their tiles in annoying ways. I am particularly aggravated by players who do a lot of mixing the tiles up before each draw. IT DOES NOT CHANGE THE OUTCOME. I also do not look kindly upon players who tap the tiles on the board as they tally their points. Why are they doing that? What really sets me over the edge, though, is when players recount my word scores after I've announced my score at the end of a turn as if I am incapable of simple math. Certainly, math is not my strong suit, but in general, I have addition under control. When this unnecessary score verification occurs, I sometimes have to sit on my hands to keep from punching a player in the face.

shame the members of my Scrabble club, several of whom were in attendance.

My opponent looked up and said, "I was in the next highest division yesterday." The gauntlet was thrown. She said it with a kind, warm smile, but she was trying to intimidate me. I could tell by the way her upper lip curled. Well played. I wondered if I could purchase adult diapers at the nearest gas station.

The tournament started, and I managed to spell my words and use the timer correctly. I got into a rhythm. I placed a bingo.[15] I was feeling good. My skin flushed warmly with early success. I started thinking I had a chance. Then Number-One Seed proceeded to wipe the board with my ass; the final score was 366–277. I smiled and shook her hand, but a small piece of my soul was destroyed. I thought, *Je suis désoleé.*

When I composed myself, I took stock of what had happened. I played decently and had two bingos overall. There was simply nothing I could do. I kept drawing terribly (JVK) and getting outplayed, and she was so damn confident the entire time. Worse yet, Number-One Seed played me better than she played the game.[16] At the beginning of the match, she asked if I was a student.[17] I said, "No, I teach writing," and she said, "Oh, I'm in trouble," pretending to be the weaker prey. Here's the thing. I play poker. I know a bluff when I see one. Once she got going, she kept smirking, letting me know her foot was leaving an ugly mark on my neck.

---

[15] A bingo is when you play all seven letters on your rack. This is one of the most coveted Scrabble plays. I am a bingo player. I have no time to learn all the three-letter words and random obscure words, so I spend most of my time going for bingos because, in addition to the points you earn from the board, you also earn a fifty-point bonus. There are twenty-three possible Scrabble words in "bingo."

[16] Don't get it twisted. Competitive Scrabble is both word chess and word poker. You need a game face, and you need to wear that game face hard.

[17] I choose to believe she asked this because I look so fresh and youthful.

I was determined to win my second match because I am that competitive and I have pride and winning feels way better than losing. My opponent was really quiet and taciturn. It was not fun playing her. I slaughtered her 403–229 and I wanted to scream I was so happy. I was very tempted to jump on the table and shout, "IN YOUR FACE." For the sake of sportsmanship, I remained quiet and polite and thanked her for the game. She coldly walked away without so much as a by-your-leave. Later, as I drove home, I did gloat. I gloated a lot.

The third match was with a woman I play regularly. She's really nice and we get along well. She always beats me, and that day would be no exception—score: 390–327. My ambitious, delusional goal of winning the tournament was faltering. There were four matches left after the break, so before resuming play, we had lunch and I ate a vegetable sandwich. I told Daiva, the woman who had introduced me to the craziness of competitive Scrabble, "I'm going to win this tournament." She gave me the saddest look, as if to say, *There, there, crazy little Scrabble baby.*

There's something to be said for the delusion of confidence. I won my next four matches (389–312; 424–244; 352–312; 396–366). I was a demon. I had my word mojo. I was seeing bingos everywhere and making smart, tight plays, blocking triple-play lanes and tracking perfectly.[18] With each win, I felt increasingly invincible. I wanted to beat my chest. I was also trying to distract myself.

---

[18] Much like in poker where you try to make an educated guess as to the cards your opponent is holding, great Scrabble players will track the letters played throughout a game. By the end of the game, you should know exactly what your opponent has on his rack. It is also important to track because it allows you to make smarter strategic decisions. It's good to know if high-value letters (J, X, Q, K, V, etc.) are in play because if there are few letters left and you're holding on to a U or an I and you know the Q is still in the bag, you want to be smart about where you play those vowels so your opponent cannot build a word with his Q unless he has the necessary vowels in his own rack.

In the middle of the night, hours before the tournament began, I received a frantic call from my mother, the kind of call, as your parents get older, you hope to never receive. My normally healthy father had to be rushed to the hospital—chest pains and shortness of breath. My first instinct was to say, "I am coming home," but fortunately, my youngest brother lives nearby and was able to be there. Throughout the tournament, I was getting updates on my father's condition, trying to reassure my mother that everything would be fine.[19] I was trying not to lose my shit[20] completely. There are 227 possible Scrabble words in "completely."

In my last match of the day, it became clear the winner of our match would win the entire tournament for our division. This is how my nemesis was born.

Henry with the beautiful, piercing blue-gray eyes was sly like a fox. At the start of the match, he kept playing two-letter words, so I did the same. We were stalking each other around a cage. You know the naked fight scene in *Eastern Promises*? It was like that, only we weren't criminals, naked, or in a Turkish bath, and I was the only one with a number of visible tattoos. He wore a T-shirt that read, "World's Best Scrabble Player." It was the T-shirt that made me extra motivated to win. The level of competition was very strong, and as the game unfolded, my excitement grew.

As the second seed, Henry the Nemesis was confident he would defeat me. I could smell the confidence on him. He reeked of it. I played three bingos during the course of the match. He tried to play TREKING[21] for 81 points, but I knew that was not

[19] Everything turned out fine.

[20] "Shit" is a valid Scrabble word.

[21] There are no bingos with the letters T, R, E, K, I, N, and G. If Henry studied, he would know that.

a word. "Trekking" takes two Ks. I challenged. He rolled his eyes like he couldn't believe I had the nerve to challenge his bad spelling. My hands shook as I typed his word into the computer. I won the challenge. By the end of the match, he was irate and I was giddy. When I won, he realized he wasn't going to win the tournament and had fallen to third place. Because I was seeded so low, his ranking was going to take a hit. He refused to shake my hand and stalked off angrily. I thought he was going to throw the table over. Male anger makes me intensely uncomfortable, so I tried to sit very still and hoped the uncomfortable moment would pass quickly. Henry's bad sportsmanship did not temper my mood for long. I won my first tournament despite being the lowest-seeded[22] player in the field and took home a small cash prize. The size of my ego for the following week was difficult to measure. It would not last, though. What Scrabble giveth, another player, at another tournament, will taketh away.

When you succeed early at an endeavor, you convince yourself you will easily replicate that success. Ask child actors.[23] Three months later, I played in another tournament, the Arden Cup, a twenty-match, two-and-a-half-day affair where I won eight games and lost twelve. I learned a lot. I especially learned that it is insane to believe you will walk into a competitive tournament, among a much larger field, with a fragile and inflated ranking, and somehow win that tournament.

Henry the Nemesis was in attendance, as was a host of equally intriguing and intense players who would get under my skin

---

[22] I ended up with an amazing ranking, high enough to almost place me a division up. In the next tournament I played, I would be seeded much higher and I would pay for that, dearly.

[23] The child actors from *Diff'rent Strokes*, among others, know a little something about this. I was thinking I would pull a Mary-Kate and Ashley. Such was not the case.

nearly as much as Henry does. My least favorite player was Donnie,[24] who tried to mansplain Scrabble because he didn't recognize me[25] and took me for a neophyte. As we sat down to start our match, he said, "Now, you just play this the same way you play Scrabble at home." I made it my life's purpose, right then, to destroy him. Another opponent asked if we should play at his board or mine. When I told him I didn't have my own set, he gave me a pitying look.[26] I quickly realized I was swimming with Scrabble sharks. I was the blood in the water.

There was one redemptive moment despite the humiliation of that tournament, one where I lost so many times the matches blended into a depressing blur, where I lost mostly to mansplainers who defined words[27] even though I did not ask for definitions, regaled me with tales of their sordid Scrabble histories, and otherwise drove me crazy. I beat Henry the Nemesis again. We played twice during the tournament—he won a game and I won a game. At the end of our second game, the one I won, he stood and pointed at me. He said, "You've won two out of three times. Two. Out. Of. Three." I looked down, bit my lower lip to keep from smiling my face off.

---

[24] Also not his name.

[25] The Scrabble community is fairly small, and once you start attending tournaments regularly, you will see the same people over and over.

[26] I have my own tournament board now as well as a timer (with pink buttons), tiles (pink), and long tile racks (sadly not available in pink). I also have a carrying case with a shoulder strap so I can rock my Scrabble board slung across my shoulders like a boss.

[27] Qoph is a Hebrew letter. My opponent not only shared the word's meaning, he also explained the origins (something about a sewing needle; frankly, I had tuned him out at that point) and pronunciation. After the exciting word lesson, he started telling me all the possible Q words one can spell without a U. I wondered, *Is there a Q in "motherfucker"?*

"I wasn't keeping track," I said.[28]

I excused myself and ran to the restroom, where in the privacy of my stall, I whispered, "I beat you, I beat you, I beat you." There was fist pumping.

And so. My third tournament started brutally and the brutality was unrelenting. I ended up winning six matches (one was a bye) and losing six and took fifteenth place. My friends told me that was a good outcome. I'm pretty sure they were just being nice given the increased fragility of my Scrabble ego.

I did not get to play my nemesis, but he was there and he performed well. I took that personally.

A new nemesis was also made early during that tournament. In my first match of the day, I was tired. I had slept for only three hours after a late night in the city with friends. I am not a morning person. I did not have time to find the nearest Starbucks. I could not find any dollar bills to buy a Diet Pepsi. I could not find my Visine. I was hungover—gin, which doesn't settle well with me the day after. My stomach kept turning uncomfortably. I was drowsy. If I closed my eyes, I would simply fall into an uncomfortable sleep. I was a mess.

I was the fifth seed in a field of twenty-one, so I was stupidly pleased with myself to still be seeded so high after the previous tournament. My opponent was unseeded and had no ranking so I mistakenly assumed she was a novice player.[29] From the outset I was certain I would win the match handily even though I was hungover and barely able to cope with the dryness of my eyeballs.

Toward the end of the match, I played BROASTED and BO

---

[28] That was a pretty little lie.

[29] I willfully ignored the memory of the outcome of my first tournament, where I won as the lowest-seeded player, without a ranking.

for a Triple Word Score. My opponent challenged, and she won. When you challenge multiple words, though, the computer only tells you if the word combination is good or bad. If the combination is bad, it will not tell you if one or all the words in the combination are bad. I thought, because I was mentally incapacitated, that BO must not be a valid word. I may not know my three-letter words, but I do know my two-letter words. I was confused. I was not at my best.

A couple moves later, I played BROASTED and BA in the same location. My opponent's eyes widened. She stared at me like I was the stupidest person alive. In that moment, I hated every last cell in her body.

"You're going to do *that* again?" she asked, but it wasn't quite a question.

It was her tone that totally set me off. I had just laid down the tiles, thereby making it crystal clear I was going to make the same, ridiculous, amateurish mistake twice. What did she fail to understand?

In my defense, I was so convinced BROASTED[30] was a word, because it actually *is* a word, that I remained unwavering in my commitment to play the word. Had I succeeded, I would have earned 87 points. As we walked to the challenge computer, I could feel her laughing at me. I wanted to cry, but my eyes were still so terribly dry, and also there is no crying at a Scrabble tournament unless you're in the bathroom and you have carefully checked all the stalls to make sure you are alone.

The next time I see New Nemesis, I must explain, "I am not the idiot you think I am, or at least I am not an idiot for the reasons you think."

The match was a massacre. The final score: 500–263. That

---

[30] "Broasting" is a proper noun, and proper nouns are not valid Scrabble words. Broasting is a trademarked method of cooking chicken.

match set the tone for the tournament. Time and again, lower-ranked players taught me painful lessons. Time and again, I was humbled. At the end of the tournament, after the prizes were handed out and we applauded each of the winners and the players who had played the highest-scoring words, we losers stood in small clumps of failure bemoaning how terribly we had played while those who played well tried not to gloat. Their modesty was good-naturedly false. We packed up our boards, and the excitement of the tournament slowly seeped out of our muscles. We shook hands and bid one another good-bye until the next club meeting or tournament. We were no longer adversaries.

[GENDER & SEXUALITY]

How to Be Friends with Another Woman

1. Abandon the cultural myth that all female friendships must be bitchy, toxic, or competitive. This myth is like heels and purses—pretty but designed to SLOW women down.

1A. This is not to say women aren't bitches or toxic or competitive sometimes but rather to say that these are not defining characteristics of female friendship, especially as you get older.

1B. If you find that you are feeling bitchy, toxic, or competitive toward the women who are supposed to be your closest friends, look at why and figure out how to fix it and/or find someone who can help you fix it.

2. A lot of ink is given over to mythologizing female friendships as curious, fragile relationships that are always intensely fraught. Stop reading writing that encourages this mythology.

3. If you are the kind of woman who says, "I'm mostly friends

with guys," and act like you're proud of that, like that makes you closer to being a man or something and less of a woman as if being a woman is a bad thing, see Item 1B. It's okay if most of your friends are guys, but if you champion this as a commentary on the nature of female friendships, well, soul-search a little.

3A. If you feel like it's hard to be friends with women, consider that maybe women aren't the problem. Maybe it's just you.

3B. I used to be this kind of woman. I'm sorry to judge.

4. Sometimes, your friends will date people you cannot stand. You can either be honest about your feelings or you can lie. There are good reasons for both. Sometimes you will be the person dating someone your friends cannot stand. If your man or woman is a scrub, just own it so you and your friends can talk about more interesting things. My go-to explanation is "I am dating an asshole because I'm lazy." You are welcome to borrow it.

5. Want nothing but the best for your friends because when your friends are happy and successful, it's probably going to be easier for you to be happy.

5A. If you're having a rough go of it and a friend is having the best year ever and you need to think some dark thoughts about that, do it alone, with your therapist, or in your diary so that when you actually see your friend, you can avoid the myth discussed in Item 1.

5B. If you and your friend(s) are in the same field and you can collaborate or help each other, do this without shame. It's not your fault your friends are awesome. Men invented nepotism and practically live by it. It's okay for women to do it too.

5C. Don't tear other women down, because even if they're not your friends, they are women and this is just as important. This is not to say you cannot criticize other women, but understand the difference between criticizing constructively and tearing down cruelly.

5D. Everybody gossips, so if you are going to gossip about your friends, at least make it fun and interesting. As a corollary, never say "I never lie" or "I never gossip" because you are lying.

5E. Love your friends' kids even if you don't want or like children. Just do it.

6. Tell your friends the hard truths they need to hear. They might get pissed about it, but it's probably for their own good. Once, my best friend told me to get my love life together and demanded an action plan, and it was irritating but also useful.

6A. Don't be totally rude about truth telling, and consider how much truth is actually needed to get the job done. Finesse goes a long way.

6B. These conversations are more fun when preceded by an emphatic "GIRL."

7. Surround yourself with women you can get sloppy drunk with who won't draw stupid things on your face if you pass out, and who will help you puke if you overcelebrate, and who will also tell you if you get sloppy drunk too much or behave badly when you are sloppy drunk.

8. Don't flirt, have sex, or engage in emotional affairs with your friends' significant others. This shouldn't need to be said, but it needs to be said. That significant other is an asshole, and you don't want to be involved with an asshole who's used goods. If you want to be with an asshole, get a fresh asshole of your very own. They are abundant.

9. Don't let your friends buy ugly outfits or accessories you don't want to look at when you hang out. This is just common sense.

10. When something is wrong and you need to talk to your

friends and they ask you how you are, don't say "Fine." They know you're lying and it irritates them and a lot of time is wasted with the back-and-forth of "Are you sure?" and "Yes?" and "Really?" and "I AM FINE." Tell your lady friends the truth so you can talk it out and either sulk companionably or move on to other topics.

11. If four people are dining, split the check evenly four ways. We are adults now. We don't need to add up what each person had anymore. If you're high rolling, just treat everyone and rotate who treats. If you're still in the broke stage, do what you have to do.

12. If a friend sends a crazy e-mail needing reassurance about love, life, family, or work, respond accordingly and in a timely manner even if it is just to say, "GIRL, I hear you." If a friend sends you like thirty crazy e-mails needing reassurance about the same damn shit, be patient because one day that's going to be you tearing up Gmail with your drama.

13. My mother's favorite saying is *"Qui se ressemble s'assemble."* Whenever she didn't approve of who I was spending time with, she'd say this ominously. It means, essentially, you are whom you surround yourself with.

Girls, Girls, Girls

A television show about my twenties would follow the life of a girl who is lost, literally and figuratively. There wouldn't be a laugh track. The show would open deep in my *lost year*—the year I drop out of college and disappear. With no ability to cope and no way to ask for help, the main character—me—is completely crazy. She makes a spectacular mess.

A lot happens in the pilot. About ten days before the start of junior year, my character gets on a plane and abandons everything. She runs away to Arizona by way of a trip to San Francisco with a much older man she has only corresponded with via the Internet. We're talking about the old-fashioned Internet, in 1994—a 2400-baud modem or some such. It is a small miracle she isn't killed. She cuts off all contact with her family, her friends, or anyone who thought they knew her. She has no money, no plan, a suitcase, and a complete lack of self-regard. It is real drama.

The rest of that first season is equally dramatic. Before long, she finds a seedy job doing about the only thing she's qualified to

do, working from midnight to eight in a nondescript office building. She sits in a little, windowless booth and talks to strangers
on the phone. She drinks diet soda from a plastic cup, sometimes
with vodka, and does crossword puzzles. It is so easy to talk to
strangers. She loves the job until she doesn't.

There is an interesting cast. Her coworkers are girls who are
also messy. They are different races, from different places, but all
lost together. They give themselves names like China and Bubbles
and Misty, and at the end of a long shift they hardly remember
who belongs to which name. My character has many different
names. She wakes up and says, "Tonight, I'm Delilah, Morgan,
Becky." She wants to be anyone else.

This is late-night television. Cable. China does heroin in the
bathroom at work. Sometimes, she leaves a burnt strip of tin-
foil on the counter. The manager calls them all into her office
and yells. The girls will never rat China out. Bubbles has baby
daddy problems. Sometimes, her man drops her off at work and
girls smoking in the parking lot watch as Bubbles and her man
yell at each other, terrible things. In another episode, the baby
daddy drops Bubbles off and they practically fuck in the front
seat. Misty has been on her own since she was sixteen. She is
very skinny and has scabs all over her arms and never seems to
wash her hair. After most shifts, the girls go to Jack in the Box
and then lie out by the pool of the house where my character is
staying. The girls tell my character how lucky she is to live in a
house with air-conditioning. They have swamp coolers and live
in crappy apartments. My character stares up at the sun from the
diving board where she loves to stretch out and thinks, bitterly,
Yes, I am so fucking lucky. She is too young to realize that compared to them she is lucky. She ran away but still has something
to run back to when she is ready. My character doesn't come to
this realization until the season finale.

Every woman has a series of episodes about her twenties, her girlhood, and how she came out of it. Rarely are those episodes so neatly encapsulated as an episode of, say, *Friends*, or a romantic comedy about boy meeting girl.

Girls have been written and represented in popular culture in many different ways. Most of these representations have been largely unsatisfying because they never get girlhood quite right. It is not possible for girlhood to be represented wholly—girlhood is too vast and too individual an experience. We can only try to represent girlhood in ways that are varied and recognizable. All too often, however, this doesn't happen.

We put a lot of responsibility on popular culture, particularly when some pop artifact somehow distinguishes itself as not terrible. In the months and weeks leading up to the release of *Bridesmaids*, for example, there was a great deal of breathless talk about the new ground the movie was breaking, how yes, indeed, women *are* funny. Can you believe it? There was a lot of pressure on that movie. *Bridesmaids* had to be good if any other women-driven comedies had any hope of being produced. This is the state of affairs for women in entertainment—everything hangs in the balance all the time.

Bridesmaids could not afford to fail, and didn't. The movie received a positive critical reception (the *New York Times* referred to the movie as "unexpectedly funny") and did well at the box office. Critics lauded the cast for their fresh performances. Some people even used the word "revolution" for the change the movie would bring for women in comedy.

A revolution is a sudden, radical, or complete change—a fundamental shift in the way of thinking about or visualizing something. Could one movie really be responsible for a *revolution*? *Bridesmaids* is a good movie, one I really enjoyed—smart humor, good acting, a relatable plot, a somewhat realistic portrayal of women in a cinematic wasteland where representations of women are generally appalling. *Bridesmaids* isn't perfect, but given the

unfair responsibility placed on the movie, the burden was shoul-
dered well. At the same time, the movie did not bring about radical change, particularly when, as Michelle Dean discusses in her
review of the movie for *The Awl*, many of the familiar tropes we
see in comedies and in the depictions of women are present in
Bridesmaids. She notes that the portrayal of Melissa McCarthy's
character, Megan, in particular, treads familiar ground: "Almost
every joke was designed to rest on her presumed hideousness,
and her ribald but unmistakably 'butch' sexuality was grounded
primarily in her body type and an aversion to makeup." Within
this context, considering *Bridesmaids* revolutionary is a bit much.

Why do we put so much responsibility on movies like *Bridesmaids*? How do we get to a place where a movie, one movie, can
be considered revolutionary for women?

There's another woman-oriented pop artifact being asked to
shoulder a great deal of responsibility these days: Lena Dunham's
Girls, a television series on HBO. The show debuted to a lot of
hype. Critics almost universally embraced Dunham's vision and
the way she chronicles the lives of four twenty-something girls
navigating that interstitial time between graduating from college
and growing up.

I am not the target audience for *Girls*. I was not particularly
enthralled by the first three episodes or the first two seasons, but
the show gave me a great deal to think about. That counts for
something. The writing is often smart and clever. I laughed a few
times during each episode and recognize the ways in which this
show is breaking new ground. I admire how Dunham's character, Hannah Horvath, doesn't have the typical body we normally
see on television. There is some solidity to her. We see her eat,
enthusiastically. We see her fuck. We see her endure the petty
humiliations so many young women have to endure. We see the
life of one kind of real girl and that is important.

It's awesome that a twenty-five-year-old woman gets to write, direct, and star in her own show for a network like HBO. It's just as sad that this is so *revolutionary* it deserves mention.

A generation is a group of individuals born and living contemporaneously. In the pilot, Hannah Horvath is explaining to her parents why she needs them to keep supporting her financially. She says, "I think I might be the voice of my generation. Or at least, a generation . . . somewhere." We have so many expectations; we're so thirsty for authentic representations of girls that we only hear the first half of that statement. We hear that *Girls* is supposed to speak for all of us.

At times, I find *Girls* and the overall premise to be forced. Amidst all the cleverness, I want the show to have a stronger emotional tone. I want to feel something genuine, and rarely has the show given me that opportunity. Too many of the characters seem like caricatures, where more nuance would better serve both the characters and their story lines. In the first season, for example, Hannah's not-boyfriend, Adam, is a depressing, disgusting composite of every asshole every woman in her twenties has ever dated. We would get the point if he were even half the asshole. The pedophile fantasy Adam shares at the beginning of the "Vagina Panic" episode is cringe-worthy. The ironic rape joke Hannah makes during her job interview in that same episode is cringe-worthy. It all feels very "Look at me! I am edgy!" Maybe that's the point. I cannot be sure. More often than not, the show is trying too hard to do too much, but that's okay. This show should not have to be perfect.

Girls reminds me of how terrible my twenties were—being lost and awkward, having terrible sex with terrible people, being perpetually broke, eating ramen. I am not nostalgic for that time. I had no money and no hope. Like the girls in *Girls*, I was never really on the verge of destitution but I lived a generally crappy life. There was nothing romantic about the experience. I understand why many young women find the show so relatable, but

watching the show makes me slightly nauseated and exceptionally grateful to be in my thirties.

As you might expect, the discourse surrounding *Girls* has
been remarkably extensive and vigorous—nepotism, privilege,
race. Dunham has given us a veritable trifecta of reasons to dissect her show.

Lena Dunham is, indeed, the daughter of a well-known artist,
and the principal cast comprises the daughters of other well-
known figures like Brian Williams and David Mamet. People
resent nepotism because it reminds us that sometimes success
really is whom you know. This nepotism is mildly annoying, but
it is not new or remarkable. Many people in Hollywood make
entire careers out of hiring their friends for every single project.
Adam Sandler has done it for years. Judd Apatow does it with
such regularity you don't need to consult IMDb to know whom
he will cast in his projects.

Girls also represents a very privileged existence—one where
young women's New York lifestyles can be subsidized by their
parents, where these young women can think about art and
unpaid internships and finding themselves and writing memoirs
at twenty-four. Many people are privileged, and again, it's easy to
resent that because the level of privilege expressed in the show
reminds us that sometimes, success really starts with where you
come from. *Girls* is a fine example of someone writing what she
knows and the painful limitations of doing so.

One of the most significant critiques of *Girls* is the relative absence of race. The New York where *Girls* takes place is much like
the New York where *Sex and the City* was set—a mythical city
completely void of the rich diversity of the very real New York.
The critique is legitimate, and people across many publications
have written deeply felt essays about why it is damaging for a

show like *Girls* to completely negate certain experiences and realities. In the second season, *Girls* tried and failed to bring race into the show in a relevant way. During the premiere, Hannah has a black boyfriend and it's handled fairly well. The boyfriend, Sandy, is conservative, and there's a clever moment in which Hannah claims she doesn't see race, thereby exposing that she is not nearly as evolved as she might believe. The episode is smart, but not smart enough because it misses the point—clever defiance does not a diversity problem address.

Every girl or once-was-girl has a show that would be best for her. In *Girls* we finally have a television show about girls who are awkward and say terribly inappropriate things, are ill equipped to set boundaries for themselves and have no idea who they're going to be in a few years. We have so many expectations for this show because *Girls* is a significant shift in what we normally see about girls and women. While critics, in their lavish attention, have said Dunham's show is speaking to an entire generation of girls, there are many of us who recognize that the show is only speaking to a narrow demographic within a generation.

Maybe the narrowness of *Girls* is fine. Maybe it's also fine that Dunham's vision of coming-of-age is limited to the kinds of girls she knows. Maybe, though, Dunham is a product of the artistic culture that created her—one that is largely myopic and unwilling to think about diversity critically.

We all have ideas about the way the world should be, and sometimes we forget how the world is. The absence of race in *Girls* is an uncomfortable reminder of how many people lead lives segregated by race and class. The stark whiteness of the cast, their upper-middle-class milieu, and the New York where they live force us to interrogate our own lives and the diversity, or lack thereof, in our social, artistic, and professional circles.

Don't get me wrong. The stark whiteness of *Girls* disturbs and disappoints me. During the first season, I wondered why Hannah and her friends didn't have at least one blipster friend or why Hannah's boss at the publishing house or one or more of the girls' love interests couldn't be an actor of color. The show is so damn literal. Still, *Girls* is not the first show to commit this transgression, and it certainly won't be the last. It is unreasonable to expect Dunham to somehow solve the race and representation problem on television while crafting her twenty-something witticisms and appalling us with sex scenes so uncomfortable they defy imagination.

In recent years, I have enjoyed looking at pictures from literary events, across the country, wondering if I will see a person of color. It's a game I play that I generally win. Whether the event takes place in Los Angeles or New York City or Austin or Portland, more often than not, the audiences at these events are completely white. Sometimes, there will be one or two black people, perhaps an Asian. At most of these literary events I attend, I am generally the only spot of color, even at a large writers' conference like Association of Writers & Writing Programs events. It's not that people of color are deliberately excluded but that they are not *included* because most communities, literary or otherwise, are largely insular and populated by people who know the people they know. This is the uncomfortable truth of our community, and it is disingenuous to be pointing the finger at *Girls* when the show is a pretty accurate reflection of many artistic communities.

There's more, though, to this intense focus on privilege and race and *Girls*. Why is *this* show being held to the higher standard when there are so many television shows that have long ignored race and class or have flagrantly transgressed in these areas?

There are so many terrible shows on television representing women in sexist, stupid, silly ways. Movies are even worse. Movies take one or two anemic ideas about women, caricature them, and shove those caricatures down our throats. The moment we see a pop artifact offering even a sliver of something different—say, a woman who isn't a size zero or who doesn't treat a man as the center of the universe—we cling to it desperately because that representation is all we have. There are all kinds of television shows and movies about women but how many of them make women recognizable?

There are few opportunities for people of color to recognize themselves in literature, in theater, on television, and in movies. It's depressingly easy for women of color to feel entirely left out when watching a show like *Girls*. It is rare that we ever see ourselves as anything but the *sassy* black friend or the nanny or the secretary or the district attorney or the magical negro—roles relegated to the background and completely lacking in authenticity, depth, or complexity.

One of the few equivalents to *Girls* we've ever had was *Girlfriends*, created by Mara Brock Akil. *Girlfriends* debuted in 2000 and ran for 172 episodes. It followed the lives and close friendships of four black women in Los Angeles—Joan (Tracee Ellis Ross), Maya (Golden Brooks), Lynn (Persia White), and Toni (Jill Marie Jones). I particularly admire how the show rarely made race its focal point. Joan, Maya, Lynn, and Toni simply lived their lives. They were all professionals (a lawyer, a writer and secretary, a real estate agent, and an artist/actress/whimsy of the week) who dealt with job stresses, romantic troubles, romantic successes, and new adventures, and tried to become better women. It took me years to appreciate *Girlfriends* and I'm not sure why, but once I fell in love with the show, I fell hard. Finally, I was able to recognize something about myself in popular culture. The writing was smart and funny, and the show did a good job of depicting the lives of women of color in their late twenties and thirties. The show wasn't perfect, but the women were human and they were portrayed humanely. *Girlfriends*, to be sure, *is* a show that never received the critical attention or audience it deserved, but it lasted for eight seasons and still has a very dedicated fan base of women who remain so relieved to see themselves in some small way.

Women of color come of age and have the same experiences Dunham depicts in her shows, but we rarely see those stories because they don't fit the popular imagination's rendering of Other girlhood, which is generally nonexistent in popular culture. At least there have been a few shows for black women to recognize themselves—the aforementioned *Girlfriends, Living Single, A Different World, The Cosby Show*. What about other women of color? For Hispanic and Latina women, Indian women, Middle Eastern women, Asian women, their absence in popular culture is even more pronounced, their need for relief just as palpable and desperate.

The incredible problem *Girls* faces is that all we want is everything from each movie or television show or book that promises to offer a new voice, a relatable voice, an important voice. We want, and rightly so, to believe our lives deserve to be new, relatable, and important. We want to see more complex, nuanced depictions of what it really means to be whoever we are or were or hope to be. We just want so much. We just need so much.

I'm more interested in a show called *Grown Women* about a group of friends who finally have great jobs and pay all their bills in a timely manner but don't have any savings and still deal with sloppy love lives and hangovers on Monday morning at work. That show doesn't exist, though, because stability holds little allure for the popular imagination and Hollywood rarely acknowledges women of a certain age. Until that show comes along or I decide to write it, we have to deal with what we have.

I Once Was Miss America

In 1984, Vanessa Williams became Miss America. She would later have to step down because of a nude photo scandal, but when she was first crowned it was an amazing moment for black girls everywhere. Williams was the first black woman to wear the Miss America crown in the pageant's sixty-three-year history. I was not the kind of girl who cared much about pageants or being a beauty queen, but watching Williams and her perfect cheekbones and glittering teeth as she accepted the crown gave girls like me ideas. That moment made us believe we too could be beautiful.

While Vanessa Williams offered black girls a new image of who the All-American Girl could be, the more traditional image of the All-American Girl could be found in Sweet Valley, an idyllic town in sunny Southern California where the lawns are perfectly manicured. Everyone is fit and beautiful and successful. As is the case in most perfect places, life in Sweet Valley is episodic. There is a narrative arc to each day or week or month, always a valuable lesson to be learned from life's experiences. The endings, in Sweet Valley, are mostly happy. The meek inherit. All good things come to those who wait. There is nowhere in the world like Sweet Valley.

Elizabeth and Jessica Wakefield are the sweethearts of Sweet Valley. They are blond and thin and perfect even with all their human flaws. The Wakefield sisters are twins—twice the perfection. Elizabeth is the good twin, and Jessica is the more rebellious twin. Jessica is a bad, bad girl, even though in Sweet Valley, a bad girl is never quite that bad. The sisters wear matching lavaliere necklaces, and they drive a red Fiat. Elizabeth and Jessica love each other and are best friends, but they are also rivals. Sisters are complicated even when they are perfect.

Elizabeth is responsible and universally adored for her sweetness and patience. She wants to be a journalist. She loves Todd Wilkins, a tall, handsome, and popular basketball player. She works on the school paper and is a cheerleader—smart and athletic, the perfect combination.

Jessica likes boys and partying. She is charming and enjoys gossip, flirting, and shopping. She loves to borrow Elizabeth's clothes, and Elizabeth puts up with it because you cannot say no to Jessica Wakefield. She's a cheerleader too, and although she comes off as a bit of an airhead, Jessica has depth and intelligence. She sometimes says unkind things, but that's because she is impulsive and has a bit of a temper. She's all emotion. Jessica is the kind of girl who gives in to her impulses, while Elizabeth controls her urges, at least most of the time.

The Wakefield twins aren't real; they are the main characters of the Sweet Valley High series. I started reading the Sweet Valley High books when I was eight or nine years old. I was cross-eyed and wore thick bifocals. Other than my younger brother, I was the only black kid in school, so I was going to be noticed even though I wanted very much to go unnoticed. I was shy and awkward and didn't know how to fix myself. My hair was wild, stood on end, earning me the inexplicable nicknames Hair, Beard, and Mustache even though I had neither a beard nor a mustache. My classmates also called me Don King. I looked nothing like Don King. He's a man, for one. I was told my parents "talked funny," which I later realized was a reference to their thick Haitian accents, which I did not hear until they were pointed out to me, and then suddenly those accents were all I heard. I read books while I walked to school. I had the strangest laugh—somewhat halted and tentative—and a bit of a bucktooth situation. I regularly wore overalls by choice and didn't *really* know any curse words, so that should give you a sense of where I was on the social ladder—reaching for the bottom rung.

When I first started reading Sweet Valley High books, I wanted girls like the Wakefield twins to love me. I wanted the handsome boys who chased girls like those Wakefield twins to love me. I wanted the popular kids to pull me into the shelter of their golden embrace and make me popular too. Popularity is contagious. Many movies from the 1980s bear this theory out. I had hope, is what I'm saying, though certainly that hope was fragile.

There was one particular group of golden, popular kids at my school. They're in every school, an interchangeable infestation of good genes and big smiles and perfect hair and Guess or Girbaud jeans. I don't remember much about grade school, but I remember the first and last names of the popular kids. If I returned to my childhood neighborhood, I could point out their houses and other geographical points of interest. I watched the popular kids all the time, trying to figure out how to breathe the air in their atmosphere. They were so *American* and, therefore, exotic because they had freedoms I did not. I was a different kind of American. I had conservative Haitian parents who wanted the best for their kids but were also very wary of American permissiveness. I was American at school and Haitian at home. This required negotiating a fine balance, and I am a clumsy person.

There is nothing more desperate and unrequited than the love an unpopular girl nurtures for the cool kids. One day, the kids in the popular clique were teasing me, about what, I do not remember. I got angrier and angrier as they taunted me, not only because they were teasing me but also because I was so painfully aware of the gaping distance between where we were and where I wanted us to be—walking through the mall, arm in arm, or sharing secrets at a slumber party, or gossiping about cute boys. I liked the mall. I had secrets. I liked cute boys.

That day, though, I needed to come up with a snappy retort to show them they couldn't push me around, to show them I was cool too, to stand my ground. I pointed my fingers at them like Miss Celie laying a curse on Mister in *The Color Purple*, and I shouted, "One day, just you wait and see. I'm going to become Miss America." That was my mother's nickname for me, Miss America. I'm her beloved firstborn, her first child born in these United States. I loved my nickname. Those popular kids laughed and laughed. For the rest of that year and into the next, they teased me mercilessly about being Miss America, asking how my campaign was going, making comments about sashes and crowns, prancing around in front of me doing the Miss America wave. They incorporated props. Those kids made it clear I didn't have a shot in hell at the crown, but I'm stubborn and Vanessa Williams had won Miss America so I began to sincerely believe I was going to become Miss America. I reminded my classmates of my belief regularly, which only fueled their petty torments. I have no idea where I was going with that strategy.

The Sweet Valley High books were extremely popular when I was young, and most girls immediately identified as an Elizabeth or a Jessica. Most of the people who knew me would assume I was an Elizabeth, minus her popularity, but I wasn't. In my head and in my heart, I was a bad girl: misunderstood and interesting. I was a Jessica—a girl who was confident and sexy and smart, a girl everyone wanted to be around. I was the future Miss America, ordained by my mother and Vanessa Williams.

I always knew there was something unnatural about Sweet Valley. I did not care. I still don't. I was well aware not everyone lives in a perfect suburb with perfect parents leading perfect lives. I had been to Haiti, seen incomprehensible poverty with my own eyes, so I knew my relatively good fortune was an accident of birth. I knew there is rarely such a thing as a happy ending. I understood that the Sweet Valley High books espouse an unrealistic, narrow ideal of beauty (blond, white, thin) and that any town where everyone looks and acts the same is not to be trusted. The one time a citizen of Sweet Valley (Steven Wakefield, the twins' older brother) dated interracially, that relationship lasted for only one book (#94) because the couple decided, in the end, that they were too different. I also knew that verdict was suspect.

Like many writers, I lived inside of books as a child. Inside books I could get away from the impossible things I had to deal with. When I read I was never lonely or tormented or scared. I read everything I could get my hands on, and my parents indulged and encouraged me. They were strict about things like television and grades, but they never censored my reading material or questioned my love of Sweet Valley. We moved around a lot for my father's job, but Sweet Valley never moved and the people never changed. The kids in Sweet Valley were a constant, and in a small, poignant way, they were my friends.

I waited for new Sweet Valley High books the way other kids waited for new comics or movie releases. Each time my mother took me to the mall, I went straight to Waldenbooks and quickly scanned the shelves in the Young Adult section, wondering what the twins and their friends and enemies would get into next. When the series began churning out thick super editions, I could have died and gone to Sweet Valley heaven. As my collection of Sweet Valley High books grew, I maintained the set meticulously, keeping the books in perfect order and pristine condition. Sometimes my brothers would sneak into my room and reorder the books. Minor skirmishes would erupt between us that often ended with me doing something like burying their favorite toys in the backyard. I was quite serious about my Sweet Valley High books.

Nostalgia is powerful. It is natural, human, to long for the past, particularly when we can remember our histories as better than they were. Life happens faster than I can comprehend. I am nearly forty, but my love of Sweet Valley remains strong and immediate. When I read the books now, I know I'm reading garbage, but I remember what it was like to spend my afternoons in Sweet Valley, hanging out with the Wakefield twins and Enid Rollins and Lila Fowler and Bruce Patman and Todd Wilkins and Winston Egbert. The nostalgia I feel for these books and these people makes my chest ache.

When I learned Francine Pascal was releasing *Sweet Valley Confidential*, an update to the Sweet Valley High series, set ten years into the future, I basically lost my shit and began obsessing about what was going down in Sweet Valley. I began marking the days until the book's release.

At 2:30 in the morning, on the day of its release, *Sweet Valley Confidential* downloaded to my Kindle. I spent the next three hours reading. There wasn't a page I turned, electronically speaking, where I didn't think *Girrrrrrrrl*, laugh aloud, or mutter "Mmmm." Reading this book was a vocal and emotional experience. I went to work, and when I got home, I read *Sweet Valley Confidential* again. The book was, as you might imagine, terrible, an insult to the memory of the original Sweet Valley High series. As I read, I kept thinking, *They could have called me. I work cheap.* "They," of course, have no idea who I am, but still, it hurt to know how many fans of Sweet Valley are out there, fans who could have written this book in the manner it deserved.

Sweet Valley Confidential makes you understand why so many people are lamenting the death of publishing. The book is bewildering. On a fundamental level, the writing is extremely bad. The word "appalling" comes to mind. The narrative structure is so deeply flawed it physically pained me. The story jumps from the present told in third person past tense to the past told in first person present tense. Sometimes the narrator changes from one twin to the next, and then other times the narrator is another, lesser character. I have spent more time than I care to admit trying to make sense of these authorial choices. Every so often, some sort of Web 2.0, social media reference is dropped into the narrative as if Pascal is saying, "Look, I'm still relevant! Twitter! Facebook! Oh my!"

The twins and their friends are all a decade older, but there is little evidence of any emotional maturity. You would expect that the twins, as women in their late twenties, would have sex lives, but most of the sex in the book is strangely antiseptic, eroticism from another room, as if the audience is still tween and teen girls. When you do see a bit of Elizabeth's or Jessica's sexual personas, it's written so you can only cringe. Many of the petty grievances from high school linger, and most of the characters come off as the very worst people in the world. The whole enterprise has the feel of caricature. The twins have been written in such a way that makes you think Pascal (who created the series but didn't write any of the original books) has no idea who the Wakefield twins are. Elizabeth and Jessica display behaviors so uncharacteristic that the simplest explanation is that Elizabeth and Jessica have both been lobotomized. I don't want to give too much away, but throughout the novel, we're supposed to feel sorry for Elizabeth. However, she is portrayed as such a self-indulgent, self-pitying sop of a woman you start to feel like she deserves her misery. Jessica, on the other hand, we're supposed to hate, but she's professionally successful and in a loving relationship and has a personality. She seems rational and interesting and as vibrant as ever. She makes mistakes but in a really human, endearing way. When you find yourself rooting for the person you're supposed to hate because of the overall plot of the novel, the narrative has taken a drastically wrong turn. (For the record, TEAM JESSICA 4 EVA!)

One thing remains gloriously the same, though: the gratuitous descriptions of Elizabeth and Jessica's beauty.

In *Sweet Valley High 1: Double Love*, the twins are described thusly:

> *With their shoulder-length blond hair, blue-green eyes, and perfect California tans, Elizabeth and Jessica were exact duplicates of one another, down to the tiny dimples in their left cheeks when they smiled. Each wore a gold lavaliere around her neck—matching presents from their parents on their sixteenth birthday last June.*

Twenty-eight years later, in *Sweet Valley Confidential*, the twins look much the same, though their description has aged finely, like wine:

> *Like the twins of that poem, Elizabeth and Jessica Wakefield appeared interchangeable, if you considered only their faces.*
>
> *And what faces they were.*
>
> *Gorgeous. Absolutely amazing. The kind you couldn't stop looking at. Their eyes were shades of aqua that danced in the light like shards of precious stones, oval and fringed with thick, light brown lashes long enough to cast a shadow on their cheeks. Their silky blond hair, the cascading kind, fell just below their shoulders. And to complete the perfection, their rosy lips looked as if they were penciled on. There wasn't a thing wrong with their figures, either. It was as if billions of possibilities all fell together perfectly.*
>
> *Twice.*

When I first read the passage from *Sweet Valley Confidential*, I woke someone up with my laughter. I literally applauded because I was so thrilled by the exquisite badness.

To be fair, *Sweet Valley Confidential* could never have satisfied the expectations of those of us who fell in love with the original Sweet Valley High series. Like I said, nostalgia is powerful and that power builds with time; it often reshapes our memories. It's not that the original Sweet Valley High books were the mark of great literature, but that to some preteen and teenage girls, the books were the most familiar and resonant expressions of our angst and our fondest wishes for ourselves, the girls we wanted to become. There is a young girl-heart still throbbing in many of us. Those of us who read *Sweet Valley Confidential* were looking to recapture some of the Sweet Valley magic from our youth.

Despite the book's flaws, the magic was very much there for me. I easily embraced the drama, the absurdity, the wild implausibilities. You would not believe what's going down in Sweet Valley and who has ended up with whom, but let me tell you, it's all a delicious scandal. Someone's gay! Someone betrayed her sister. Someone's living in New York City. Someone got married to a wealthy but controlling man and lived in Europe until she escaped. Someone is engaged to be married and everyone's talking. A guy we all thought was a prince of a man is really just a man. Someone has turned into a real bitch. Someone uses baking to sublimate her sorrow. Someone had cancer. Someone became a real asshole. Someone hasn't changed one little bit. Someone got filthy rich. Someone got filthier rich. Someone died. Someone loves someone else in a tragic, unrequited way. Amidst all the drama, some things in Sweet Valley don't change. There are many happy endings. As mindless, escapist entertainment, *Sweet Valley Confidential* delivers.

I was never going to become Miss America. I know that now. Vanessa Williams and her glittering teeth could only do so much. Nonetheless, I continue to have a very active fantasy life. In one of my more elaborate, embarrassing flights of fancy, I win an Oscar for writing the Best Adapted Screenplay based on my bestselling novel, which has graced the *New York Times* bestseller list for at least fifty-seven weeks. At the Oscar ceremony I am wearing something flawless by a designer with a long, exotic name. My hair and face are beat. I don't trip when I walk up the stairs in my Louboutins to accept my honor. My date is my husband, who is the most handsome, famous movie star in the world. He is madly, uxoriously in love with me, and he beams as I stare into the audience. He will win Best Actor later in the evening because he starred in my movie. That's how we met. In my acceptance speech, I thank my parents and my agents and my famous movie-star husband and my friends. I thank Francine Pascal for creating the land of Sweet Valley and Vanessa Williams for teaching me I could be beautiful. Then I call out the names of the golden, popular kids who never loved me. I raise my Oscar over my head with one hand, and I point my fingers at a camera with the other, once again like Miss Celie laying a curse on Mister. I say, "I once told you I was going to become Miss America. This isn't the Miss America crown, but it's pretty damn close."

As a black girl, as a Haitian girl, I was not supposed to see myself in the Sweet Valley High books, but I did. Perhaps it was because I too lived in the suburbs, perhaps it was because I was looking for the way toward a perfect life and becoming Miss America, but I felt the Sweet Valley stories deeply. I read and reread the books countless times. The drama, recycled plots, and ludicrous circumstances spoke to me profoundly. This may also explain why in high school I become utterly devoted to *Beverly Hills 90210*, which took the Sweet Valley High formula and elevated it to high art. *Sweet Valley Confidential* reminded me of my most awkward years and the silly promise I made to a silly group of kids. The book reminded me of the solace, escape, and quiet joy I found in Sweet Valley. Some experiences are universal. A girl is a girl whether she lives in West Omaha or Sweet Valley. Books are often far more than just books.

Garish, Glorious Spectacles

The green girl likes to watch herself suffer.

—KATE ZAMBRENO, *Green Girl*

In her groundbreaking book *Gender Trouble*, Judith Butler asserts that gender is a performance, an unstable identity that forms through how it is performed over and over. She writes,

> Gender ought not to be construed as a stable identity or locus of agency from which various acts follow; rather, gender is an identity tenuously constituted in time, instituted in an exterior space through a stylized repetition of acts. The effect of gender is produced through the stylization of the body and, hence, must be understood as the mundane way in which bodily gestures, movements, and styles of various kinds constitute the illusion of an abiding gendered self.

While our conceptions of gender have evolved since the publication of *Gender Trouble*, there is a lot to be said for Butler's theory, particularly when it comes to the ways in which women, knowingly or unknowingly, perform femininity and the ways in which women are sometimes trapped by how they are expected to perform their gender.

In popular culture, the world often feels like a stage on which women perform, and no novel in recent memory has captured this performance and how fraught it can be better than Kate Zambreno's *Green Girl*.

The best word to describe *Green Girl* is "searing." The novel is at once a compelling narrative about a young American woman living in London and an indictment of what ails our culture—rampant consumerism, shallow human connection, and, most of all, the cult of beauty and the unbearable and impossible constraints of gender—a culture where women wear their faces as masks, their bodies as shields. Throughout the novel, the green girl is as foolishly bold as she is vulnerable. She inhabits her contradictions in deeply seductive ways.

If, as Butler believes, gender is a performance, *Green Girl* is a novel about a young woman who is learning how to perform her femininity, who is learning the power of it, the fragility. Her education is, at times, painful. The green girl is as vicious as she is vulnerable, and Zambreno deftly exposes both this viciousness and vulnerability in her protagonist. *Green Girl* reveals the intimate awareness many women have about the ways they are on display when they move in public, about the ways they perform their roles as women: "The awareness on the train, the fashion show. The men are always looking, always looking with their flirty eyes. One can shop but does not have to buy. But sometimes life in the spotlight can be difficult. Sometimes she wants to be invisible."

In *Green Girl*, Ruth is playing the part of girl. Her performance, at times, stands in place of her identity. As Ruth realizes, "Sometimes she is struck by the sense that she is someone else's character, that she is saying someone else's lines." The green girl also does one thing and feels another because "the passivity of the green girl masquerades as politeness." She wants to put her fist through a window but doesn't because she knows that's not what is expected of a green girl. She knows she is beautiful but does not necessarily feel her beauty inside. Throughout the novel, these tensions are brightly exposed over and over. At times, the novel makes it seem that to be a green girl is to be in a rather hopeless predicament.

Ruth is a shopgirl responsible for selling a perfume, Desire. She is always on display at work while also part of the scenery. One morning at work, she observes a group of teenage girls: "The girls slinking up the aisles have a rehearsed quality to them, their purses positioned just so on their shoulders, their eyes downcast yet somehow watchful. They cannot escape this self-awareness. They are playing the role of young girls, girls younger than Ruth." There is an irony in Ruth's observations. Throughout the novel, she plays the role of the young woman and her self-awareness (and, at times, self-loathing) is palpable and as inescapable as the self-awareness she sees in those teenage girls.

Zambreno demonstrates the self-absorption and vanity of the green girl, her insecurities, the mask(s) she wears, her conflicting desires. At times, Ruth wants to shield herself from the gaze of strangers. She closes in on herself, tries to occupy as little space as possible whether walking down the street or taking the tube. At other times, she wants to be seen, desired, loved. She is, at one point, willing to exploit herself to an unnamed former lover: "She prays to be preyed upon. She is a deer standing in the middle of the forest road, knees buckling, begging for a predator." Ruth, like so many of us, wants everything, all at once.

Though this is a novel about women, there are, indeed, men in *Green Girl*: the man at work Ruth longs for, the brutal former lover she longs for, the seemingly platonic lover she yearns for until they consummate their relationship at which point she longs for something else. Ruth has desires, but those desires seem largely removed, lacking in immediacy, and rarely do those desires come into sharp relief. When Ruth has sex, it is often in a detached manner, her partners rather incidental to the act, Ruth herself incidental to the act. Ruth has an assignation with a bartender in the supply room of the bar, her detachment finely honed. "She is the voyeur of herself," Ruth observes. And later, when Ruth and the bartender are fucking, "she has seen it all before, as if in a dream. But she is not really there. Not really."

In "The Laugh of the Medusa," Hélène Cixous states, "Woman must put herself into the text—as into the world and into history— by her own movement." *Green Girl* is fascinating for the ways Zambreno puts woman into the text, physically and emotionally:

> *Ruth wants to escape. She wants to escape outside of herself. Everywhere she goes she wants to confide: Do you know what it's like not to be able to shake your own quality? She doesn't want to be. She doesn't want to live. She wants to lose herself, lose herself in the crowd. She is somehow numbed to the horrors of everyday. Images, other images haunt her brain. The violence of life, she observes blankly.*

More than anything, *Green Girl* is relentless in what it reveals about the green girl and her inner life, the emptiness and loneliness, the naked violence of it, how she must swallow it "deep deep inside." The novel makes it seem like there is a green girl inside all of us, as desperately fragile as she is resilient. The green girl is able to understand the damage she does to herself even if she does nothing to prevent it.

If Ruth is woman as green girl rising, Maria Wyeth in Joan Didion's equally scorching *Play It as It Lays* is the green girl as she falls, the green girl as she tires of playing the part of girl, the green girl as she decides to stop playing the part of girl because she no longer has any need (or, perhaps, desire) to do it. Even though *Play It as It Lays* was published in 1970, little has changed when it comes to woman as spectacle. Maria Wyeth is tormented and a bit tragic, but there is tenacity about her. The novel chronicles Maria's descent into madness after having an abortion at the bidding of her estranged husband; her descent is more controlled than you might imagine.

Play It as It Lays reveals a complex web of relationships among Maria and her husband, Carter; their friends Helene and BZ; her lover, Les Goodwin; and her former lover, Ivan Costello, and it also discloses how these people break themselves against one another in rather terrible ways. There is also a young daughter, Kate, suffering from an unspecified condition and living at a facility away from home, a daughter Maria openly yearns for and who is the one person in the novel for whom she demonstrates genuine affection.

Like Ruth, the green girl, Maria, as a never-quite-model-and-actress, is always on display and aware of it, craving the attention as much as she despises it. Living in Hollywood, she is, like Ruth in the store where she works, just another part of the scenery of desperate and drugged women who, as Maria refers to her own beauty, "looked all right" and move through their lives playing the proper parts. Like Ruth, Maria is self-absorbed and selfish, but she has a stronger awareness of these flaws. She enjoys watching a movie she starred in because "the girl on the screen seemed to have a definite knack for controlling her own destiny." Just as Ruth often feels like she is someone else's character, Maria, as an actress, has had opportunities to become someone else's character to similar effect.

As a fading green girl, Maria remains detached. She loves her daughter and mourns her mother, but like with Ruth in *Green Girl*, she approaches most of her relationships clinically, with a bemused detachment. She rarely indicates a genuine interest in preserving her marriage and has little tolerance for the men in her life. When her lover, Les, leaves three messages, she asks her answering service to tell him she hasn't picked up her messages because "she had nothing to say to any of them." After she has an abortion, she meets Les Goodwin and he asks what's wrong with her. She says, "I am just very very very tired of listening to you all." What the people in her life label, throughout the novel, as insanity or selfishness reads quite clearly as weariness—a weariness of playing her part properly, of being on display, of being the ingenue and good green girl.

The literature of abortion is complex. Certainly, there are novels like Richard Brautigan's *The Abortion* and John Irving's *Cider House Rules*, among others. These literary treatments of abortion often struggle to strike the proper balance between narrative and political message. Didion's treatment of the subject is far more nuanced—the *message* does not subsume the story. This is a story about abortion, but it is also a story about what happens to the green girl who changes but does not necessarily become any less powerless, empty, filled with longing.

During the procedure, Maria is dispassionate: "No moment more or less important than any other moment, all the same: the pain as the doctor scraped signified nothing beyond itself, no more constituted the pattern of her life than did the movie on television in the living room of this house in Encino." It is only after, when she realizes she has, perhaps, done something she would rather not have, that the emotional significance begins to affect her, and even then, she does not seem to know what to do with those emotions so she dulls them through the liberal use of barbiturates.

Even though her desires are often muted, Ruth has them. She longs for things even if she does nothing to reach for her desires.

Maria Wyeth longs for things she could not possibly reach for—a dead mother, a sick daughter, an aborted fetus.

Like Ruth, Maria is willing to make herself prey, willing to be woman as victim. In a parking lot where several boys are vandalizing cars, Maria walks right toward them:

> *She kept her eyes steady, her pace even, and when she found herself unlocking the car under their blank gaze it was with extreme deliberation. As she slid into the driver's seat she stared directly at each of them, one by one, and in that instant of total complicity one of them leaned across the hood and raised a hand in recognition of what had passed between them, his palm out, inscribing an arc in the still air.*

When Maria emerges from such situations unscathed, there is a sense of disappointment, that she cannot be freed from her weariness.

Toward the end of *Play It as It Lays*, Maria has a one-night stand with an actor she doesn't even like. As dispassionate as Ruth fucking the bartender, Maria lies still beneath the actor. When he falls asleep, Maria takes his Ferrari and drives to Vegas, near where she is pulled over by a highway patrolman for speeding. The agent she shares with her husband, Freddy, comes to rescue her and finds Maria is "still wearing the silver dress and she was still barefoot and her face was streaked with dust." On the flight back to Los Angeles, Freddy says he doesn't understand *girls* like Maria. He says, "I mean there's something in your behavior, Maria, I would almost go so far as to call it . . . Almost go so far as to call it a very self-destructive personality structure." Maria doesn't bother to respond, and why should she? Freddy only has one idea about *girls like Maria*. He's not interested in trying to understand her as an actual person.

We are left with Maria Wyeth in a psychiatric facility. She has committed a terrible crime. The people in her life think she is crazy, selfish, *self-destructive.* Maria is probably the sanest person in her sad group of lovers and friends. She wants nothing more than to get out and take her daughter and raise her. As the fallen green girl, Maria knows something Ruth could never know. In trying to explain herself, Maria says, "I know what 'nothing' means, and keep on playing."

If Ruth is woman as green girl rising, and Maria Wyeth is the green girl in fall, the women of reality television are the green girls interrupted, green girls at their most garishly exposed, cut open for the cameras, performing the best and worst parts of themselves for attention, to be seen, for love, to be adored, for fame, to be wanted.

Reality television often gives the impression that, like gender, the whole of life is a performance. I love watching that performance—one where people reveal how we are willing to compromise ourselves for something as fleeting as fame. The Los Angeles mansion or the tropical jungle or the fading rock star's tour bus is the stage, and what a stage it is—brightly lit, lurid, encouraging us to see the garish spectacle of life at its most artificially real. I watch it all—the faux highbrow fare of Bravo, the booze-soaked MTV programming, the glossy competition shows on CBS, the sleazy exploitative fare of VH1, and even the off-brand shows on lesser cable networks, like *Bad Girls Club* and *Sister Wives.*

No one shines more luridly on this faux-real stage than a woman. Whether it's a modeling competition, a chance to *compete* for love, a weight-loss challenge, or a look into the lives of an aging magazine publisher's harem, women are often the brightly polished trophies in the display case of reality television. The genre has developed a very successful formula for reducing women to an awkward series of stereotypes about low self-esteem, marital desperation, the inability to develop meaningful relationships with other women, and an obsession with an almost pornographic standard of beauty. When it comes to reality television, women, more often than not, work very hard at performing the part of woman, though their scripts are shamefully, shamefully warped.

Reality Bites Back: The Troubling Truth about Guilty Pleasure TV, by Jennifer Pozner, skewers reality television for its sexist, racist, and dehumanizing tactics in nearly every genre of reality television. While I think of myself as media literate and a feminist, I don't know that any book I've read this year has made me as uncomfortable as *Reality Bites Back* for its incisive examination of what I have often thought of as harmless entertainment programming. I had to question what it says about me that I take so much pleasure in the drama of *The Real Housewives of Beverly Hills* or the drunken, weave-snatching antics of *Rock of Love* or *Flavor of Love.* I, like many others, take pleasure in what Pozner brands "the cathartic display of other people's humiliations." These shows exist because audiences need reminders of the wrong turns our lives might take.

In her analysis, Pozner reveals the many tropes reality television exploits—women as "catty, bitchy, manipulative, and not to be trusted," for example—and how these tropes are coded into every aspect of these shows, from marketing to how the shows are scripted. The green girls interrupted are manipulated into becoming the worst versions of themselves, and while certainly anyone who goes on a reality television show in this day and age has a certain level of reality sophistication, one gets the impression, from Pozner's critique, that these green girls do not have the intimate self-awareness of a Ruth or a Maria Wyeth. They don't have an opportunity to develop this self-awareness because the "reality" of reality television is so heavily constructed these women can only be aware of the artifice surrounding them and the parts they are scripted to play within that artifice.

Perhaps no reality television better exemplifies the green girl interrupted, the green girl wholly aware of the artifice surrounding her and somewhat complicit in maintaining that artifice, than VH1's now defunct "Celebreality" shows *Rock of Love* and *Flavor of Love*. In *Rock of Love*, women vied for the affections of fading rock star Bret Michaels, while in *Flavor of Love*, the women vied for the affections of has-been hype man Flavor Flav of Public Enemy. In each of these shows, the women deftly play the part of bad (green) girl or good (green) girl or good (green) girl gone bad—each pretending the former star is the center of the romantic universe amid freely flowing alcohol, forced interactions designed to create artificial but vicious conflict, writhing on stripper poles, and other luridly spectacular scenes. In *Flavor of Love*, the women don't even keep their real names. Instead, Flav, as the women call him, assigns each woman a new name of his choosing because he cannot be bothered to see the green girl interrupted for who she really is. The names range from the silly (Smiley) to the degrading (Thing 1 and Thing 2). The show's artifice allows these women to easily step into constructed identities through this renaming. The women are undoubtedly exploited, but they often seem resigned to it and willing to revel in that exploitation rather than challenge it.

In both shows, across multiple seasons, these green girls interrupted go through the motions of looking for true love with men who are contributing to the artifice by spouting hollow sentiments and platitudes as a means of seduction while metaphorically winking at the camera to let us know *they* know how unreal their reality is—usually during the unscripted confessionals. The exploitation, and these women's participation in it, continued when many of the women from both shows went on to appear on spin-offs with equally artificial premises like *Rock of Love: Charm School, Charm School with Ricki Lake, I Love Money*, several shows for former *Flavor of Love* contestant New York (a.k.a. Tiffany Pollard), and on and on. During each of these shows, these women rarely demonstrate any self-awareness. Instead, they reveal how intimately aware they are of the artifice around them and what that artifice will bring them (attention, a modicum of fame, money). These green girls interrupted are the parts they must play, and within the context of these shows, they do not evolve beyond those roles. They remain interrupted.

If reality television has any connection to reality, it is that women are often called upon to perform their gender, whether through how they present themselves and their sexuality, how they behave, and how they conform (or don't) to society's expectations for women. The repetition of gender acts in reality television becomes grossly stylized through artificially tanned skin, elaborate hair extensions, dramatic makeup, surgically enhanced bodies, and chemically injected faces. The acts become grossly stylized through bad behavior, often carefully orchestrated by producers. Under the persistent glare of the camera, these women have little choice but to sacrifice themselves for our entertainment. The women of reality television are, perhaps, the greenest of girls, women who revel in watching themselves suffer because they have been so irrevocably interrupted they do not know what else they should do. We can't look away. These women—these interrupted Ruths and Marias—look at their ruin. They are such garish, glorious spectacles.

At the end of *Green Girl*, Ruth wants some kind of rebirth, some way of making herself clean. She wants to "smash that thing that houses me inside of myself." She decides, "I want to go to a church and direct my eyes up high and open my arms open my arms up to the ceiling. And scream. And scream. And scream." She wants to scream in both agony and ecstasy. She wants to lose herself as much as she wants to find herself. The same thing could be said for Maria Wyeth. And, perhaps, the same thing could be said for the women of reality television as they break themselves against one another, against the camera, against the ways they are expected to perform their gender.

What may be most terrifying is just how real reality television is, after all. We say we watch these shows to feel better about ourselves, to have that reassurance that we are not that desperate. We are not that green. But perhaps we watch these shows because in the green girls interrupted, we see, more than anything, the plainest reflections of ourselves, garishly exposed but unfettered.

Not Here to Make Friends

My memory of men is never lit up and illuminated like my memory of women.
—MARGUERITE DURAS, *The Lover*

In my high school yearbook there is a note from a girl who wrote, "I like you even though you are very mean." I do not remember the girl who wrote this note. I do not remember being mean to her, or to anyone, for that matter. I do remember that I was feral in high school, socially awkward, emotionally closed off, completely lost.

Or maybe I don't want to remember being mean because I've changed in the twenty years between then and now. Around my junior year, I went from being quiet and withdrawn to being mean, where mean was saying exactly what I thought and making sarcastic comments relentlessly. Sincerity was dead to me.

I had so few friends it didn't really matter how I behaved. I had nothing to lose. I had no idea what it meant to be likable, though I was surrounded by generally likable people—or, I suppose, I was surrounded by people who were very invested in projecting a likable facade, people who were willing to play by the rules. I had likable parents and brothers. I was the anomaly as a social outcast. Even from a young age I understood that when a girl is unlikable, a girl is a problem. I also understood that I wasn't being intentionally mean. I was being honest (admittedly, without tact), and I was being human. It is either a blessing or a curse that those are rarely likable qualities in a woman.

Inevitably on every reality television program, someone will boldly declare, "I'm not here to make friends." These people do so to establish that they are on a given program to win the nebulous prize or the bachelor's heart or to get the exposure they need to begin their unsteady rise to a modicum of fame. They make this declaration by way of explaining their unlikability or the inevitably unkind edit they're going to receive from the show's producers. It isn't that they are terrible, you see. It's simply that they are not participating in the show to make friends. They are freeing themselves from the burden of likability, or they are, perhaps, freeing us from the burden of guilt for the dislike and eventual contempt we might hold for them.

In the movie *Young Adult*, Charlize Theron stars as Mavis Gary. Nearly every review of the movie raises her character's unlikability, painting her with a bright scarlet *U*. Based on this character's critical reception, an unlikable woman embodies any number of unpleasing but entirely human characteristics. Mavis is beautiful, cold, calculating, self-absorbed, full of odd tics, insensitive, and largely dysfunctional in nearly every aspect of her life. These are, apparently, unacceptable traits for a woman, particularly given the sheer number working in concert. Some reviews go so far as to suggest that Mavis is mentally ill, because there's nothing more reliable than armchair diagnosis by disapproving critics. In his review, Roger Ebert lauds *Young Adult* screenwriter Diablo Cody for making Mavis an alcoholic because "without such a context, Mavis would simply be insane." Ebert and many others require an explanation for Mavis's behavior. They require a diagnosis for her unlikability in order to tolerate her. The simplest explanation, of Mavis as human, will not suffice.

In many ways, likability is a very elaborate lie, a performance, a code of conduct dictating the proper way to be. Characters who don't follow this code become unlikable. Critics who criticize a character's unlikability cannot necessarily be faulted. They are merely expressing a wider cultural malaise with all things unpleasant, all things that dare to breach the norm of social acceptability.

Why is likability even a question? Why are we so concerned with whether, in fact or fiction, someone is likable? *Unlikable* is a fluid designation that can be applied to any character who doesn't behave in a way the reader finds palatable. Lionel Shriver notes, in an essay for the *Financial Times*, that "this 'liking' business has two components: moral approval and affection." We need characters to be lovable while they do right.

Some might suggest that this likability question is a by-product of an online culture in which we reflexively click "Like" or "Favorite" on every status update and bit of personal trivia shared on social networks. Certainly there is a culture of relentless affirmation online, but it would be shortsighted to believe that this desire to be liked, this desire to express what or whom we like, begins or ends with the Internet. I have no doubt that Abraham Maslow has some ideas about this persistent desire, in so many of us, to be liked and, in turn, to belong, to have our deftness at following the proper code of conduct affirmed.

As a writer and a person who has struggled with likability—being likable, wanting to be liked, wanting to belong—I have spent a great deal of time thinking about likability in the stories I read and those I write. I am often drawn to unlikable characters, to those who behave in socially unacceptable ways, say whatever is on their mind, and do what they want with varying levels of regard for the consequences. I want characters to do bad things and get away with their misdeeds. I want characters to think ugly thoughts and make ugly decisions. I want characters to make mistakes and put themselves first without apologizing for it.

I don't even mind unlikable characters whose behavior is psychopathic or sociopathic. This is not to say I condone, for example, murder, but Patrick Bateman, in *American Psycho*, is a very interesting man. There is a psychiatric diagnosis for his unlikability, a deviant pathology, but he has his charms, particularly in his scathing self-awareness. Serial killers are people too, and sometimes they are funny. "My conscience," Bateman thinks in the novel, "my pity, my hopes disappeared a long time ago (probably at Harvard) if they ever did exist."

I want characters to do the things I am afraid to do for fear of making myself more unlikable than I may already be. I want characters to be the most honest of all things—human.

That the question of likability even exists in literary conversations is odd. It implies that we are engaging in a courtship. When characters are unlikable, they don't meet our mutable, varying standards. Certainly we can find kinship in fiction, but literary merit shouldn't be dictated by whether we want to be friends or lovers with those about whom we read.

Frankly, I find "good," purportedly likable characters rather unbearable. Take May Welland in Edith Wharton's *The Age of Innocence.* May's likability is, to be fair, deliberate, a choice Wharton has made so Newland Archer's passion for Countess Olenska is ever more fraught and bittersweet. Still, May is the kind of woman who always does everything right, everything that is expected of her. She is a perfect society lady. She knows how to keep up appearances. Meanwhile, everyone looks down on May's unspoken rival and cousin, the Countess Olenska, a woman who dares to defy social conventions, who dares to not tolerate a terrible marriage, who dares to want real passion in her life even if that passion is found with an unsuitable man.

We're not supposed to like her, but Countess Olenska intrigues me because she is interesting. She stands apart from the blur of social conformity. We're supposed to like, or at least respect, May for being the proper and sweet innocent she carries herself as; but in Wharton's skilled hands, we eventually see that May Welland is as human, and therefore as unlikable, as anyone else. This question of likability would be far more tolerable if all writers were as talented as Edith Wharton, but alas.

Far more pernicious than the characters whose likability serves a greater purpose within a narrative are the characters who are flatly likable. It's a bit silly, but I spend a great deal of time, even now, lamenting the perfection of one Elizabeth Wakefield, one of the two golden twins prominently featured in the popular Sweet Valley High young adult series. Elizabeth is the good girl who always makes the right choices, even when she has to sacrifice her own happiness. She gets good grades. She's a good daughter, sister, and girlfriend. It's boring. Elizabeth's likability is downright loathsome. I am Team Jessica. I prefer Nellie Olesen over Laura Ingalls Wilder.

This matter of likability is largely a futile one. Oftentimes, a likable character is simply designed as such to show that he or she is one who knows how to play by the rules and cares to be seen as playing by the rules. The likable character, like the unlikable character, is generally used to make some greater narrative point.

Often in literary criticism, writers are told that a character isn't likable, as if a character's likability is directly proportional to the quality of a novel's writing. This is particularly true for women in fiction. In literature, as in life, the rules are all too often different for girls. There are many instances in which an unlikable man is billed as an antihero, earning a special term to explain those ways in which he deviates from the norm, the traditionally likable. The list, beginning with Holden Caulfield in *The Catcher in the Rye*, is long. An unlikable man is inscrutably interesting, dark, or tormented, but ultimately compelling, even when he might behave in distasteful ways. This is the only explanation I can come up with for the popularity of, say, the novels of Philip Roth, who is one hell of a writer but who also practically revels in the unlikability of his men, with their neuroses and self-loathing (and, of course, humanity) boldly on display from one page to the next.

When women are unlikable, it becomes a point of obsession in critical conversations by professional and amateur critics alike. Why are these women daring to flaunt convention? Why aren't they making themselves likable (and therefore acceptable) to polite society? In a *Publishers Weekly* interview with Claire Messud about her novel *The Woman Upstairs*, which features a rather "unlikable" protagonist, Nora, who is bitter, bereft, and downright angry about what her life has become, the interviewer said, "I wouldn't want to be friends with Nora, would you? Her outlook is almost unbearably grim." And there we have it. A reader was here to make friends with the characters in a book and she didn't like what she found.

Messud, for her part, had a sharp response for her interviewer.

For heaven's sake, what kind of question is that? Would you want to be friends with Humbert Humbert? Would you want to be friends with Mickey Sabbath? Saleem Sinai? Hamlet? Krapp? Oedipus? Oscar Wao? Antigone? Raskolnikov? Any of the characters in The Corrections? *Any of the characters in* Infinite Jest? *Any of the characters in anything Pynchon has ever written? Or Martin Amis? Or*

*Orhan Pamuk? Or Alice Munro, for that matter? If you're reading
to find friends, you're in deep trouble. We read to find life, in all its
possibilities. The relevant question isn't "Is this a potential friend for
me?" but "Is this character alive?"*

Perhaps, then, unlikable characters, the ones who are the most
human, are also the ones who are the most alive. Perhaps this
intimacy makes us uncomfortable because we don't dare be so
alive.

In *How Fiction Works*, James Wood says,

*A great deal of nonsense is written every day about characters in
fiction—from the side of those who believe too much in character
and from the side of those who believe too little. Those who believe
too much have an iron set of prejudices about what characters are: we
should get to "know" them; . . . they should "grow" and "develop";
and they should be nice. So they should be pretty much like us.*

Wood is correct, in part, but the ongoing question of character likability leaves the impression that what we're looking for in
fiction is an ideal world where people behave in ideal ways. The
question suggests that characters should be reflections not of us,
but of our better selves.

Wood also says, "There is nothing harder than the creation
of fictional character." I can attest to this difficulty, though with
perhaps less hyperbole. I have, indeed, found several other tasks
harder over the years. Regardless, characters are hard to create
because we need to develop people who are interesting enough
to hold a reader's attention. We need to ensure that they are
some measure of credible. We need to make them distinct from
ourselves (and, in the best of all words, from those in our lives,

unless of course there is a need to settle scores). Somehow they need to be well developed enough to carry a plot, or carry a narrative without a plot, or endure the tribulations we writers tend to throw at them with alacrity. It's no wonder so many characters are unlikable, given what they have to put up with.

It is a seductive position writers put the reader in when they create an interesting, unlikable character—they make the reader complicit, in ways that are both uncomfortable and intriguing.

If people with messy lives are the point of certain narratives, if unlikable women are the point of certain narratives, novels like *Battleborn*, *Treasure Island!!!*, *Dare Me*, *Magnificence*, and many others exhibit a delightful excess of purpose, with stories filled with women who are deemed unlikable because they make so-called bad choices, describe the world exactly as they see it, and are, ultimately, honest and breathtakingly alive.

These novels depict women who are clearly not participating in their narratives to make friends and whose characters are the better for it. Freed from the constraints of likability, they are able to exist on and beyond the page as fully realized, interesting, and realistic characters. Perhaps the saying "the truth hurts" is what lies at the heart of worrying over likability or the lack thereof—how much of the truth we're willing to subject ourselves to, how much we are willing to hurt, when we immerse ourselves in the safety of a fictional world.

Sara Levine's *Treasure Island!!!* features a narrator who is unlikable in curious ways. She is utterly self-obsessed, acts without considering consequences, and always makes choices that will benefit herself over others. She is intensely preoccupied with the book *Treasure Island* and sets out to live her life by the book's core values: BOLDNESS, RESOLUTION, INDEPENDENCE, and HORN-BLOWING. As the narrator careens from one self-created disaster to another, she is unrepentant. There is no redemption or lesson learned from misdeeds. There is no apology or moral to the story, and that makes an already incisive and intelligent novel even more compelling.

When you think about it, these core values the narrator in *Treasure Island!!!* seeks to live by—BOLDNESS, RESOLUTION, INDEPENDENCE, and HORN-BLOWING—are characteristics that define how supposedly unlikable women lead their fictional lives.

In Pamela Ribon's *You Take It from Here*, a woman, Smidge, is dying of lung cancer and wants her best friend, Danielle, to essentially finish the job of raising her daughter and being her husband's companion in grief. The book's premise is an interesting one, but what really stands apart is how deeply unlikable Smidge is. She is the kind of person who, it might seem, shouldn't have any friends—bossy, intense, controlling, unrepentant, and manipulative. And yet. She has a best friend, a daughter, a husband, and a community of people who will deeply mourn her when she is gone. Ribon's steadfastness in this character's lack of likability is admirable. She never panders by making Smidge somehow have some kind of epiphany of character simply because she is dying. Ribon is unwavering in what she shows us of Smidge, and the novel is the better for it.

A customer review of *You Take It from Here* on Amazon .com from Danae Savitri states, "I never warmed up to Smidge as a character, thought she suffered from borderline personality disorder, common among people who are charismatic narcissistics, who alternately bully, manipulate, and charm others around them." Instead of judging the book, she calls into question a woman's likability. Again, there is an armchair diagnosis of mental disease. Pathologizing the unlikable in fictional characters is an almost Pavlovian response.

Dare Me, by Megan Abbott, is a book about high school cheerleaders, but it is nothing like what you might expect. Populated by women who act with boldness, resolve, independence, and a prioritizing of the self, these mighty principles from *Treasure Island!!!*, *Dare Me* is both engaging and terrifying because it reveals the fraught intimacy between girls. It's a novel about bodies and striving for perfection and ambition and desire so naked, so palpable, you cannot help but want the deeply flawed women in the book to get what they want, no matter how terribly they go about getting it. The young women at the center of the novel, Beth and Addy, are friends as much as they are enemies. They betray each other and they betray themselves. They commit wrongs, and still they are each other's gravitational center. On the phone, after a drunken night, Beth asks Addy if she remembers

> *how we used to hang on the monkey bars, hooking our legs around each other, and how strong we got and how no one could ever beat us, and we could never beat each other, but we'd agree to each release our hands at the count of three, and that she always cheated, and I always let her, standing beneath, looking up at her and grinning my gap-toothed, pre-orthodontic grin.*

It is a moment that shows us how Addy has always seen Beth plainly, and understood her and loved her nonetheless. Throughout the novel Beth, and Addy to an extent, remains unlikable, remains flawed, but there is no explanation for it, no clear trajectory between cause and effect. Traditional parameters of likability are deftly avoided throughout the novel in moments as honest and no less poignant as these.

Susan Lindley, a widow, has to move on after her husband's tragic death in Lydia Millet's *Magnificence*. From the outset, we know she was unfaithful to her husband. She inherits her uncle's mansion, filled with a rotting taxidermy collection, and sets about making some kind of order, both in the mansion and in her own life. She has a daughter who is involved with her boss and a boyfriend who is married to another woman. She feels responsible for her husband's death but is matter-of-fact in reconciling herself to this. "Was she relieved, slut that she was?" Susan thinks. "Was there something in her that was relieved by any of this? If anyone could admit such a thing, she should be able to. She was not only a slut but a killer." Susan does go on to acknowledge that she feels a profound absence in the loss of her husband, a "freedom of nothing," and throughout the novel she indulges in this freedom; she embraces it.

So much of *Magnificence* is grounded solely in Susan's experiences, her awkward perceptions of the world she has created and continues to create for herself. We also have the pleasure of seeing a woman in her late forties as a deeply sexual being who is equally unashamed in her want for material things as she becomes more and more attached to the mansion she has inherited. Though the prose often gives over to lush excess and meditation, what remains compelling is this woman who reveals little remorse for her infidelities and the ways she tends to fail the people in her life. In a lesser novel, such remorse would be the primary narrative thrust, but in *Magnificence* we see how a woman, one deemed unlikable by many, is able to exist and be part of a story that expands far beyond remorse and the kinds of entrapments that could hold likable characters back. We are able to see just what the freedom of nothing looks like.

The short story collection *Battleborn*, by Claire Vaye Watkins, contains many stories with seemingly unlikable women. As much as the stories are about place, all set, in some form, in the desert of the American West, several stories are about women and their strength, where their strength comes from, and how that strength can fail in unbearably human ways. The phrase "battle born" is, in fact, Nevada's state motto—meant to represent the state's strength, forged from struggle. In perhaps the most powerful story, "Rondine al Nido," there is an epigraph at the beginning. Normally, I do not care for epigraphs. I don't want my reading of a story to be framed by the writer in such an overt way. This story's epigraph, though, is from the *Bhagavad Gita*, and reads, "Now I am become Death, the destroyer of worlds." From the outset we know that only ruin lies ahead, and the story becomes a matter of learning just how that ruin comes about. We learn of a woman who "walks out on a man who in the end, she'll decide, didn't love her enough, though he in fact did love her, but his love wrenched something inside him, and this caused him to hurt her." Really, though, this is a story about when the woman was a girl, sixteen, with a friend, Lena, the kind who would follow the narrator, "our girl," wherever she went. There is an evening in Las Vegas, and an incident in a hotel room with some boys the girls meet, one that will irrevocably change the friendship, one that could have been avoided if a flawed young woman didn't make the wrong choice, the choice that makes the story everything.

Perhaps the most unlikable woman in recent fictional memory is Amy in Gillian Flynn's *Gone Girl*, a woman who goes to extraordinary lengths—faking her own murder and framing her husband, Nick—to punish his infidelity and keep him within her grasp. Amy was so excessively unlikable, so unrepentant, so shameless, that at times this book is intensely uncomfortable. Flynn engages in a clever manipulation in which we learn more and more about both Nick and Amy in small moments, so that we never quite know how to feel about them. We never quite know if they are likable or unlikable, and then we do know that they are both flawed, both terrible, and stuck together in many ways, and it is exhilarating to see a writer who doesn't blink, who doesn't pull back.

There is a line of anger that runs throughout *Gone Girl*, and for Amy, that anger is born of the unreasonable burdens women are so often forced to bear. The novel is a psychological thriller, but it is also an exquisite character study. Amy is, by all accounts, a woman people should like. She's "a smart, pretty, nice girl . . . with so many *interests* and *enthusiasms*, a cool job, a loving family. And let's say it: money." Even with all these assets, Amy finds herself single at thirty-two, and then she finds Nick.

The most uncomfortable aspect of *Gone Girl* is the book's honesty and how desperately similar many of us likely are to Nick and Amy in the ways they love and hate each other. The truth hurts. It hurts, it hurts, it hurts. When we finally begin to see the truth of Amy, she says of the night she met Nick,

> *That night at the Brooklyn party, I was playing the girl who was in style, the girl a man like Nick wants: the Cool Girl. Men always say that as* the *defining compliment, don't they?* She's a cool girl. *Being the Cool Girl means I am a hot, brilliant, funny woman who adores football, poker, dirty jokes, and burping, who plays video games, drinks cheap beer, loves threesomes and anal sex, and jams hot dogs and hamburgers into her mouth like she's hosting the world's biggest culinary gang bang while somehow maintaining a size 2, because Cool Girls are above all hot. Hot and understanding . . . Men actually think this girl exists. Maybe they're fooled because so many women are willing to pretend to be this girl.*

This is what is so rarely said about unlikable women in fiction—that they aren't pretending, that they won't or can't pretend to be someone they are not. They have neither the energy for it nor the desire. They don't have the willingness of a May Welland to play the part demanded of her. In *Gone Girl*, Amy talks about the temptation of being the woman a man wants, but ultimately she doesn't give in to the temptation to be "the girl who likes every fucking thing he likes and doesn't ever complain." Unlikable women refuse to give in to that temptation. They are, instead, themselves. They accept the consequences of their choices, and those consequences become stories worth reading.

How We All Lose

Discussions about gender are often framed as either/or propositions. Men are from Mars and women are from Venus, or so we are told, as if this means we're all so different it is nigh impossible to reach each other. The way we talk about gender makes it easy to forget Mars and Venus are part of the same solar system, divided by only one planet, held in the thrall of the same sun. Unfortunately, many books released in 2012 did little to productively reframe the cultural conversation about gender. Instead, these books offered rather narrow insights into women and men and were, at times, disappointing for the opportunities they missed to bring nuance to how we think about gender.

If women's fortunes improve, it must mean men's fortunes will suffer, as if there is a finite amount of good fortune in the universe that cannot be shared equally between men and women. This is certainly how I felt while reading Hanna Rosin's interesting and intelligent, but ultimately frustrating, *The End of Men:*

And the Rise of Women. What does it even mean to suggest that the end of men is explicitly connected to the rise of women? There's no denying women are doing better than they ever have, but is that really saying much? When you consider what life was like for women before suffrage, before Title IX, before the Equal Pay Act, before *Roe v. Wade*, before any number of changes that made life merely tolerable, most any success women encountered would seem like a rise in circumstance.

Rosin has clearly done a great deal of research and makes compelling arguments. I particularly appreciated the way she tried to advance the conversation about gender by upending our expectations. So often when we talk about gender, we have tunnel vision, where we can only understand the lives of women as being grounded in disadvantage (the endless "having it all" debate, for example). Rosin complicates that notion by revealing the many ways women are gaining the upper hand in education, several industries, and the culture at large.

I was skeptical as I read *The End of Men*, but Rosin makes it easy to respect many of her ideas. At the same time, it's pretty easy to frame an argument convincingly by being selective in the data presented. No writer or critic is free from this selectivity, but at times it stands out as problematic in *The End of Men*. In the chapter "Pharm Girls: How Women Remade the Economy," Rosin discusses the rise of women in the pharmaceutical industry. She notes that "in 2009, for the first time in American history, the balance of the workforce tipped toward women, who continue to hover around 50 percent." This is an encouraging, important statistic, but according to 2010 census data, women still earn 77 percent of what men earn and that cannot be ignored. We make up half the workforce but pay a pretty steep price for that privilege.

Throughout the chapter, Rosin highlights the great strides women have made as pharmacists, how they are practically dominating the field, and it is truly inspiring to see how far we've come in a field once entirely male-dominated. At the same time, this is only one field. For every argument there is a counterargument. Women are doing well in pharmacy, but the statistics are starkly different in, say, the sciences and most engineering disciplines.

One of the recurrent themes throughout *The End of Men* is that of female ambition—women are working harder, are more focused, and are willing to do what it takes to fulfill their responsibilities, both personally and professionally. At many colleges and universities women are the majority, while men are choosing not to enroll or not to finish their college degrees. Rosin doesn't do enough, though, to explore why this trend has emerged. She highlights the fact that there was a time when men didn't have to go to college—they could work in manufacturing or learn a trade and make a good living for themselves and their families. As more manufacturing jobs have gone overseas and the economy has collapsed, however, nothing has replaced these jobs. Men haven't adapted. What goes unsaid is that women might be more ambitious and focused because we've never had a choice. We've had to fight to vote, to work outside the home, to work in environments free of sexual harassment, to attend the universities of our choice, and we've also had to prove ourselves over and over to receive any modicum of consideration. Women are rising but Hillary Clinton, a former secretary of state and potential presidential candidate in 2016, still must answer questions about fashion. CNN feels comfortable publishing an article suggesting women's votes might be influenced by their hormones.

And then Rosin discusses violence, the increase in female aggression, and notes that "women today are far less likely to get murdered, raped, assaulted, or robbed than at any time in recent history." This is excellent news, but there's a curious aside when Rosin continues: "A 2010 White House report on women and girls laid out the latest statistics straightforwardly, to the great irritation of many feminists," but doesn't provide any evidence of this supposed feminist irritation. It is hard to accept at face value that feminists would be irritated that there's a decline in violence against women, as if the rise of women is somehow antithetical to the "feminist agenda." Rosin goes on to cite several other statistics without acknowledging how much abuse and sexual violence goes unreported. The truth is that we'll never have a truly accurate statistical count for the violence women, or men for that matter, experience. We can only make best guesses.

Another advance Rosin touts is how the "definition of rape has expanded to include acts that stop short of penetration—oral sex, for example—and circumstances in which the victim was too incapacitated (usually meaning too drunk) to give meaningful consent." This has been a critical improvement in acknowledging the breadth of sexual violence, but we also have to consider the many different kinds of rape we have learned about over the past few years as conservative politicians blunder through trying to explain their stances on sexual violence and abortion.

For instance, Indiana treasurer Richard Mourdock, running for the US Senate in 2012, said, in a debate, "I struggled with it myself for a long time, and I realized that life is a gift from God, and I think even when life begins in that horrible situation of rape, that it is something God intended to happen." I've been obsessing over these words, and trying to understand how someone who purports to believe in God can also believe that anything born of rape is God-intended. Just as there are many different kinds of rape, there are many different kinds of God. I am also reminded that women, more often than not, are the recipient of God's intentions and must also bear the burdens of these intentions.

Mourdock is certainly not alone in offering up opinions about rape. Former Missouri representative Todd Akin believes in "legitimate rape" and the oxymoronic "forcible rape," not to be confused with all that illegitimate rape going on. Ron Paul believes in the existence of "honest rape," but turns a blind eye to the dishonest rapes out there. Former Wisconsin State representative Roger Rivard believes some girls, "they rape so easy." Lest you think these new definitions of rape are only the purview of men, failed Senate candidate Linda McMahon of Connecticut has introduced us to the idea of "emergency rape." Given this bizarre array of new rape definitions, it is hard to reconcile the belief that women are rising when there is still so much in our cultural climate working to hold women down. We can, I suppose, take comfort in knowing that none of these people is in a position of power anymore.

The paperback of *The End of Men* offers a new epilogue. A great deal of the piece antagonizes the feminists Rosin imagines gleefully reveling in the suffering of all us downtrodden women. Rosin implores feminists to accept that the patriarchy is dead, which is so patently absurd that the hashtag #RIPPatriarchy quickly flourished on Twitter in response. In the epilogue, she picks a pointless fight with an audience that simply isn't paying her any mind.

Rosin is not wrong that life has improved in measurable ways for women, but she is wrong in suggesting that better is good enough. Better is not good enough, and it's a shame that anyone would be willing to settle for so little. I cannot think of clearer evidence of how alive and well the patriarchy remains (see above).

It's a shame, really, because the epilogue and its tone do such a disservice to a reasonably good book. There's also blatantly incorrect information like the suggestion that women compose a third of Congress. Women represent 18.3 percent of the 535 seats in the 113th Congress.

We don't need to get petty, though. The patriarchy, if that's what we're calling it today, is alive and well. The tech industry is consistently embroiled in one misogyny-related controversy or another. At TechCrunch's 2013 Disrupt, two programmers shared the TitStare app, which is exactly what you think it is.

Something so puerile is hardly worth anyone's time or energy, but it's one more example of the cultural stupidity that is fueled by misogyny. That same year, Harvard introduced Riptide, a project that will examine how journalism collapsed under the pressure of digital advances. Unfortunately, most of the people interviewed for the project were white men, offering, as usual, a narrow perspective on an issue that would benefit from a more diverse set of voices. Fix the Family, a conservative, Catholic "family values" organization, published a list of reasons why families should not send their daughters to college. The list is not satirical.

These are relatively small things, though—symptoms, not the disease. These situations are irritants that pale in comparison to the more significant issues women face both in the United States and around the world. We could talk about the retraction of reproductive freedom in North Carolina and Texas and Ohio, or we could conjure up a lot of statistics about domestic and sexual violence or women living in poverty. If the patriarchy is dead, the numbers have not gotten the memo.

Rosin suggests that feminists are holding on to a grudge, that feminists are willfully holding on to this notion of patriarchal dominance as if we would be unable to function if we weren't suffering. I'm only one feminist, but I'm confident we'd be just fine if all were right with the world. Rosin writes, "The closer women get to real power, the more they cling to the idea that they are powerless. To rejoice about feminist victories these days counts as betrayal." The flaw here is the same as the flaw in *The End of Men*—an all-or-nothing outlook, and an unwillingness to consider nuance. Some women being empowered does not prove the patriarchy is dead. It proves that some of us are lucky.

It is far more important to discuss power than to exhaustively regurgitate the harmful cultural effects of power structures where women are consistently marginalized. We already know the effects. We live them and try to overcome them. But let's talk about power. There are bright shining stars like Marissa Mayer and the other twenty women who are CEOs of the Fortune 500—a whopping 4 percent. In the updated epilogue, Rosin blithely references this number as if to say, *Leave me within my delusion. I am busy.* We can also talk about how no woman has ever been president of the United States and how, as of July 2013, there were only nineteen women presidents and prime ministers throughout the entire world.

In some ways, Rosin—who in the book says she is neither a radical feminist nor anti-feminist—makes a clever rhetorical move. No matter how you respond, she places you in the position of seeming like you do, in fact, have a grudge, that you are holding on to anger and unwilling to see the *truth* as she frames it. Disagreement, however, is not anger. Pointing out the many ways in which misogyny persists and harms women is not anger. Conceding the idea that anger is an inappropriate reaction to the injustice women face backs women into an unfair position. Nor does disagreement mean we are blind to the ways in which progress has been made. Feminists are celebrating our victories and acknowledging our privilege when we have it. We're simply refusing to settle. We're refusing to forget how much work there is yet to be done. We're refusing to relish the comforts we have at the expense of the women who are still seeking comfort.

In Caitlin Moran's *How to Be a Woman*, she suggests that, historically speaking, women haven't accomplished much at all, that women have not yet risen. Moran says,

> *Even the most ardent feminist historian, male or female—citing Amazons and tribal matriarchies and Cleopatra—can't conceal that*

women have basically done fuck-all for the last 100,000 years. Come on—let's admit it. Let's stop exhaustingly pretending that there is a parallel history of women being victorious and creative, on an equal with men, that's just been comprehensively covered up by The Man.

According to Moran, women simply haven't had the chance to achieve greatness the way men have because of a number of sociocultural factors that have favored male dominance.

How to Be a Woman, a memoir cum feminist text, also approaches gender matters in a selective manner, one grounded in a narrow brand of feminine experience. This is a book where the main thesis revolves around asking if men are worrying about the things women worry about. It's a catchy idea. One of the most oft-quoted excerpts is:

And it's asking this question: "Are the men doing it? Are the men worrying about this as well? Is this taking up the men's time? Are the men told not to do this, as it's 'letting our side down'? Are the men having to write bloody books about this exasperating, retarded, time-wasting bullshit?"

Who wouldn't want to be on board with this succinct philosophy? There's so much in this book that demands we reconcile casual insensitivity and narrow cultural awareness for the sake of funny feminist (albeit dated) thinking. Again, we have to deal with selectivity because while people love quoting the question "Are the men doing it?," they ignore what Moran says farther down the page about her stance on burkas. "It was the 'Are the boys doing it?' basis on which I finally decided I was against women wearing burkas." This is an odd, glaring statement because I'm not sure what Moran's stance on burkas has to do with anything. Laurie Balbo notes in an article about an Egyptian news anchor choosing to wear the hijab during a newscast,

"There's no difference between forcing women to wear hijab and forcing them to not wear. The ultimate decision must be that of the individual." Western opinions on the hijab or burkas are rather irrelevant. We don't get to decide for Muslim women what does or does not oppress them, no matter how highly we think of ourselves.

In *How to Be a Woman*, Moran also says, "I want to reclaim the phrase 'strident feminist' in the same way the hip-hop community has reclaimed the word 'nigger.'" This is a baffling statement because there is simply no reality where the phrase "strident feminist" can be reasonably compared to the N-word. I am fascinated by the silence surrounding this statement, how people will turn a blind eye to casual racism for the sake of funny feminism. For the most part, lavish praise has been heaped on the book. The *New York Times* raves, "'How to Be a Woman' is a glorious, timely stand against sexism so ingrained we barely even notice it."

More than one review has noted the dearth of humor in feminist texts given, you know, that we love the narrative of feminists as humorless. As such, they are that much more appreciative of the humor in Moran's book. Once again, we can overlook cultural ignorance so long as we're made to laugh. Time and again Moran undermines her ideas by thinking she should apply her outlook to cultural experiences she knows nothing about. She blithely writes, "All women love babies—just like all women love Manolo Blahnik shoes and George Clooney. Even the ones who wear nothing but sneakers, or are lesbians, and really hate shoes, and George Clooney." Again, this is funny, but it is also untrue, and to try to generalize about women for the sake of humor dismisses the diversity of women and what we love. Moran undermines herself by privileging feminism as something that can exist in isolation of other considerations. Her feminism exists in a very narrow vacuum, to everyone's detriment. It's a shame because the book could have been so much more if Moran had looked just a bit beyond herself. Given the popularity of *How to Be a Woman*, I can't help but feel this was a missed opportunity.

But then there is writing about gender that is unapologetically sprawling, that reaches both backward and forward and tries to explode the vacuum of cultural conversations. We should start at the end of *Heroines* where Kate Zambreno writes, "For my criticism came out of, has always come out of, *enormous feeling.*" What intrigues me most about Zambreno's writing is how it so richly embodies the ethos she espouses. In *Heroines*, Zambreno has created a hybrid text that is part manifesto, part memoir, and part searing literary criticism. This hybridity is the book's strongest feature, and the way she moves among these different ambitions works very well. Not only does she try to elevate the conversations we have about gender, she leads by example.

Her criticism rises from emotion. It is appealing to see a writer so plainly locate the motivations behind her criticism. All too often, criticism is treated rather antiseptically under the auspices of objectivity. There is no such distance in *Heroines*. Zambreno revels in subjectivity.

Zambreno shifts between the personal and the political at a brisk pace, but the narrative style works because it so clearly embodies what Zambreno calls for at the end of the book when she says, "A new sort of subjectivity is developing online—vulnerable, desirous, well-versed in both pop culture and contemporary writing and our literary ancestors." The nature of the book also rises out of how much of the book comes from her blog, *Frances Farmer Is My Sister*, where Zambreno chronicles certain aspects of her life and her cultural and critical interests.

They say every writer has an obsession, and in *Heroines*, that obsession is reclamation or, perhaps, breaking new ground where women can be feminist and feminine and can resist the labels and forces that all too often marginalize, silence, or erase female experiences. Zambreno discusses her personal life and romantic relationship, the challenges of acclimating to Akron, Ohio, where she moved with her partner, what it meant to follow her partner, and intersperses these personal observations with examinations of women writers and artists who have, in various ways, been marginalized, silenced, or erased.

Heroines is not a perfect book. There are silences, particularly surrounding race and class and heterosexual privilege. What does it say when the majority of a woman's heroines are white, heterosexual women? No book can be everything to everyone, but it would have been nice to see what Zambreno, with such electric thinking and writing, would do if she extended her reach, if she exploded the vacuum of cultural conversations even more.

I was conflicted about Junot Díaz's collection *This Is How You Lose Her.* There is no denying Díaz's talent. The man writes exceptionally well. His stories are vivid and memorable, intelligent and intense. He understands how to work within the short form and brings a real elegance to the structures of his stories. Díaz grounds his writing in a rich cultural context and is able to capture the authenticity of his characters by allowing them to be unapologetically flawed. These nine interconnected stories follow Yunior, his family, the women he has loved, lost, and scorned, and how, in the end, he ends up alone, amidst the ruins of his misdeeds. I have been conflicted about this book because I loved these stories, the richness of the details, the voice, the way the stories pull the reader from beginning to end. These are stories with gravity. They hold the reader in place.

"Otravida, Otravez," about a woman who works as a laundress and is in a relationship with a married man, Yunior's father, speaks so beautifully to the immigrant experience, to the choices women make in love, to what they tolerate from men, to how closely they hold their hopes. "Otravida, Otravez" is, without a doubt, one of the finest stories I have ever read.

There is, indeed, something to admire in each story. In "Invierno," I could not forget the description of a long, desolate winter when Yunior, his brother, and their mother are first brought to the United States, what snow felt like on Yunior's bare head. In "Miss Lora," Díaz makes it easy to sympathize with both Yunior, sixteen and mourning the loss of his brother, and Miss Lora, the middle-aged woman he has an affair with. The collection ends with "The Cheater's Guide to Love," a story filled with regret and sorrow as Yunior details the years after his fiancée breaks up with him because of his serial cheating. The story is naked, intensely confessional, a rending of the self, Yunior trying to purge himself of his wrongdoings.

Then there is the sexism, which is at times virulent. In an interview with NPR, Díaz says he grew up in a world where "I wasn't really encouraged to imagine women as fully human. I was in fact pretty much—by the larger culture, by the local culture, by people around me, by people on TV—encouraged to imagine women as something slightly inferior to men." The influence of that world is plainly apparent throughout *This Is How You Lose Her*. Women are their bodies and what they can offer men. They are pulled apart for Yunior's sexual amusement. There's nothing wrong with that, the fact that Yunior is a misogynist of the highest order, that he is a product of a culture that routinely reduces women, that he is unable to remain faithful to his women, that none of the men in this book is very good to women. This is fiction, and if people cannot be flawed in fiction there's no place left for us to be human.

Still, I keep coming back to the relative impunity with which the men in *This Is How You Lose Her* get to behave badly, and to the tone of the critical reception to these stories, which are not only stories but confessions, lamentations of misdeeds. We have all been influenced by a culture where women are considered inferior to men, and I would have loved to see what a writer of Díaz's caliber might do if he allowed his character to step out of the constraints of the environment he grew up in, one to which readers are all subjected.

In response to these limited ways in which we talk, write, and think about gender, these vacuums in which we hold cultural conversations, no matter how good our intentions, no matter how finely crafted our approach, I cannot help but think, *This is how we all lose.* I'm not sure how we can get better at having these conversations, but I do know we need to overcome our deeply entrenched positions and resistance to nuance. We have to be more interested in making things better than just being right, or interesting, or funny.

Reaching for Catharsis:
Getting Fat Right (or Wrong) and Diana Spechler's *Skinny*

I went to fat camp once, the summer after my sophomore year in high school. I went to fat camp mostly against my will. I thought I was too old to be going to a camp of any kind. I told myself I wasn't *really* fat enough for fat camp. For the three previous years, however, I had been eating everything in sight. Finally, forty pounds heavier, people were beginning to notice. My boyfriend made annoying comments about my moderately expanding hips when we were lying on his twin bed at boarding school. One of my classmates said, "Damn, girl," when she noticed an extra shake in my ass.

I would come home for holiday breaks, and my parents noticed a new roundness to my figure. They did not approve. They gave me all kinds of advice about exercising self-control and eating properly. *Moderation*, my father would say, is the key to everything. "Moderation" is pretty much his favorite word. My parents meant well. They worried because I had always been thin, kind of lanky, and then I wasn't. There was an incident with some boys in the woods, and suddenly, I was stuffing my face with Twinkies or ordering a pizza late at night, trying to fill this ragged, ugly thing inside me that couldn't be filled or quieted. I ignored my parents and their worry entirely. All I wanted to do was eat. My body grew, became more significant, more noticeable and more invisible at the same time. Most important, though, the bigger I made my body, the safer I felt. Bad things, I'd decided years earlier, could not happen to big bodies. I was not necessarily incorrect in my thinking. Eating was, in part, a survival instinct.

I was reminded of my stint at fat camp as I read Diana Spechler's *Skinny*. I mostly read this book because I am not skinny. The novel tells the story of Gray Lachmann, a woman in her twenties who runs away to work as a fat camp counselor in North Carolina while grieving her father, who has died. There's a complex history between Gray and her father, from whom she was estranged prior to his death. For tenuous reasons, she blames herself for her father's passing. When she runs away to fat camp in North Carolina, Gray leaves behind a longtime boyfriend in New York, Mikey, a comedian who loves her, and a mother who also has a troubled relationship with food.

Despite everything she leaves behind, Gray neglects to abandon her lifelong obsession with her body and being skinny and binge eating. At the fat camp, run by an incompetent group of people who have no business looking after anyone's children, let alone fat campers, Gray has ample opportunity to continue to indulge her unhealthy behaviors. She has ample time to try to satisfy her own ragged hungers. She makes halfhearted attempts to bond with the campers even though they much prefer the time and attentions of Sheena, the younger, "cool" counselor. When Gray sees problems with the campers, she tries to bring them to the attention of the camp director, Lewis. Given how woefully unsuited she is to the task of serving as a camp counselor, she does as well as can be expected. Gray isn't that different from most summer camp counselors.

There are other things going on in *Skinny* beyond grief and self-loathing and Gray trying to regain control over her body. Gray believes she has a half sister, a camper named Eden whom Gray found via the Internet after she was appointed as the executor of her father's estate and learned that a sum of money was bequeathed to Eden's mother. Gray spends the summer trying to insert herself into Eden's good graces with little luck because Eden is a teenager and teenagers are often hard to get close to. Though she has a boyfriend back in New York, Gray also begins a complicated affair with Bennett, the camp's physical trainer, who is not really a physical trainer. None of the camp's staff members, in fact, are at all prepared to fill the roles they've been assigned, but they make do, unless they don't. Bennett is very physically fit and so Gray's obsession with her body only intensifies as she tries to whittle her body down to nothing but bone.

She spends her nights sneaking off to see Bennett, using sex to forget about her exhausting interior monologue. She spends her days trying to make herself beautiful, as if through beauty she will find happiness. "I spent my free periods doing important things: folding Crest Whitestrips over my teeth, rubbing self-tanner into my breasts, trying on my jeans that were now too big, rolling the waistband down to admire the jut of my hipbones." The book is almost hypnotic in how intimately we are immersed in Gray's self-absorption. At one point, Bennett and Gray are having a conversation and he says, "It's like you're . . . I don't know, in love with yourself," and she replies, "Self-absorption is different from self-love."

The camp I attended was nestled in the Berkshire Mountains on what I was told were beautiful grounds, but beauty is in the eye of the beholder and beauty I did not behold. I thought the camp was the worst place on earth. I went there for six expensive, excruciating weeks. It was hot and there was no air-conditioning. We had to walk everywhere and there were great distances between all the buildings. The cabins were high on a hill, and when I say "hill," what I really mean is "mountain." If you wanted to change clothes or lie down for a minute or if, God forbid, you forgot something in your bunk, you had to scale the fat camp kid's version of Everest. It was exhausting, which was, I suppose, the point. We spent a cruel amount of time outdoors, hiking and swimming and being eaten by mosquitoes. The weigh-ins were a humiliating affair where you removed your shoes and stepped on the scale and held your breath as the director kept sliding whatever those things are called back and forth until the scale settled on your weight. If you did well, you were congratulated and encouraged to do better. If you didn't do well, you received a stern lecture and a disappointed look. None of the campers really gave a damn one way or the other because kids at fat camp don't care about being really fat or sort of fat or on the verge of fat. Their parents do.

Like at most summer camps, in addition to all the exercise and dieting, there were activity nights and we wrote letters home and we gossiped and hooked up. You know what I really learned at fat camp? I learned how to smoke. I fell madly in love with smoking. I learned how to make myself throw up. I learned how to stand on the edges of the scale to throw my weight off a little. After the younger kids had their curfew, most of the counselors, a motley crew of college students not much older than us, some of whom had once been campers themselves, would gather behind one of the cabins to drink and smoke and make out.

When we hovered around their circle, the counselors rarely protested and often encouraged us to join in the fun. There is a certain thrill in corruption even though, for most of us, our corruptions had started long before we arrived at camp. The first cigarette I ever smoked was a Benson & Hedges menthol. I felt like quite the sophisticate sitting on a log, inhaling deeply, exhaling slowly, pretending I had been smoking for years. The habit would stay with me for the next eighteen years, so in some ways, fat camp had a very lasting effect.

It makes perfect sense that many of us obsess over our bodies. There is nothing more inescapable. Our bodies move us through our lives. They bring pleasure and pain. Sometimes our bodies serve us well, and other times our bodies become terribly inconvenient. There are times when our bodies betray us or our bodies are betrayed by others. I think about my body all the time—how it looks, how it feels, how I can make it smaller, what I should put into it, what I am putting into it, what has been done to it, what I do to it, what I let others do to it. This bodily preoccupation is exhausting. There is no one more self-absorbed than a fat person, and *Skinny* exposes just how obsessive people are when they are unhappy with their bodies. This is not to say all fat people are unhappy with their bodies, but many are. Most of my friends are equally obsessive even though they are thin—hating themselves or specific parts of themselves: their arms, their thighs, their chins, their ankles. They do crazy diets and starve themselves and run themselves ragged trying to maintain some semblance of control over things that are somewhat out of our control. I don't think I know any woman who doesn't hate herself and her body at least a little bit. Bodily obsession is, perhaps, a human condition because of its inescapability.

Skinny speaks well to how inescapable our bodies really are and how easy it is to lose control. As the summer progresses, Gray becomes, for all intents and purposes, anorexic. What starts as a desire to lose excess weight becomes a singular focus. She takes to eating nothing and exercising all the time, running, doing aerobics, pushing herself to extremes, reveling in the dramatic way her body changes, with jutting bones everywhere and loose clothing and the airy high of starvation. When Gray is having sex with Bennett, she marvels at how athletic and fit they both are and how their bodies *fit* together:

> *I would straddle him, kneeling, holding the handles of his ears. Or I would lean all the way back, my spine arched, my hair spreading over his feet. Or I would lie supine as he knelt above me, his legs as sturdy as Corinthian columns, my head hanging off the edge of the bed, a heel on each of his shoulders.*

Gray drowns herself in her affair with Bennett so she can avoid confronting herself or her grief. Their relationship is born, primarily, of opportunity. Gray thinks about her boyfriend, Mikey, occasionally but shows little remorse for how she betrays the man who loves her and how she betrays herself. She is grieving, after all, and in grief, there is a certain amount of indulgence for bad behavior. Sorrow allows us a freedom happiness does not. As Gray's body thins, the writing soars with euphoria, almost as if the writer herself feels freer.

I enjoyed *Skinny* because it reminded me of the misery of fat camp and because it's rare to read well-written fiction about matters of size. At the same time, I struggled with this book. It was hard to take Gray seriously because she clearly wasn't that overweight. The body is a personal territory and every person's weight struggle should be taken seriously, but there's overweight and there's *overweight*. If you're the latter, it is difficult to take the former seriously, right or wrong. No one who shops at Lane Bryant or the Avenue or Catherines is going to feel empathy for someone who is thirty pounds overweight. It's not going to happen. There are two significant weaknesses with this book, and the way thirty pounds of excess weight is treated like it is three hundred pounds of excess weight is one of them.

It can be hard, at times, to separate the writer from the writing. I didn't know anything about Diana Spechler prior to reading *Skinny*. After reading the book, I used Google's image search to see if she was fat. I was curious to see if she wrote from experience or if she was writing what she imagined to be the interior life of a fat person. I have to believe I am not the only one who did this. I know better, I do, but I couldn't help myself. Photographic evidence reveals that Diana Spechler is a gorgeous, thin woman with long hair. She may not have always been this way. Her appearance does not matter, but it does. It matters because we're talking about bodies and fat and the petty betrayals of the flesh.

In graduate school, a classmate said she took a book about race more seriously when she learned a white woman wrote the book. I wanted to slam that woman's face into the table because it offended me, to my core, that she thought a white woman deserved more respect and held more authority for broaching complex issues of race. I thought of that day with a tiny bit more understanding as I read *Skinny* and was willing to take the book more seriously if it had been written by a really fat woman, someone corpulent, wallowing in rolls of flesh, someone who would truly *know* what being fat is like, the overwhelming omnipresence of it, and be able to write that experience authentically. I wanted a lot from this book and its writer. I chose to ignore the ways in which I know better.

In *Skinny*, Gray has gained the thirty pounds that distress her so much because her father is dead. There's more to the story, but the most immediate explanation for Gray's weight concerns is grief. When it comes to fat, there has to be a reason. We need to be able to trace the genealogy of obesity. Without that genealogy, we are simply mystified. People need an explanation for how a person can lose such control over her body. They want to know if you come from a fat family or if you have some kind of medical condition or if you are simply weak and *really* love food that much. In *Skinny*, we see some of the genealogy of Gray's fat but, perhaps, not enough for the story to feel as credible as it should.

I watch all the televised fat-shaming porn as penance and motivation—*The Biggest Loser* and *Ruby* and *Heavy*, some of those off-brand fat people shows on lesser cable channels, and recently *Extreme Makeover: Fat People Edition*. It is perversely thrilling to see the gorgeous, perfectly fit trainers yelling at and shaming the fat contestants until their vocal cords bleed, shaming the fat people into working out for eight hours a day while consuming only twelve hundred calories so the fat people can become an instantly gratificatory success story, however temporary that success might be. At some point in each episode, the trainers or the producers will get shallowly psychological with the contestants, trying to figure out *why* the contestants weigh 280 pounds, 357 pounds, or nearly 600 pounds, trying to uncover the fat genealogy as if all it takes to solve a weight problem is a tearful, heartfelt conversation about what went wrong or who did wrong and when and why.

There are dead husbands and dead babies and divorced parents and absent fathers and terrible abuse and all the painful things that happen to a person and the body over the course of a lifetime, the kinds of things that can be appeased, or at least numbed in part, by a quart of cold ice cream or the hot, melted cheese of a pizza. Sometimes the contestants say, "I don't know how I got this way," but they do. There's always a reason. Jillian Michaels, one of the *Biggest Loser* trainers, loves to force her contestants into dramatic catharses. It makes for good television. In *Skinny*, you get the sense that Gray is reaching for catharsis too. She's pushing herself in every way she possibly can to reach some kind of emotional break-through. I'm not sure she ever quite finds it.

Sometimes, a bold, sort of callous person will ask me how I got *so* fat. They want to know the *why*. "You're so smart," they say, as if stupidity is the only explanation for obesity. And of course, there's that bit about having such a pretty face, what a shame it is to waste it. I never know what to tell these people. There is the truth, certainly. This thing happened and then this other thing happened and it was terrible and I knew I didn't want either of those things to happen again and eating felt safe. French fries are delicious and I'm naturally lazy too so that didn't help. I never know what I'm supposed to say, so I mostly say nothing. I don't share my catharsis with these inquisitors.

Throughout *Skinny*, Gray writes letters to fat people. These letters, which the campers also have to write, are an opportunity for soul-searching and truth-telling and all that. Anyone who has spent time in therapy is familiar with the tool of letter writing as a step toward healing. Fat is about the mind more than it is about the body, isn't it? Lewis, the camp director, wants the campers to write these letters to fat people to explain why they hate fat people. "You all hate fat people," Lewis declares. These letters are the first step, he says, to help the campers accept their bodies and begin to change their bodies. The letters are full of the cruelties (or truths?) everyone thinks about fat people.

For example, Gray writes, "Excuses are worthless. Either change your life, stop slinging blame, stop stuffing food into the cracks in your heart, or give yourself over to the shortened, uncomfortable, sweaty life of the obese." These letters are clearly supposed to add something to the narrative. They are deliberate, didactic moments. They get the job done in that you can't help but have a reaction, but the novel would have worked just as well, or even better, without these interludes, so you have to wonder why they were included. The letters are somewhat forced, like those shallowly psychological moments in extreme weight-loss television programming, as if the letters are intended as opportunities for the reader to reach a cathartic place too, for the reader to nod and say, "Yes, I think these things about fat people too," so they might ultimately reach a place of empathy and understanding.

At times, these letters feel hollow and indulgent because they seem to be written by a skinny person imagining only one possible existence for a fat person, imagining that the fat life is somehow markedly different from the skinny life. It is but it isn't, save that the wardrobe of the skinny is generally better and the people around you are generally kinder.

There's a letter where Gray writes, "Dear Fat People, I see you in motorized wheelchairs, in bus seats that don't accommodate you. I see you taking breaks when you walk, pretending to admire the scenery." I recognize what's going on in that letter. I'm fat but I have eyes and I judge people too. The other day I was in a clothing store, and there were three very fat people on motorized carts congregating near the cash register, laughing merrily, and I thought, *How can they be so happy when they are immobile?* Then I felt guilty. I considered all the terrible things people must think when they judge me. We're all complicit in these matters, and these letters function, in part, to remind us of that complicity.

It's not that I expected these letters, or even this novel, to address the full spectrum of the fat experience. Is that even a thing? It's more that the letters speak to the lowest common denominator, nothing more. It's disappointing that Gray cannot possibly imagine that perhaps some fat people have amazing, athletic sex, just like she does. Perhaps they aren't sitting around miserably stuffing their faces next to someone who doesn't love them.

Earlier, I noted that there were two weaknesses in this book—
the implausibility of all this drama over a mere thirty pounds
of excess weight and, of course, these Dear Fat People letters.
Really, though, these issues are symptoms of the same weakness.
It's as if the author's understanding of fat people is such that the
fattest she could imagine Gray as still desirable and interesting
to Mikey, to Bennett, to the reader, is with only thirty pounds of
excess weight. This book would have been stunningly improved
if Gray were a hundred pounds overweight, maybe more, but I
got the sense that the writer was afraid to go *there*. The Dear Fat
People letters are purportedly from Gray, but as the book goes
on, you get the impression they are actually from the author herself confessing her sins, reaching for catharsis from within her
own personal prejudices about fat.

By the end of *Skinny*, everything has fallen apart. The camp is
shut down. The campers return to their lives, skinnier, certainly,
but only by happenstance. They haven't confronted their issues
or learned about healthy eating and healthy ways of dealing with
difficult circumstances. They haven't acquired the tools to prevent their bodies from further expanding. Bennett returns to his
home, and Gray returns to New York, though not to her relationship with Mikey. She regains most of the weight she lost. The
ending is a bit rushed, so it's hard to know if Gray has learned
much of anything. At the end, Gray is sitting in an empty room
with Bennett. There is a new distance between them even though
he does not know it yet. "And for just a second, I forgot where
I was. I forgot the things I always wished to forget. And I felt a
remarkable lightness." We are led to believe something profound
has happened in this moment, but the moment is not convincing.

In the last Dear Fat People letter, Gray writes, "You wonder
why we hate you? You are the visible manifestation of the parts
of ourselves we hide." There is truth in that too. Fat people wear
their shit on the outside, with sagging breasts and swollen ankles

and heavy thighs. Unlike a heroin addict, who might be able to cover track marks with long sleeves, a fat person cannot hide the fact that something has gone awry. Fat people have secrets, and you may not know what those secrets are, but they can be plainly seen. By the end of *Skinny*, we know many of Gray's secrets but we don't seem to know or see the secrets that matter.

When I left fat camp, I had lost the weight I needed to lose, mostly because the food at camp was terrible and there was so much walking. Anyone can lose weight if her only culinary options are Jell-O and salad with light dressing and grilled chicken breasts and she's never given a minute to sit and relax. In the first few weeks after fat camp, it was fun to feel like myself again, to feel light and somehow freed. When I returned to school, there were compliments and other expressions of appreciation for my much thinner body. That felt good too. But then I started eating again, worked even harder to make my body fill as much space as possible, tried to fill that ragged need inside of me. Very little had changed. I had not really found catharsis. Oh, how I hungered.

The Smooth
Surfaces of Idyll

Happiness is not a popular subject in literary fiction. We struggle, as writers, to make happiness, contentment, and satisfaction interesting. Perfection often lacks texture. What do we say about that smooth surface of idyll? How do we find something for narrative to hold on to? Or, perhaps, we fail to see how happiness can have texture and complexity so we write about unhappiness. That at least seems easier for me. I am probably too comfortable *going there*, wallowing in darkness, suffering, unhappiness. Misery loves company. In fiction, we can be unhappy together.

I have been thinking about happy endings. I am always thinking about happy endings. I am always thinking about happiness.

During an interview, I was asked if I ever write happy stories or happy endings. I considered that question for days. I hear it a lot from people I'm close to as well. Almost every story I write is a happy story, a fairy tale of some kind. Yes, you'll find death and loss and betrayal and darkness and violence in my stories, but there's often also a happy ending. Sometimes, people are unable to recognize happiness because all they see is the darkness. I look at many of my stories and I see a woman who has found some kind of salvation after enduring seemingly unsalvageable circumstances, a hero who helps her to that place of peace, however incomplete that peace might be. The details change, but that underlying structure, that fairy tale, is often there. I'm as intrigued by happy endings as I am by the deeply flawed ways people treat one another, even if I don't quite know what to do with that behavior.

Fairy tales have happy endings. There are often lessons to be learned, and sometimes those lessons are learned the hard way, but in the end, there is happiness, at least in the fairy tales I like best. My novel, *An Untamed State*, is in its own way about fairy tales. The story follows a woman who was living a fairy tale and then she is kidnapped and her fairy tale ends. Every story can usually be broken down to what it's *really* about in one sentence. I thought it would be interesting to start with the happy ending and see how that might unravel. It didn't just unravel. In the novel, Mireille Duval's happy ending comes all the way apart and then I had to figure out how to put the pieces back together, how to get my characters back to something resembling happiness.

I really enjoyed writing *An Untamed State*. I learned so much about pushing myself to write the same project every day and how to tell a story in long form and how to really slow the story down and give it the room it needs. The first draft of *An Untamed State* did not have a happy ending, but I received feedback indicating a happy ending of some kind, however imperfect, was needed to make things seem less hopeless. I tried my best. As I started thinking about the next novel, one that's about motherhood and surrogacy and a marriage of convenience and the incomplete choices we make when we're too young to know we're doing the wrong thing, I decided that no matter what, no matter how implausible it might seem, this book was going to have a very happy ending. I have no idea how I'm going to get there in a way that doesn't defy credulity, but I am going to try. Maybe it won't be completely realistic and maybe that's okay. Realism is relative. My fantasy life often feels quite real.

Contemporary art often unites the real and the fantastic. Contemporary art inspires, often because it is so difficult to explain or contextualize. In 2011, I saw the brilliantly curated exhibit *Hard Truths*, at the Indianapolis Museum of Art, featuring the artwork of Thornton Dial. It's hard to define Dial's style: he works across many mediums—sculpture, drawings, assemblages, collage, much of it socially conscious, all of it gorgeous, passionate, visceral.

Born in 1928, Dial grew up in the rural South and endured a great deal of economic hardship. He began working full-time at the age of seven. He experienced a great deal of racism, the untenable burden of segregation. The indelible mark of racism can be seen throughout much of his work—torment, anger, sadness, pain are all palpable. Unhappiness as muse is not solely the purview of writers.

The scale of Dial's art is often imposing. Most of his pieces are massive, taking up entire walls or floors, like he needs that much room to best express himself. My, and how he does. The scale of the art really reinforces the scale of the dark, emotional influence. That scale certainly made me feel grateful art exists as an outlet.

Trophies (Doll Factory) is one of the first pieces in the *Hard Truths* exhibit. Women raised Thornton Dial, and their feminine influence marks a great deal of his art. In *Trophies*, the dolls are garishly painted, half dressed, many of them painted gold like trophies. It's an interesting commentary on modern womanhood, perhaps even more interesting given that the commentary comes from a man. There is so much to look at in *Trophies*, in all of Dial's pieces. The level of detail is remarkable. I would have been content standing in only one of the many rooms of the exhibit because there was that much to see. The way the dolls are splayed across the canvas, how their breasts are bared, legs spread amid the chaos of the rest of the assemblage, really sets the tone for the exhibit. As I moved on, I thought, *There won't be any happy stories here.*

Dial imbues his work with suffering. The companion volume to the *Hard Truths* exhibit, edited by Joanne Cubbs and Eugene W. Metcalf, details how Dial's art functions as social commentary on race, class, gender, war, politics, all human concerns. In 1993, Dial was interviewed by Morley Safer for *60 Minutes.* He thought the interview was going to be about his art, but instead, Safer took the opportunity to do an "exposé" on how southern black vernacular artists were being exploited by white art dealers. Dial was and felt ambushed and misled and misrepresented by Safer. He carried a lot of anger about the incident for years, anger you can see in *Strange Fruit: Channel 42.* Dial's work really gave me the opportunity to think about art as a narrative. In *Strange Fruit: Channel 42,* you see Dial as the man hanging in effigy, self as strange fruit, and the TV antenna (channel 42 was the station that aired the Safer interview where Dial lived). There are smaller details you can't see unless you are standing in front of the piece, but they all work in concert to tell the story of Dial's anger and frustration. He was angry for many reasons, but mostly because he thought the *60 Minutes* interview was going to be his big break, that finally his work was going to be recognized. There's a bitter humor to the piece that holds the weight of the artist's disappointment. Dial also created another piece in response to the interview; this one, *Looking Good for the Price*, is much darker and angrier: a slave auction scene with a macabre white auctioneer, everything abstract and quite tortured, the images spread across the canvas at awkward angles. *Looking Good for the Price* tells another story about the artist's anger, his sense of humiliation, another story about unhappiness, one without a happy ending.

The exhibit, as a whole, was overwhelming. As I moved from room to room, I thought about how much pain Dial bleeds onto his canvas and how he works with that pain in culturally savvy and responsive ways. Given Dial's life story, it's understandable that his work is a reflection of the difficulties he has experienced. I could not imagine that a happy ending would be possible.

And yet.

Room after room after room of the exhibit was filled with these massive art pieces, sculptures, drawings, most of them created using found materials and lived experiences. The last room of the exhibit, though, was saturated in bright color. It was startling to enter the room and see . . . redemption, salvation, triumph, hope, happiness, a happy ending after a long, sorrowful journey. The pieces in the last room of the exhibit reflected Dial's spirituality and how he overcame serious illness. Everything about the artwork was vibrant, almost ecstatic, in a much different way from the rest of the exhibit. Dial's *The Beginning of Life in the Yellow Jungle* is an explosion of yellow, an artistic musing on life and how it evolves. The assemblage has fake plants, flowers made from plastic soda bottles, a doll serenely composed, and because of how these elements are held together, with Splash Zone epoxy, you get the sense that everything is connected, both literally and figuratively. It was inspiring and refreshing to see an artist willing to explore happiness as much as he was willing to explore pain, anger, darkness, unhappiness. Dial's art argues that both light and dark can rise from an artist's experiences.

I have been thinking about happy endings in life, in art, in literature.

Dawn Tripp's *Game of Secrets* is, as you might imagine, a novel about secrets—secrets among the novel's characters and secrets the author withholds from the reader. Most of the plot hinges on Tripp doling out pieces of these secrets a little at a time. The story begins with an affair and a decades-old murder—sex, betrayal, death—the stuff of many interesting stories.

There's some mystery to *Game of Secrets*, but mostly, a man is dead and we know it, even if we don't know how he came to such a pass. The dead man was a father and an estranged husband and a lover. *Game of Secrets* is about many things, but mostly it revolves around the aftermath of this man, Luce Weld's, death and how, for decades, it affects many residents in a small New England town. We think we know who did it—Silas Varick, the husband of Ada Varick, with whom Luce Weld was having an affair—but we can't be sure.

The story is told from multiple perspectives across several decades, but the two main characters are Marne Dyer and her mother, Jane Dyer, who is the daughter of Luce Weld. Throughout the novel, Marne is engaged in the fragile beginnings of a relationship with Ray Varick, Ada's son, and Jane is playing a game of Scrabble with Ada. In small towns, you can't really escape secrets or Scrabble, and what makes *Game of Secrets* so readable is that, as a reader, you start to see that everyone knows a little something. Tripp makes it easy to piece together what everyone knows in order to see the whole story. The premise makes a happy ending seem nearly impossible because there are so many secrets that have been held close for so long.

In such an atmosphere, there's bound to be unhappiness, sorrow, darkness, but these emotions don't overwhelm the story. Instead, the awkwardness of these secrets creates a mournful tone. As I neared the end, I wondered how the story could have a happy ending for anyone involved. Because I was invested, I wanted that happy ending for everyone. I wanted the people in this town to find their way out of the darkness, to reach a place of redemption, salvation, triumph, hope, happiness, a happy ending after a long, sorrowful journey, even if I couldn't see how that could be possible.

And yet.

There are happy endings in *Game of Secrets* for almost everyone involved, even though those happy endings may not look the way we expect happy endings to look. Just before his death, a man recognizes his son. A daughter finally begins to understand the mother who has long confounded her, and that daughter is able to grow, able to show her mother kindness. A husband tells his daughter his wife was the only one, has always been the only one, without regret. A woman makes peace with moving back to her hometown and tries to allow herself to love. A man remains open to love even when he is pushed away. The happy endings in *Game of Secrets* are subtle and incomplete but they are there, and it works because happiness itself is often subtle and incomplete.

Sometimes, and especially as a writer, I feel like I have no idea what happiness is, what it looks like, what it feels like, how to show it on the page.

I have no problem with darkness, sorrow, pain, or unhappiness. I have no intention of straying from these themes in my writing. But. In considering the Dial exhibit and *Game of Secrets*, I wonder how we can complicate these themes that pervade fiction and art so we can also achieve a more complete, complex understanding of happiness. Happiness is not uninspiring if we don't allow our imaginations to fail us. I want to believe there is substance to fairy tales. I want to believe there's something to hold on to, even when dealing with the slick smoothness of idyll, of joy.

The Careless Language
of Sexual Violence

There are crimes and then there are crimes and then there are atrocities. These are matters of scale. I was shaken by an article in the *New York Times* about an eleven-year-old girl who was gang-raped by eighteen men in Cleveland, Texas. The levels of horror to this story are many, from the victim's age, to what is known about what happened to her, to the number of attackers, to the public response in that town, to how the story was reported. There is video of the attack too because this is the future. The unspeakable will be televised.

The article was entitled "Vicious Assault Shakes Texas Town," as if the victim in question were the town itself. James McKinley Jr., the article's author, focused on how the men's lives would be changed forever, how the town was being ripped apart, how those poor boys might never be able to return to school. There was discussion of how the eleven-year-old girl, the child, dressed like a twenty-year-old, implying that there is a realm of possibility where a woman can "ask for it" and that it's somehow understandable that eighteen men would rape a child. There were even questions about the whereabouts of the girl's mother, given, as we all know, that a mother must be with her child at all times or whatever ill befalls the child is clearly the mother's fault. Strangely, there were no questions about the whereabouts of the father while this rape was taking place.

The overall tone of the article was what a shame it all was, how so many lives were affected by this one terrible event. Little word space was spent on the girl, the child. It was an eleven-year-old girl whose body was ripped apart, not a town. It was an eleven-year-old girl's life that was ripped apart, not the lives of the men who raped her. It is difficult to make sense of how anyone could lose sight of that fact, and yet it isn't.

We live in a culture that is overly permissive where rape is concerned. While there are certainly many people who understand rape and the damage of rape, we also live in a time that necessitates the phrase "rape culture." This phrase denotes a culture where we are inundated, in different ways, by the idea that male aggression and violence toward women is acceptable and often inevitable. As Lynn Higgins and Brenda Silver ask in their book *Rape and Representation*, "How is it that in spite (or perhaps because) of their erasure, rape and sexual violence have been so ingrained and so rationalized through their representations as to appear 'natural' and inevitable, to women as to men?" This is an important question, trying to understand how we have come to this.

We have also, perhaps, become immune to the horror of rape because we see it so often and discuss it so often, many times without acknowledging or considering the gravity of rape and its effects. We jokingly say things like "I just took a rape shower" or "My boss totally just raped me over my request for a raise." We have appropriated the language of rape for all manner of violations, great and small. It is not a stretch to imagine why James

McKinley Jr., in his reportage, was more concerned about eighteen men than one girl.

The casual way in which we deal with rape may begin and end with television and movies where we are inundated with images of sexual and domestic violence. Can you think of a dramatic television series that has not incorporated some kind of rape story line? There was a time when these story lines had a certain educational element to them, à la "A Very Special Episode." I remember, for example, the episode of *Beverly Hills 90210* where Kelly Taylor discusses being date-raped, at a slumber party, surrounded, tearfully, by her closest friends. For many young women that episode created a space where they could have a conversation about rape as something that was not just perpetrated by strangers. Later in the series, when the show was on its last legs, Kelly would be raped again, this time by a stranger. We watched the familiar trajectory of violation, trauma, disillusion, and finally vindication, seemingly forgetting we had sort of seen this story before.

Nearly every other movie aired on Lifetime or Lifetime Movie Network features some kind of violence against women. The violence is graphic and gratuitous while still being strangely antiseptic, where more is implied about the actual act than shown. We consume these representations of violence and do so eagerly. There is a comfort, I suppose, to consuming violence contained in ninety-minute segments, muted by commercials for household goods and communicated to us by former television stars with feathered bangs.

While rape as entertainment fodder may have also once included an element of the didactic, such is no longer the case. Rape is good for ratings. In Season 4 of ABC's *Private Practice*, Charlotte King, an iron-willed, independent, and sexually adventurous doctor, is brutally raped. This happened, of course, just as February sweeps were beginning. The depiction of the assault was as graphic as you might expect from prime-time network television. For several episodes we saw the attack and its aftermath, the narrative arc of how the once vibrant Charlotte became a shell of herself, how she became sexually frigid, how her body bore witness to the physical damage of rape. Another character on the show, Violet, bravely confesses she too had been raped. The show was widely applauded for its sensitive treatment of a difficult subject. The episode that began the arc, "Did You Hear What Happened to Charlotte King?," was the highest-rated episode of the season.

General Hospital, like most soap operas, incorporates a rape story line every five years or so when it needs an uptick in viewers. Emily Quartermaine was raped, and before Emily, Elizabeth Webber was raped, and long before Elizabeth, Laura of the infamous "Luke and Laura" was raped by Luke, but that rape was okay because Laura married Luke so her rape doesn't really count. Every woman, *General Hospital* wanted us to believe, loves her rapist. In 2010, the rape story line on the soap offered a twist. The victim was a man, Michael Corinthos III, son of Port Charles mob boss Sonny Corinthos, himself no stranger to violence against women. While it was commendable to see the show's producers trying to address the issue of male rape and prison rape, the subject matter was still handled carelessly, was still a source of titillation, and was still packaged neatly between commercials for cleaning products and baby diapers.

Of course, if we are going to talk about rape and how we are inundated by representations of rape and how, perhaps, we've become numb to rape, we have to discuss *Law & Order: SVU,* which deals, primarily, in all manner of sexual assault against women, children, and, once in a great while, men. Each week the violation is more elaborate, more lurid, more unspeakable. When the show first aired, Rosie O'Donnell, I believe, objected quite vocally when one of the stars appeared on her show. O'Donnell said she didn't understand why such a show was needed. People dismissed her objections and the incident was quickly forgotten. The series is in its fifteenth season and shows no signs of ending anytime soon. When O'Donnell objected to *SVU*'s premise, when she dared to suggest that perhaps a show dealing so explicitly with sexual assault was unnecessary and too much, people treated her like she was the crazy one, the prude censor. I watch *SVU* religiously and have seen every episode more than once. I am not sure what that says about me.

It is rather ironic that only a couple of weeks before publishing "Vicious Assault Shakes Texas Town," the *Times* ran an editorial about the "War on Women." This topic matters to me. I once wrote an essay about how, as a writer who is also a woman, I increasingly feel that writing is a political act whether I intend it to be or not because we live in a culture where McKinley's article is permissible and publishable. I am troubled by how we have allowed such intellectual distance between violence and the representation of violence. We talk about rape, but we don't carefully talk about rape.

We live in a strange and terrible time for women. There are days when I think it has always been a strange and terrible time to be a woman. Womanhood feels more strange and terrible now because progress has not served women as well as it has served men. We are still stymied by the issues our forbears railed against. It is nothing less than horrifying to realize we live in a culture where the "paper of record" can write an article that comes off as sympathetic to eighteen rapists while encouraging victim blaming. Have we forgotten who an eleven-year-old is? Perhaps people do not understand the trauma of gang rape. While there's no benefit to creating a hierarchy of rape where one kind of rape is worse than another because rape is, at the end of the day, rape, there is something particularly insidious about gang rape, about the idea that a pack of men feed on one another's frenzy and both individually and collectively believe it is their right to violate a woman's body in such an unspeakable manner and watch the others take turns.

Gang rape is a difficult experience to survive physically and emotionally. There is the exposure to unwanted pregnancy and sexually transmitted diseases, vaginal and anal tearing, fistulae and vaginal scar tissue. The reproductive system is often irreparably damaged. Victims of gang rape, in particular, have a higher chance of miscarrying a pregnancy. Psychologically, there are any number of effects, including PTSD, anxiety, fear, coping with the social stigma and coping with shame, and on and on. The aftermath can be far-reaching and more devastating than the rape itself. We rarely discuss these things, though. Instead, we are careless. We delude ourselves that rape can be washed away as neatly as it is on TV and in the movies, where the trajectory of victimhood is neatly defined.

I cannot speak universally, but given what I know about gang rape, the experience is wholly consuming. There is little point in pretending otherwise. Perhaps McKinley is, like so many people today, anesthetized or somehow willfully distanced from such brutal realities. Despite this inundation of rape imagery, where we are immersed in a rape culture—one that is overly permissive toward all manner of sexual violence—not enough victims of gang rape speak out about the toll the experience exacts. The right stories are not being told, or we're not writing enough about the topic of rape in the right ways. Perhaps we too casually use the term "rape culture" to address the very specific problems that rise from a culture mired in sexual violence. Should we, instead, focus on "rapist culture" because decades of addressing "rape culture" has accomplished so little?

In her essay "Your Friends and Rapists," Sarah Nicole Prickett writes, "Yes, I am tired of rape stories. I think rape stories are boring. I am sick of rape stories on CNN and sicker of rape stories on Jezebel. I would like instead to see national, televised debates and full episodes of morning radio shows and several long-form podcasts and a portion of the next State of the Union address dedicated to determining whether men should be allowed to keep their dicks." The weariness and rage of this statement is palpable, but it is also important. Prickett is suggesting that we reframe the conversation about rape. It is a call to address "dick culture," which Prickett refers to as "the inordinate pride men feel in owning and wielding their dicks."

I am approaching this topic somewhat selfishly. I am concerned about rape culture and how we perpetuate it, intentionally or not, but I also write about sexual violence in my fiction. The why of this writerly obsession doesn't matter, but I return to the same stories. Writing is cheaper than therapy or drugs. When I read articles such as McKinley's, I consider my responsibility as a writer and what writers can do to critique rape culture intelligently and illuminate the realities of sexual violence without exploiting the subject.

In Margaret Atwood's short story "Rape Fantasies," a woman, Estelle, shares her rape fantasies—ones where she gets away from a would-be rapist instead of being ravished. Atwood exposes the glossy treatment of rape in women's magazines, the casual, flitty way in which rape fantasies might be talked about over lunch with friends. The story explicitly addresses the sense of the inevitable fostered by rape culture—a question of when a woman will be raped, rather than if—and uses dark humor brilliantly. Atwood offers an intriguing way of upholding a writer's responsibility without compromising her artistic integrity. "Rape Fantasies" was first published in 1977, but the story's commentary would be just as timely were it published today. Rape culture, it seems, doesn't really change.

This responsibility of the writer was always on my mind as I wrote my debut novel, *An Untamed State*. It's the story of a brutal kidnapping in Haiti, and part of the story involves gang rape. Writing that kind of story requires going to a dark place. At times, I nauseated myself in the writing and by what I am capable of writing and imagining, my ability to *go there*.

As I write any of these stories, I wonder if I am being gratuitous. I want to *get it right*. But how do you get this sort of thing right? How do you write violence authentically without making it exploitative? I worry I am contributing to the cultural numbness that would allow an article like the one in the *Times* to be written and published, that allows rape to be such rich fodder for popular culture and entertainment. We cannot separate violence in fiction from violence in the world no matter how hard we try. As Laura Tanner notes in her book *Intimate Violence*, "the act of reading a representation of violence is defined by the reader's suspension between the semiotic and the real, between a representation and the material dynamics of violence which it evokes, reflects, or transforms." She also goes on to say that "the distance and detachment of a reader who must leave his or her body behind in order to enter imaginatively into the scene of violence make it possible for representations of violence to obscure the material dynamics of bodily violation, erasing not only the victim's body but his or her pain." The way we currently represent rape, in books, in newspapers, on television, on the silver screen, often allows us to ignore the material realities of rape, the impact of rape, the meaning of rape.

While I have these concerns, I also feel committed to telling the truth. These violences happen even if bearing such witness contributes to a spectacle of sexual violence. When we're talking about race or religion or politics, it is often said we need to speak carefully. These are difficult topics where we need to be vigilant not only in what we say but also in how we express ourselves. That same care must extend to how we write about violence and sexual violence in particular.

In the *Times* article, the phrase "sexual assault" is used, as is the phrase "the girl had been forced to have sex with several men." The word "rape" is used only twice and not really in connection with the victim. That is not a careful use of language. Language in this instance, and far more often than makes sense, is used to buffer our sensibilities from the brutality of rape, from the extraordinary nature of such a crime. Feminist scholars have long called for a rereading of rape. Higgins and Silver note that "the act of rereading rape involves more than listening to silences; it requires restoring rape to the literal, to the body: restoring, that is, the violence—the physical, sexual violation." We need to find new ways, whether in fiction or creative nonfiction or journalism, for rewriting rape, ways of rewriting that restore the actual violence to these crimes and make it impossible for men to be excused for committing atrocities and make it impossible for articles like McKinley's to be written, to be published, to be considered acceptable.

An eleven-year-old girl was raped by eighteen men. The suspects ranged in age from middle schoolers to a twenty-seven-year-old. There are pictures and videos. Her life will never be the same. The *New York Times*, however, would like you to worry about those boys, who will have to live with this for the rest of their lives, and the poor, poor town. That is not simply the careless language of sexual violence. It is the criminal language of sexual violence.

What We Hunger For

All too often, representations of a woman's strength overlook the cost of that strength, where it rises from, and how it is called upon when needed most.

The Hunger Games, released in 2008, is the first book in a trilogy by Suzanne Collins. *Catching Fire* and *Mockingjay*, the next two books, were released in 2009 and 2010. The franchise was an instant success. More than 2.9 million copies of the books are in print. There are more than twenty foreign editions. *The Hunger Games* was on the *New York Times* bestseller list for one hundred weeks. There are special editions. There is merchandise, including a Katniss Barbie, which Katniss would absolutely hate. In March 2012, the movie was released and earned nearly $460 million worldwide.

The series tells the story about a young woman, Katniss Everdeen, who doesn't know her own strength until she is confronted by her need for that strength. She is a tough young woman who is forced to become even stronger in circumstances that might otherwise break her. She is a young woman who has no choice but to fight for survival—for herself, her family, her people.

I have found myself inexplicably drawn to these books, the complex world Collins has created, and the people she has placed in that world.

I am not the kind of person who becomes so invested in a book or movie or television show that my interest becomes a hobby or intense obsession, one where I start to declare allegiances or otherwise demonstrate a serious level of commitment to something fictional I had no hand in creating.

Or, I didn't used to be that kind of person.

Let me be clear: Team Peeta. I cannot fathom how one could be on any other team. Gale? I can barely acknowledge him. Peeta, on the other hand, is everything. He frosts things and bakes bread and is unconditional and unwavering in his love, and also he is very, very strong. He can throw a sack of flour, is what I am saying. Peeta is a place of solace and hope, and he is a good kisser.

In December 2011, I didn't know much about *The Hunger Games*. Given my abiding interest in pop culture, I'm not sure how I missed the books. Then a friend suggested that *The Hunger Games* would be a great book to teach in my novel-writing class, so I decided to check it out.

I do most of my leisure reading at the gym. I hate exercise. Yes, it's good for you and weight loss and whatever, but normally, I work out and want to die. I knew I was in love with *The Hunger Games* when I did not want to get off the treadmill. The book captivated me. I wanted to stay in the world Collins created. More than that, *The Hunger Games* moved me. There was so much at stake, so much drama, and it was all so intriguing, so hypnotizing, so intense and dark. I particularly appreciated what the book got right about strength and endurance, suffering and survival. I found myself gasping and hissing and even bursting into tears, more than once. I looked insane but I did not care. I was completely without shame.

After finishing *The Hunger Games*, I quickly read the next two books in the trilogy—my obsession, at this point, was raging and white hot. I was so invested I couldn't stop talking about the books. I daydreamed about Katniss, Peeta, and, I suppose, sometimes Gale, as well as the other compelling characters—Cinna, Rue, Thresh, Haymitch, Finnick, Annie. I wanted the best for these characters even when all seemed hopeless, was hopeless.

This obsession intensified well before I realized the first movie would be released. That development took things to a whole new level.

I started counting down to the movie well before opening day. I could hardly contain myself. I attended the midnight showing even though I had to teach the next (same) morning. I warned my gentleman friend that he couldn't mock me for how I reacted during the movie because I knew I was going to get close to the rapture and didn't want to be judged. I live in a small town, so I expected that there wouldn't be many people attending the midnight opening, but AMC screened *The Hunger Games* on all ten screens and every screening was sold out. My friends and I joked that we were probably some of the oldest people in the auditorium. It was no small relief when we saw some silver-haired folk among us.

As we waited, the teenagers and tweens chattered energetically about the books and the casting and whatever else young people talk about these days. Nearly all of them were staring at electronic devices. I thought, *Don't they have school tomorrow?* The movie began, and I held my breath. I had so many expectations, and I didn't want those expectations, those hopes, destroyed by Hollywood, a known killer of dreams.

I was not disappointed. I had *feelings* throughout the movie, true, mad, deep *feelings*. Had I been alone, I would have embarrassed myself with vulgar displays of enthusiasm. At times I wanted to spontaneously break into applause to celebrate the thrill of seeing the book I've read so many times playing out twenty feet high. There was just so much to look at—the set design, the costumes, the glittery cast. The movie was almost cerebral and meticulously faithful to the book when it needed to be. The production values were impeccable with only a few missteps (whatever the hell was going on with Katniss's flaming outfits, for example). The actors acquitted themselves well. I became even more fervently a member of Team Peeta. I left the movie thrilled with the overall experience of the movie.

As a critic, I recognize the significant flaws, I do, but *The Hunger Games* is not a movie I am able to watch as a critic. The story means too much to me.

The Hunger Games books are not perfect. While the writing is engaging and well paced, the quality of the prose weakens with each successive book. Many of the secondary characters aren't well developed, and at times the plot strains credulity. The third book is rather rushed, and some of Collins's choices feel almost gratuitous, particularly with regard to the characters she chose to kill off. The complete erasure of sexuality is problematic. Intimacy is conveyed through a great deal of kissing to the point that it becomes laughable. It is disturbing that within the world of the Hunger Games, it is perfectly acceptable for teenagers to kill one another and die or otherwise suffer in really violent ways, but it is not at all acceptable for them to explore their sexuality.

I was struck, consistently, by the sheer brutality, and yet the undeniable heart of the story, of the characters, of my dearest Peeta and his devotion for Katniss, and how toward the end, even when it seemed hopeless, they found their way to each other. The books' imperfections are easily forgiven because the best parts of the books are the truest—that sometimes, the one you love best is the one who has always been right by your side, even when you didn't notice.

I am fascinated by strength in women.

People tend to think I'm strong. I'm not. And yet. I identify with Katniss because throughout the trilogy, the people around Katniss expect her to be strong and she does her best to meet those expectations, even when it costs her a great deal.

I come from a loving, tight-knit, imperfect but great family. My parents have always been involved in my life even when I pushed them away. I have wanted for little. One of my biggest weaknesses, one that has always shamed me, is that I have always been lonely. I've struggled to make friends because I can be socially awkward, because I'm weird, because I live in my head. When I was young, we moved around a lot, so there was rarely any time to get to know a new place, let alone new people. Loneliness was the one familiar thing, making me this bottomless pit of need, open and gaping and desperate for anything to fill me up.

I should not be this way but I am.

When I was in middle school, when I was young—old enough to like a boy but young enough to have no clue what that meant—there was a boy who I thought was my boyfriend and who said he was my boyfriend but who also completely ignored me at school. It's a sad, silly story lots of girls know. It was fine because when we were together, he made me feel like he could fill my gaping void. He was terrible, but he was also charming and persuasive. I was nerdy and friendless, all lanky limbs and crazy hair, and he was beautiful and popular. I accepted the state of affairs between us.

When we were together, he'd tell me what he wanted to do to

me. He wasn't asking permission. I was not an unwilling participant. I was not a willing participant. I felt nothing one way or
the other. I wanted him to love me. I wanted to make him happy.
If doing things to my body made him happy, I would let him do
anything to my body. My body was nothing to me. It was just
meat and bones around that void he filled by touching me. Tech-
nically, we didn't have sex, but we did everything else. The more
I gave, the more he took. At school, he continued looking right
through me. I was dying but I was happy. I was happy because
he was happy, because if I gave enough, he might love me. As an
adult, I don't understand how I allowed him to treat me like that.
I don't understand how he could be so terrible. I don't understand how desperately I sacrificed myself. I was young.

I was always a good girl. I was a straight-A student, top of my
class. I did as I was told. I was polite to my elders. I was good to
my siblings. I went to church. It was very easy to hide how very
bad I was becoming from my family, from everyone. Being good
is the best way to be bad.

It never crossed my mind to say no or that I should say no, that
I could say no. He started pressuring me to have sex. I didn't say
no but I didn't say yes and I did not want to say yes. I wanted to
say no but could not because I would lose him. I would be nothing again.

One day we were riding our bikes in the woods. About a mile
deep, there was an abandoned hunting cabin often used by teenagers to do the things teenagers do when they're hiding out in the
woods. It was disgusting—small, a dirt floor littered with empty
beer cans and used condom wrappers and discarded cigarette
packs. There was a small bench. The glass in the windows was
broken, brown with age. Several of his friends from school were
there. I didn't know them well, had mostly seen them in the halls.
They were all popular, handsome. They would never have reason
to know a girl like me, quiet, shy, awkward.

I did not understand, not at first. I was very naïve despite what I thought I knew. Once I realized what was going on, I assumed this boy wanted me to give his friends blow jobs. I did not want to do that, to share what I thought was private between this boy and me, but I would have. I could have, if only to make him happy. I told him I wanted us to leave, to continue on our bike ride. I did that. I did try to save myself. I did understand I was not safe. They were all so much bigger and I finally felt something. I felt fear but I didn't know how to say no. I tried to leave, to run out of that cabin, but they grabbed me just past the threshold. I screamed. I opened my mouth and I screamed and my voice echoed through the woods and no one came for me. Not one person heard me. We were too far deep.

The boy I thought was my boyfriend pushed me to the ground. He took my clothes off, and I lay there with no body to speak of, just a flat board of skin and girl bones. I tried to cover myself with my arms but I couldn't, not really. The boys stared at me while they drank beer and laughed and said things I didn't understand because I knew things but I knew nothing about what a group of boys could do to kill a girl.

I was a good girl who went to church. I had faith. I believed in God back then, so I prayed. I prayed for God to save me because I could not save me. I whispered Our Father because it was the only prayer I knew by heart. I begged God to change those boys' minds. He didn't. And then I did say no, I found my voice, and it didn't matter and I wasted my first love, my first everything, on a boy who thought so very little of me.

They kept me there for hours. It was as bad as you might expect. The repercussions linger. I walked home alone, pushing my stupid bike, hating myself for thinking this boy loved me. I was a good girl, so that's what my parents saw when I came home a completely different person and went to my room and tried to pull myself together well enough to be the girl everyone knew. I had to hide what happened because I didn't want to get in trouble, because my parents were strict, because you're not allowed to have sex before marriage, because I was a good girl, so that's what I did. I swallowed the truth, which only made that gaping void of need inside me yawn wider.

Just because you survive something does not mean you are strong.

The worst of it was going to school the next day. I didn't want to but I had no choice. I was a good girl. I went to French class and sat in the second-to-last row. It was uncomfortable in every way. Just as class was about to begin, the boy behind me grabbed my shoulder and I felt a surge of adrenaline, then terror. He stood and leaned into me. He said, "You're a slut," and everyone heard and they snickered. Everyone started calling me a slut. When the teacher came in and stood at the front of the room, she looked at me differently. If she could have, she would have called me a slut too. I was mortified and trapped. I sat perfectly still and tried to concentrate, but all I could hear was the hiss of the word "slut." That shame was one of the worst things I have ever known. "Slut" was my name for the rest of the school year because those boys went and told a very different story about what happened in the woods.

In June 2011, Meghan Cox Gurdon wrote, in the *Wall Street Journal*, about how Young Adult fiction has taken too dark a turn, has unnecessarily exposed young readers to complex, difficult situations before they are mature enough to make sense of those situations. She wrote,

> *If books show us the world, teen fiction can be like a hall of funhouse mirrors, constantly reflecting back hideously distorted portrayals of what life is. There are of course exceptions, but a careless*

young reader—or one who seeks out depravity—will find himself
surrounded by images not of joy or beauty but of damage, brutality
and losses of the most horrendous kinds.

She is correct in noting that there is darkness in some Young Adult fiction, but she largely ignores the diversity of the genre and the countless titles that aren't grounded in damage, brutality, or loss. More troubling, though, is the suggestion that somehow reality should be sanitized for teen readers.

The critical response to Gurdon's article was swift and passionate from writers and readers alike. Sherman Alexie wrote, "There are millions of teens who read because they are sad and lonely and enraged. They read because they live in an often-terrible world. They read because they believe, despite the callow protestations of certain adults, that books—especially the dark and dangerous ones—will save them."

I learned a long time ago that life introduces young people to situations they are in no way prepared for, even good girls, lucky girls who want for nothing. Sometimes, when you least expect it, you become the girl in the woods. You lose your name because another one is forced on you. You think you are alone until you find books about girls like you. Salvation is certainly among the reasons I read. Reading and writing have always pulled me out of the darkest experiences in my life. Stories have given me a place in which to lose myself. They have allowed me to remember. They have allowed me to forget. They have allowed me to imagine different endings and better possible worlds.

Perhaps I loved the Hunger Games trilogy because the books were, in their own way, a fairy tale and I am always, always in search of a fairy tale.

As I read the Hunger Games series, I thought of Gurdon's article because I was struck, more than once, by the intensity of the traumas the characters were put through, the relentlessness of that trauma, and the visible effects. At times, I thought, *This is too much*, but I know something of the world now, and there are rarely limits to suffering. In this trilogy, suffering has few limits, and suffering has consequences that, all too often, we forget when narratives neatly imply that everything turns out okay, when narratives imply that *it gets better* without demonstrating what it takes to get to better. In the Hunger Games, it takes everything.

My love for these books, at its purest, is not really about Peeta or anything silly and girly. I love that a young woman character is fierce and strong but human in ways I find believable, relatable. Katniss is clearly a heroine, but a heroine with *issues*. She intrigues me because she never seems to know her own strength. She isn't blandly insecure the way girls are often forced to be in fiction. She is brave but flawed. She is a heroine, but she is also a girl who loves two boys and can't choose which boy she loves more. She is not sure she is up to the task of leading a revolution, but she does her best, even as she doubts herself.

Katniss endures the unendurable. She is damaged and it shows. At times, it might seem like her suffering is gratuitous, but life often presents unendurable circumstances people manage to survive. Only the details differ. The Hunger Games trilogy is dark and brutal, but in the end, the books also offer hope—for a better world and a better people and, for one woman, a better life, a life she can share with a man who understands her strength and doesn't expect her to compromise that strength, a man who can hold her weak places and love her through the darkest of her memories, the worst of her damage. Of course I love the Hunger Games. The trilogy offers the tempered hope that everyone who survives something unendurable hungers for.

The Illusion of Safety/
The Safety of Illusion

When I see men who look like him or his friends. When I smell beer on a man's breath. When I smell Polo cologne. When I hear a harsh laugh. When I walk by a group of men, clustered together, and there's no one around. When I see a woman being attacked in a movie or on television. When I am in the woods or driving through a heavily wooded area. When I read about experiences that are all too familiar. When I go through security at the airport and am pulled aside for extra screening, which seems to happen every single time I travel. When I'm having sex and my wrists are unexpectedly pinned over my head. When I see a young girl of a certain age.

When it happens, a sharp pang runs right through the center of my body. Or I feel sick to my stomach. Or I vomit. Or I break into a cold sweat. Or I feel myself shutting down, and I go into a quiet place. Or I close my fingers into tight fists until my knuckles ache. My reaction is visceral and I have to take a deep breath or two or three or more. I have to remind myself of the time and distance between then and now. I have to remind myself that I am not the girl in the woods anymore. I have to convince myself I never will be again. It has gotten better over the years.

It gets better until it doesn't.

The first congressional hearing on television violence was held in 1954, and in the ensuing years, the debate about television and violence has been ongoing. The Telecommunications Act of 1996 dictated that televisions needed to include a chip to monitor program ratings. The current television parental guidelines went into effect on January 1, 1997. These guidelines were designed to help parents monitor what their children were watching and get some sense of the appropriateness of a given television program.

The guidelines rated television content by age appropriateness from G (all audiences) to MA (mature audiences only). There are also a second set of guidelines designed to protect children from violence, coarse language, and sexual themes. These guidelines, of course, only work if someone is monitoring what children are watching and is able to enforce a set of standards about what children can watch. Cable boxes and most televisions now allow parents to lock certain channels or shows with ratings they consider inappropriate for their children, but there is only so much a parent can control.

How effective, then, are these ratings and guidelines? In "Ratings and Advisories: Implications for the New Ratings System for Television," Joanne Cantor et al. note how research shows that "parental discretion warnings and the more restrictive MPAA ratings stimulate some children's interest in viewing programs," and "the increased interest in restricted programs is more strongly linked to children's desire to reject control over their viewing than to their seeking out violent content." Even children want a taste of forbidden fruit. Or at the very least, children don't want to be told they cannot taste that fruit.

Television ratings are like airport security—an act of theater, an illusion designed to reassure us, to make us feel like we control the influences we allow into our lives.

We want our children to be safe. We want to be safe. We want and need to pretend this is possible.

When I see the phrase "trigger warning," I am far more inclined to read whatever follows. I myself enjoy the taste of forbidden fruit.

I also know trigger warnings cannot save me from myself.

Trigger warnings are, essentially, ratings or protective guidelines for the largely unmoderated Internet. Trigger warnings provide order to the chaos of the interwebs; they are a signal that the content following the warning may be upsetting, may trigger bad memories or reminders of traumatic or sensitive experiences. Trigger warnings allow readers a choice: steel yourself and continue reading, or protect yourself and look away.

Many feminist communities use trigger warnings, particularly in online forums when discussing rape, sexual abuse, and violence. By using these warnings, these communities are saying, "This is a safe space. We will protect you from unexpected reminders of your history." Members of these communities are given the illusion they *can* be protected.

There are a great many potential trigger warnings. Over the years, I have seen trigger warnings for eating disorders, poverty, self-injury, bullying, heteronormativity, suicide, sizeism, genocide, slavery, mental illness, explicit fiction, explicit discussions of sexuality, homosexuality, homophobia, addiction, alcoholism, racism, the Holocaust, ableism, and Dan Savage.

Life, apparently, requires a trigger warning.

This is the uncomfortable truth: everything is a trigger for someone. There are things you cannot tell just by looking at someone.

We all have history. You can think you're *over* your history. You can think the past is the past. And then something happens, often innocuous, that shows you how far you are from *over it*. The past is always with you. Some people want to be protected from this truth.

I used to think I didn't have triggers because I told myself I was tough. I was steel. I was broken beneath the surface, but my skin was forged, impenetrable. Then I realized I had all kinds of triggers. I simply had buried them deep until there was no more room inside me. When the dam burst, I had to learn how to stare those triggers down. I had a lot of help, years and years of help.

I have writing.

Every so often debates about trigger warnings flare hotly and both sides are resolute. Trigger warnings are either ineffective and impractical or vital for creating safe online spaces.

It has been suggested, more than once, that if you don't believe in trigger warnings, you aren't respecting the experiences of rape and abuse survivors. It has been suggested, more than once, that trigger warnings are unnecessary coddling.

It is an impossible debate. There is too much history lurking beneath the skin of too many people. Few are willing to consider the possibility that trigger warnings might be ineffective, impractical, and necessary for creating safe spaces all at once.

The illusion of safety is as frustrating as it is powerful.

There are things that rip my skin open and reveal what lies beneath, but I don't believe in trigger warnings. I don't believe people can be protected from their histories. I don't believe it is at all possible to anticipate the histories of others.

There is no standard for trigger warnings, no universal guidelines. Once you start, where do you stop? Does the mention of the word "rape" require a trigger warning, or is the threshold an account of a rape? How graphic does an account of abuse need to be before meriting a warning? Are trigger warnings required anytime matters of difference are broached? What is graphic? Who makes these determinations?

It all seems so futile, so impotent and, at times, belittling. When I see trigger warnings, I think, *How dare you presume what I need to be protected from?*

Trigger warnings also, when used in excess, start to feel like censorship. They suggest that there are experiences or perspectives too inappropriate, too explicit, too bare to be voiced publicly. As a writer, I bristle when people say, "This should have had a trigger warning."

I do not understand the unspoken rules of trigger warnings. I cannot write the way I want to write and consider using trigger warnings. I would second-guess myself, temper the intensity of what I have to say. I don't want to do that. I don't intend to ever do that.

Writers cannot protect their readers from themselves, nor should they be expected to.

There is also this thought: maybe trigger warnings allow people to avoid learning how to deal with triggers and getting help. I say this with the understanding that having access to professional resources for getting help is a privilege. I say this with the understanding that sometimes there is not enough help in the world. That said, there is value in learning, where possible, how to deal with and respond to the triggers that cut you open, the triggers that put you back in terrible places, that remind you of painful history.

It is untenable to go through life as an exposed wound. No matter how well intended, trigger warnings will not stanch the bleeding; trigger warnings will not harden into scabs over your wounds.

I don't believe in safety. I wish I did. I am not brave. I simply know what to be scared of; I know to be scared of everything. There is freedom in that fear. That freedom makes it easier to appear fearless—to say and do what I want. I have been broken, so I am prepared should that happen again. I have, at times, put myself in dangerous situations. I have thought, *You have no idea what I can take.* This idea of unknown depths of endurance is a refrain in most of my writing. Human endurance fascinates me, probably too much because more often than not, I think of life in terms of enduring instead of living.

Intellectually, I understand why trigger warnings are necessary. I understand that painful experiences are all too often threatening to break the skin. Seeing or feeling yourself come apart is terrifying.

This is the truth of my trouble with trigger warnings: there is nothing words on the screen can do that has not already been done. A visceral reaction to a trigger is nothing compared to the actual experience that created the trigger.

I don't know how to see beyond this belief to truly get why trigger warnings are necessary. When I see trigger warnings,

I don't feel safe. I don't feel protected. Instead, I am surprised there are still people who believe in safety and protection despite overwhelming evidence to the contrary.

This is my failing.

But.

I do recognize that in some spaces, we have to err on the side of safety or the illusion thereof. Trigger warnings aren't meant for those of us who don't believe in them, just like the Bible wasn't written for atheists. Trigger warnings are designed for the people who need and believe in that safety.

Those of us who do not believe should have little say in the matter. We can neither presume nor judge what others might feel the need to be protected from.

But still.

There will always be a finger on the trigger. No matter how hard we try, there's no way to step out of the line of fire.

The Spectacle of
Broken Men

Though I've lived all over the country, I have spent many years, off and on, living in Nebraska, both as a child and as an adult. Nebraska is Husker country. There is God and there are the Huskers, and sometimes their order of importance is, well, unclear. On game day, Memorial Stadium is the third-largest city in Nebraska. Even though he has long since retired as coach, a position he held for twenty-five years, there is Tom Osborne, seated at the right hand of the Holy Father. He is the current athletic director at the University of Nebraska–Lincoln. He handily won his congressional district and served in Congress for six years. At the height of Nebraska football, during the 1990s, Nebraska won the national championships in 1994 and 1995, and captured part of the championship in 1997. Osborne ascended somewhere above God. To Nebraskans, Tom Osborne is much like Joe Paterno is to the people of Penn State. Amen.

In the 1990s, the unnecessary roughness of many Nebraska

players was well known. Lawrence Phillips was probably the hottest mess on that team, always getting in trouble for one thing or another. His crimes, more than once, involved violence against women, but he was such a fine running back and that mattered more than the woman's face he threatened to break. In those years, Nebraska players were getting arrested so much it was as if criminality had become a second letter sport for the players. The media would halfheartedly question Osborne about these "thugs," and he'd talk about how he was able to see the good in flawed men. More often than not, these players were forgiven for drug and alcohol infractions and assault and rape allegations because they could move the football down the field. They could fill Memorial Stadium week after week. They could take *our* team to the championship game, over and over. They could take us to church. Amen.

Nebraska certainly was not and is not unique. Neither is Penn State. College and professional athletes get away with all kinds of criminal behavior, and we must be comfortable with that criminal behavior because week in and week out we tune in to the football games and baseball games and basketball games and hockey games that showcase broken men carrying the hopes of millions on their backs. We cheer and buy jerseys and make rich men or soon-to-be rich men richer. When the truth about Jerry Sandusky and the Penn State football program was revealed, we were outraged, and rightly so, but there's plenty more to be outraged about where athletes, coaches, criminality, and silence are concerned. We live in a culture where athletes are revered, and overlooking terrible, criminal behavior is the price we are seemingly willing to pay for our reverence. Amen.

We're supposed to give accused criminals the benefit of the doubt. We are supposed to at least consider the possibility that someone accused of a crime is, actually, innocent. It's hard to do what we're *supposed* to do sometimes.

In high-profile cases such as the Sandusky case, it is very difficult to give the accused the benefit of the doubt. Being tried in the court of public opinion is the price highly visible figures must pay when they are accused of wrongdoing. Their penance begins well before they ever enter the courtroom.

I was marginally willing to give Jerry Sandusky the benefit of the doubt before I watched his interview with Bob Costas on *Rock Center* at the end of 2011. I was willing to do so because I don't want to believe a man is capable of sexually assaulting several children, for more than a decade. I don't want to believe that same man is capable of getting away with such heinous crimes because of the prestige and power of his position. I don't want to believe a coach who positioned himself as a paragon of moral virtue in a football program widely lauded for having a moral compass enabled such criminal and corrupt behavior. I certainly don't want to believe a grown man watched a young boy getting raped and, instead of trying to stop the rape or notifying the authorities, called his father and then called his boss and did nothing more. I don't want to believe a university would work to cover up this crime for years and years.

There's a certain crassness to an alleged pedophile being allowed to defend himself on national television. While our justice system is predicated upon the notion of the presumption of innocence until the establishment of guilt, there should be limits to what a highly visible figure can do to establish that innocence outside of the court of law. There aren't, though, not really.

Like most people, I gather what legal knowledge I have from a little show called *Law & Order*. My grasp on most legal concepts is tenuous at best. On *Law & Order*, most defense attorneys strongly discourage their clients from taking the stand in their own defense. They also discourage clients from talking to the media. Innocent or guilty, it is too easy for accused criminals to incriminate themselves when their words are not managed and mediated by someone else. With the hellstorm that surrounded Jerry Sandusky, you have to wonder what kind of attorney would let that man speak to the media.

I watched the *Rock Center* interview between Bob Costas and Jerry Sandusky. Beyond my general disgust for the proceedings, I realized Sandusky sounded like a broken, broken man. If he is guilty of the crimes he has been accused of—and yes, I surely do believe he is guilty, as does a court of law—Sandusky has been a broken man for a very long time. In that interview, he chose to reveal the ways in which he is broken, laid himself bare, however unintentionally.

Or, perhaps, he sounded so desperately broken because he got caught, because he no longer has unfettered access to young boys and an elite athletic program. After more than fifteen years, the loss of that lifestyle must have been quite a blow. You never can tell what it takes to break a man down.

If you ever want to know what guilt sounds like, listen to Sandusky try to explain his untoward actions with young boys over the years. His voice is haunting—weakened, I hope, by the gravity of his crimes. He talks of showering with the boys and roughhousing and touching them as if such behavior is normal. When asked, "Are you sexually attracted to young boys?," Sandusky repeats the question. Instead of simply saying, "No," which is what most people would say whether they were guilty or innocent, he says, "Am I sexually attracted to young boys? I enjoy young people. I love to be around them. But no, I'm not sexually attracted to young boys." The denial is an afterthought.

I give the victim the benefit of the doubt when it comes to allegations of rape and sexual abuse. I choose to err on that side of caution. This does not mean I am unsympathetic to the wrongly accused, but if there are sides to be chosen, I am on the side of the victim. I am glad such decisions are not left up to me because I don't know how to be impartial. It's all too close.

There is no easy way out of this situation for anyone involved. Either Sandusky sexually abused young men or he didn't, and the damage in either case is irreparable and runs deep. There are Sandusky and those surrounding him, a constellation of broken men—the victims and the men who enabled him, the men who looked the other way, year after year, men who would have to be broken to commit such inexplicable acts of silence and collusion.

After the interview aired, more victims stepped forward and accused Sandusky of sexual abuse. Sandusky and his legal team continued to cast aspersions upon the victims while offering a hollow defense. They chose the age-old "blame the victim" strategy, which is, all too often, how broken men respond to these situations, making it seem as if the damage lies elsewhere even though their own fractures are plain to see.

During Sandusky's trial, we saw just how broken he really is and how he has, in turn, broken far too many others. The details that came out of that Pennsylvania courtroom are as repulsive as they are heartbreaking. There might be some small measure of justice for the victims—it's too soon to tell. We can hope. The damage, though, has been done and it cannot be undone. The trial ended. Penn State will rebuild itself. A new football season will always start in Happy Valley and in Lincoln and in college towns all across the country, casting a wholesome veneer over ugly truths. Young men will break their bodies against one another while we cheer them on. Off the field, who knows what those young men will do. We will forget about Jerry Sandusky and his victims, even if we don't mean to. This is how it goes. There's always some new fracture in humanity to focus on.

On Saturday, June 9, 2013, a father in central Texas found a man sexually abusing his daughter. The father beat that man to death, broke him so badly there was no coming back from it.

There won't be a trial. Justice, in this case, was swift and applied brutally. Many are calling this father a hero. Many of us would do the same thing, would get caught in a moment of blind fury in the face of such a violation. That father was remorseful. He wasn't trying to kill a man. He was trying to save his daughter and he did, or at least, he saved what he could. He was not charged. Mostly, this story shows us how broken men are everywhere—on ranches in central Texas, in elite football programs, both on the field and on the sidelines. And alongside these broken men are the women who all too often become broken too. It's a spectacle in every way.

A Tale of Three
Coming Out Stories

We are still in that time in our history when public figures come out of invisible closets largely built by a public insatiable in its desire to know all the intimate details of the private lives of very public people.

We want to know everything. In this information age, we are inundated with information, so now we feel entitled. We also like taxonomy, classification, definition. Are you a man or a woman? Are you a Democrat or a Republican? Are you married or single? Are you gay or straight? We don't know what to do when we don't know the answers to these questions or, worse, when the answers to these questions do not fall neatly into a category.

When public figures don't provide outward evidence of their sexuality, our desire to classify intensifies. Any number of celebrities are dogged by "gay rumors" because we cannot quite place them into a given category. We act like placing these people in categories will have some impact on our lives, or that creating these categories is our responsibility, when, most of the time, such taxonomy won't change anything at all. For example, there is nothing in my life that is impacted by knowing Ricky Martin is gay. The only thing satisfied by that information is my curiosity.

Sometimes, this zeal to classify has resulted in public figures being outed against their will. In particular, politicians who have gone on record for legislation that suppresses civil rights have found themselves in the glare of the spotlight. Congressman Edward Schrock was outed in 2004 because he voted for the Marriage Protection Act. There have been many others. When people have been forcibly outed, those doing the outing have said they were acting for the greater good or working to reveal hypocrisy, as if the right to privacy and the right to determine if and when to come out is only afforded to those who are infallible.

This is, in part, a matter of privacy. What information do we have the right to keep to ourselves? What boundaries are we allowed to maintain in our personal lives? What do we have a right to know about the lives of others? When do we have a right to breach the boundaries others have set for themselves?

People with high public profiles are allowed very few boundaries. In exchange for the erosion of privacy, they receive fame and/or fortune and/or power. Is this a fair price? Are famous people aware of how they are sacrificing privacy when they ascend to a position of cultural prominence?

There are many ways we have surrendered privacy in the information age. We willingly disclose what we've eaten for breakfast, where we spent last night and with whom, and all manner of trivial information. We submit personal information when registering for social media accounts and when making purchases online. We often surrender this information without question or reflection. These disclosures come so freely because we've long been conditioned to share too much with too many.

In his book *Privacy*, Garret Keizer explores privacy through a series of essays that consider privacy legally, from the feminist perspective, through the lens of class, and more. He demonstrates a real concern for how little privacy we have, how cavalier we can be with our privacy, and how unthinkingly we might infringe on the privacy of others. He says,

> *We speak of privacy as a right but we might also think of it as a test, as a canary in the mine of our civilization. It lives or dies to the extent that we remain willing to believe that the human person, body and soul—our blood relative in his or her flesh, and beyond reduction in his or her grandeur and nobility—is sacred, endowed with inalienable rights, and a microcosm of us all.*

We tend to forget that culturally prominent figures are as sacred to those they love as the people closest to us. We tend to forget that they are flesh and blood. We assume that as they rise to prominence, they shed their inalienable rights. We do this without question.

One of the most striking arguments Keizer makes is that privacy and class are intrinsically bound together. He asserts that people with privilege have more access to privacy than people who don't. Keizer notes, "Social class is defined in large part by the degree of freedom one has to move from private space to public space, and by the amount of time one spends in relative privacy."

This relationship between privacy and privilege extends to race, gender, and sexuality. When a woman is pregnant, for example, there's increasingly less privacy because, as she reaches full term, her condition becomes more and more visible. Keizer remarks, with regard to pregnant women, that

> *her condition is an unequivocally public statement of a very private experience, begun in circumstances of intimacy and continued within*

the sanctum of her own body—yet there is no hiding it for her, nor any denying the feeling we have that somehow she belongs to us, that she embodies our collective future and represents our individual pasts.

Any time your body represents some kind of difference, your privacy is compromised to some degree. A surfeit of privacy is just one more benefit the privileged class enjoys and often takes for granted.

Heterosexuals take the privacy of their sexuality for granted. They can date, marry, and love whom they choose without needing to disclose much of anything. If they do choose to disclose, there are rarely negative consequences.

In recent years, celebrities have started coming out with little fanfare by way, perhaps, of an interview where a man might casually mention his male partner or refer to himself as a gay man, or a woman might thank her partner in an award acceptance speech. The public reacts when celebrities come out quietly, but the spectacle is somewhat muted. When celebrities come out in this manner, they are generally saying, "This is simply one more thing you now know about me."

In July 2012, popular journalist Anderson Cooper came out of one of those invisible closets built by someone else's hands in an e-mail to the *Daily Beast*'s Andrew Sullivan, who published the message on his blog.

Cooper wrote:

The fact is, I'm gay, always have been, always will be, and I couldn't be any more happy, comfortable with myself, and proud.

I have always been very open and honest about this part of my life with my friends, my family, and my colleagues. In a perfect world, I don't think it's anyone else's business, but I do think there is value in standing up and being counted.

There was a range of responses to Cooper's coming out. Many people shrugged and said Cooper's sexuality was presumed, an open secret. Others insisted it was important and even necessary for Cooper to come out and to, as he puts it, stand up and be counted.

This is often what is said when public figures do or do not come out in this day and age: there is a greater obligation that must be met beyond what that person might ordinarily choose to meet. We make these demands, though, without considering how much less privacy that person might have as a public figure who is also part of an underrepresented group. I am not suggesting that we cry for the celebrity who enjoys a lush lifestyle; I am saying we should give thought to the celebrity who would prefer to keep his marriage to a man private for whatever reason, but isn't allowed that right, a right that is, for heterosexuals, inalienable.

In *Privacy*, Keizer notes, "The public obligations of prominently powerful people can also constrain their private lives." We see these constraints time and again when celebrities and other prominent figures sidestep questions about their personal lives they are unwilling to answer. They may be hesitant for any number of reasons—protecting their privacy, protecting their careers and social standing, protecting loved ones. The public rarely seems to care about those reasons. They—we—need to know.

At the same time, we live in a complex cultural climate, one where seventeen states allow same-sex marriage but twenty-nine states have constitutions forbidding marriage equality. Things are improving, but we are inching too slowly to equal rights for all. The world we live in is not as progressive as we need it to be. When a celebrity comes out, it is still news. The coming out is still culturally significant. When a man like Anderson Cooper comes out, it's a step forward in achieving civil rights for everyone. At the very least, it is one more person saying, "I am here. I matter. I demand to be recognized." Cooper is, by many standards, the "right kind of gay"—white, handsome, successful, masculine. Many celebrities who have successfully come out in recent years fit that profile—Neil Patrick Harris, Matt Bomer, Zachary Quinto, and so on. These men are held up as examples—not too flamboyant, not *too* gay.

Still, prominent gay people need to stand up and be counted because the word "gay" is still used as a slur. Nine out of ten LGBT teenagers report being bullied at school. LGBT youth are two to three times more likely to commit suicide. The bullying and harassment of LGBT youth are so pervasive that, in 2010, Dan Savage and his partner, Terry Miller, created a YouTube video to show LGBT youth how life can, indeed, get better beyond the torments of adolescence. That video spawned countless other videos and a foundation dedicated to continuing this project of showing LGBT youth there is a light at the end of an often very dark tunnel.

Celebrities like Cooper also need to stand up and be counted because there is only a handful of states where gay marriage is legal. It was only in 2013 that the Supreme Court invalidated the Defense of Marriage Act, passed in 1996. The Defense of Marriage Act denied gay couples 1,138 federally preserved rights afforded to heterosexual couples. More than twenty states have constitutional provisions explicitly defining marriage as a union between a man and a woman. There are states where LGBT people cannot adopt children. Depending on where they live, members of the LGBT community may lose their jobs because of their sexual orientation. They may face ostracism from family, friends, and community. Things get better, perhaps, but slowly and certainly not universally.

LGBT people are the victims of hate crimes. There is the

young lesbian couple in Texas, Mary Kristene Chapa and Mollie Olgin, who were both shot in the head by an unknown assailant and left to die. A gay couple in northeast DC was attacked two blocks from their apartment by three assailants who were shouting homophobic slurs. One, Michael Hall, was hospitalized; he had no health insurance and had a fractured jaw. In Edmond, Oklahoma, a gay man's car was vandalized with a homophobic slur and set on fire. In Indianapolis, Indiana, there was a drive-by shooting of a gay bar. Hate is everywhere.

It gets better, sort of. It gets better unless you're in the wrong place at the wrong time. Sometimes the wrong place is your home, the one place where you should be able to feel safe no matter what the world is like.

Sally Ride, the first woman astronaut, who died in July 2012 at the age of sixty-one, was survived by her female partner of twenty-seven years. At the time of her death, Ride's widow was not able to receive the federal benefits normally given to a surviving spouse. Sally Ride was able to fly into space and reach the stars, but here on earth, her long-term relationship went largely unrecognized. The 2012 Republican presidential hopeful Mitt Romney tweeted, "Sally Ride ranks among the greatest pioneers. I count myself among the millions of Americans she inspired with her travel to space." Music group the Mountain Goats replied, "Kind of despicable and grotesque that her partner of twenty-seven years will be denied her federal benefits, don't you think?" Despicable and grotesque, indeed, but in her death, Sally Ride stood up and was counted. She became even more of a hero than she already was.

It's a problem, though, that there's a right kind of gay, that there are LGBT people who are warmly encouraged to step out of the closet while others who don't fit certain parameters go largely ignored. It's easy enough for a man like Anderson Cooper, living in fairly liberal New York City, to come out. He will likely continue to be very successful. He has a supportive family and a welcoming community to embrace him. Coming out stories for everyday people are often far different, complicated and difficult. We forget what it's like to come out in the so-called flyover states. It's not easy.

In July 2012, musician Frank Ocean, a celebrity with a lower profile than Cooper but with, perhaps, more to lose, came out via Tumblr as having once loved a man by sharing some of the liner notes for his critically acclaimed album *Channel Orange*. Once again, cultural observers noted that Ocean's coming out was significant.

As a black man coming out as gay or bisexual, particularly as part of the notoriously homophobic R&B and hip-hop community, Ocean was taking a bold step, a risk. He was trusting that his music would transcend the prejudices of his audience. So far, that risk seems to have paid off. Many celebrities vocalized their support of Ocean, including Russell Simmons, Beyoncé, 50 Cent, and others. He is standing up to be counted. *Channel Orange* was a critical and commercial success.

Of course, Ocean is also part of the Odd Future collective. His friend and collaborator Tyler, the Creator's debut album, *Goblin*, contains 213 gay slurs. Tyler, the Creator continues to assert he's not homophobic with that old canard of having gay friends. He stepped up his defense by also claiming his gay fans were totally fine with his use of the term "faggot" over and over and over— immunity by association. I do not know the man. Maybe he is homophobic, maybe he isn't. I do know he doesn't think about language very carefully. He believes that just because you can say something, you should. He is not shamed by using slurs 213 times on one album, no matter how that frequency reflects a lack of imagination.

For every step forward, there is some asshole shoving progress back.

Despite our complex cultural climate and what needs to be done for the greater good, it is still an unreasonable burden that someone who is marginalized must bear an extra set of responsibilities. It is unfair that prominent cultural figures who come out have to forge these inroads on our behalf; they carry the hopes of so many on their shoulders. They stand up and are counted so that someday things might actually be better for everyone, everywhere, not just the camera- or radio-ready celebrities for whom coming out is far easier than most.

I am reminded of the Iowa lesbian couple whose son, Zach Wahls, testified in 2011 before the Iowa House Judiciary Committee about how a child raised by two women turns out. He spoke in support of gay marriage in Iowa. He was passionate and eloquent and a real credit to his parents. The video clip of his testimony was shared across the Internet. Every time I saw it I was both thrilled and angry—angry because queer people always have to fight so much harder for a fraction of the recognition. No one ever asks heterosexual parents to ensure that their children are models of citizenry. The bar for queer parents is unfairly, unnecessarily high, but young men like this one keep vaulting that bar nonetheless.

Perhaps we expect gay public figures and other prominent queer people to come out, to stand and be counted, so they can do the work we're unwilling to do to change the world, to carry the burdens we are unwilling to shoulder, to take the stands we are unwilling to make. As individuals, we may not be able to do much, but when we're silent when someone uses the word "gay" as an insult, we are falling short. When we don't vote to support equal marriage rights for all, we are falling short. When we support musicians like Tyler, the Creator, we are falling short. We are failing our communities. We are failing civil rights. There are injustices great and small, and even if we can only fight the small ones, at least we are fighting.

Too often, we fail to ask ourselves what sacrifices we will make for the greater good. What stands will we take? We expect *role models* to model the behaviors we are perfectly capable of modeling ourselves. We know things are getting better. We know we have far to go. In *Privacy*, Keizer also says, "The plurality of intrusions on our privacy has the cumulative effect of inducing a sense of helplessness." We are willing—even anxious—to see prominent figures in a state of helplessness as they sacrifice their privacy for the greater good. How helpless are *we* willing to be for the greater good? That question interests me most.

Beyond the Measure of Men

Here we are again.

In the *New York Times Book Review*, Meg Wolitzer addresses the matter of "women's fiction" in her essay "The Second Shelf." She highlights the ongoing, fraught conversation about men, women, the books they write, and the disparity in the consideration these books receive.

It is a shame that I can point to any number of essays that take up issues of gender, literary credibility, and the relative lack of critical acceptance and attention women receive from the (male) literary establishment, with equal skill and precision as Wolitzer does. It is absurd that talented writers continue to have to spend their valuable time demonstrating just how serious, pervasive, and far-reaching this problem is instead of writing about more interesting topics.

When we look beyond publishing and consider that the United States is a country where we're still having an incomprehensible debate about contraception and reproductive freedom, it becomes clear women are dealing with trickle-down misogyny. What starts with the legislature reaches everywhere. The cocreator of *Two and a Half Men* flippantly said, with regard to women-oriented television, "Enough, ladies. I get it. You have periods," and "We're approaching peak vagina on television, the point of labia saturation." The 2012 National Magazine Award finalists were announced, and there were no women included in several categories—reporting, feature writing, profile writing, essays and criticism, and columns and commentary. Every single day there's a new instance of gender trouble. Some men aren't interested in the concerns of women, not in society, not on television, not in publishing, not anywhere.

The time for outrage over things we already know is over. The call-and-response of this debate has grown tightly choreographed and tedious. A woman dares to acknowledge the gender problem. Some people say, "Yes, you're right," but do nothing to change the status quo. Some people say, "I'm not part of the problem," and offer up some tired example as to why this is all no big deal, why this is all being blown out of proportion. Some people offer up submission queue ratios and other excuses as if that absolves responsibility. Some people say, "Give me more proof," or "I want more numbers," or "Things are so much better," or "You are wrong." Some people say, "Stop complaining." Some people say, "Enough talking about the problem. Let's talk about solutions." Another woman dares to acknowledge this gender problem. Rinse. Repeat.

The solutions are obvious. Stop making excuses. Stop saying women run publishing. Stop justifying the lack of parity in prominent publications that have the resources to address gender inequity. Stop parroting the weak notion that you're simply publishing *the best writing, regardless.* There is ample evidence of the excellence of women writers. Publish more women writers. If women aren't submitting to your publication or press, ask yourself why, deal with the answers even if those answers make you uncomfortable, and then reach out to women writers. If women don't respond to your solicitations, go find other women. Keep doing that, issue after issue after issue. Read more widely. Create more inclusive measures of excellence. Ensure that books by men and women are being reviewed in equal numbers. Nominate more *deserving* women for the important awards. Deal with your resentment. Deal with your biases. Vigorously resist the urge to dismiss the *gender problem*. Make the effort and make the effort and make the effort until you no longer need to, until we don't need to keep having this conversation.

Change requires intent and effort. It really is that simple.

The term "women's fiction" is so wildly vague it is mostly useless. The book covers are often marked by pastels, the silhouettes of well-accessorized women, or a few body parts ambiguously splayed. In the *New York Times Book Review* Chloë Schama writes, "A plague of women's backs is upon us in the book cover world." She goes on to cite an alarming number of recent book covers featuring a woman's back, her nape exposed, as if we dare not see a woman's face. Schama concludes, "Sex sells, and this reference to the body without obvious objectification must appeal to an industry that overwhelmingly attracts and employs women." "Women's fiction" is a label designed to sell a certain kind of book to a certain kind of reader. As writers, we have little control over how our books are marketed or the covers our books receive. And let's be clear: "women's fiction" and the accompanying, often cloying cover designs are marketing choices meant to either encompass the subject matter of a book or its author, or both. We are beholden to these arbitrary categories that are, in many ways, insulting to men, women, and writing.

There are books written by women. There are books written by men. Somehow, though, it is only books by women, or books about certain topics, that require this special "women's fiction" designation, particularly when those books have the audacity to explore, in some manner, the female experience, which, apparently, includes the topics of marriage, suburban existence, and parenthood, as if women act alone in these endeavors, wedding themselves, immaculately conceiving children, and the like. Women's fiction is often considered a more intimate brand of storytelling that doesn't tackle the *big* issues found in men's fiction. Anyone who reads knows this isn't the case, but that misperception lingers. As Ruth Franklin notes, "The underlying problem is that while women read books by male writers about male characters, men tend not to do the reverse. Men's novels about suburbia (Franzen) are about society; women's novels about suburbia (Wolitzer) are about women."

Narratives about certain experiences are somehow legitimized when mediated through a man's perspective. Consider the work of John Updike or Richard Yates. Most of their fiction is grounded in domestic themes that, in the hands of a woman, would render the work "women's fiction." While these books may be tagged as "women's fiction" on Amazon.com, they are also categorized as literary fiction. These books are allowed to be more than what they are by virtue of the writer's gender, while similar books by women are forced to be less than what they are, forced into narrow, often inaccurate categories that diminish their contents.

James Salter's excellent short story collection *Last Night* is a book filled with stories about men and women and marriage and the infinite ways people fail one another. It is a gorgeous book, one that is often concerned with the experiences of women. In one story, a wife demands her husband end an affair with his gay lover, and the muted agony of the situation is palpable. In another story, a group of friends catch up on their lives, and at the end, we learn that one of them is dying, doesn't know how to share that news, and so she tells a stranger, her cabdriver, who, in the wake of her confession, frankly assesses her appearance. A woman meets a poet at a party and becomes fixated on his dog. These stories are not so radically different from stories by, say, Elizabeth Strout.

There are more similarities between the writing of men and women than there are differences. Aren't we all just trying to tell stories? How do we keep losing sight of this fact?

When did men become the measure? When did we collectively decide writing was more worthy if men embraced it? I suppose it was the "literary establishment" that made this decision when, for too long, men dominated the canon, and it was men whose work was elevated as worthy, who received the majority of the prestigious literary prizes and critical attention.

Male readership shouldn't be the measure to which we aspire. Excellence should be the measure, and if men and *the establishment* can't (or won't) recognize that excellence, we should leave the culpability with them instead of bearing it ourselves. As long as we keep considering male readership the goal, we're not going to get anywhere.

The label "women's fiction" is often used with such disdain. I hate how "woman" has become a slur. I hate how some women writers twist themselves into knots to distance themselves from "women's fiction," as if we have anything to be ashamed of as women who write what we want to write.

I don't care if my fiction is labeled as women's fiction. I know what my writing is and what it isn't. Someone else's arbitrary designation can't change that. I don't care if men don't read my books. Don't get me wrong. I want men to read my books. I want everyone to read my books, but I'm not going to desperately pine for readers who aren't interested in what I'm writing.

If readers discount certain topics as unworthy of their attention, if readers are going to judge a book by its cover or feel excluded from a certain kind of book because the cover is, say, pink, the failure is with the reader, not the writer. To read narrowly and shallowly is to read from a place of ignorance, and women writers can't fix that ignorance no matter what kind of books we write or how those books are marketed.

This is where we should start focusing this conversation: how men (as readers, critics, and editors) can start to bear the responsibility for becoming better, broader readers.

Reading remains one of the purest things I do. As anyone who follows me on Twitter knows, I derive a great deal of joy from reading—highbrow, lowbrow, I'm into all of it. Nearly every day I chatter happily about the books I'm reading to my Twitter feed, and it's great to be able to talk about books without worrying about all the problems of publishing. It's great to remember that reading is my first love.

I don't want us to lose sight of the joy of reading because we're all too focused on the bitter realities of how our reading material finds its way into the world and struggles to have a fighting chance.

Though we are a relatively small community invested in these issues, we keep having these difficult conversations about gender and publishing, no matter where we stand, because we carry a raw and stupid hope that someday we will have acted with enough intent and effort, we will have created enough change, we will have created better measures. We continue having these conversations so someday there is nothing left to talk about but the joy and complexity of the stories we write and read. I want that joy to be the only thing that matters.

Great books remind me that when we spend more time talking about publishing than we talk about books themselves, we're forgetting what matters most.

Some Jokes Are Funnier Than Others

When I was in the sixth grade, a kid in my class—we'll call him James—was really funny, the class clown. James joked about everything and we all loved him for it because his wit was so sharp, even at such a young age. You never wanted James to turn his humor against you, but you always wondered what he might say next. You always laughed.

On January 28, 1986, the space shuttle *Challenger* lifted off at 10:38 in the morning. We were watching television in science class and it was a big deal to have our traditional class activities set aside to watch the launch. Our science teacher was particularly excited. He loved anything science-related and was a deeply engaged teacher. He was also personally invested because Christa McAuliffe, a teacher from New Hampshire, was one of the seven astronauts hurtling toward space. The mysteries of outer space felt a little more within his reach that day. He was the kind of man who wanted to touch the stars.

Shortly after liftoff, the *Challenger* exploded. We watched on the small television screen as the shuttle burst into flames and thick, spiraled plumes of smoke filled the air. Debris began falling into the ocean. It did not seem real. The classroom was silent. We were stunned. Our science teacher's eyes reddened, and he kept trying to speak but could only clear his throat. My classmates and I stared at one another uncomfortably. The newscasters began to report what few facts they knew. James snickered and said, "I guess there are a lot of dead fish now." Our science teacher lost it completely and gave James a serious dressing-down. The rest of the year was rough for James. He had finally crossed an invisible line about what one can or cannot joke about. I've never forgotten that day or how James suddenly became an outcast because he went too far, because it was too soon, because joking about a tragedy was too much.

Inappropriate humor is often the best kind. Everyone knows at least one joke she finds funny even though she shouldn't. I am not always proud of the things that make me laugh, but I genuinely admire a comedian who can both make me laugh and make me uncomfortable. Such contradictions are thought provoking. In a profile of the late Patrice O'Neal for *New York* magazine, Adrian Nicole LeBlanc wrote about how O'Neal was deliberate and merciless in testing boundaries and saying the unspeakable. She characterized his willingness to do this by saying, "The transformative power of the ugly truth was, for O'Neal, a form of grace." Most comedians seem to be reaching for that form of grace, trying to talk about the complexity of these lives we lead in ways that can make us laugh and think and feel.

Many of O'Neal's fans said they laughed with him even when they disagreed. They said he could joke about anything because of how he did it. For O'Neal and many comics, there are no lines they are unwilling to cross, no subjects that are taboo, and they get away with these transgressions because they know how to walk that very fine, always moving line.

I am not a fan of Daniel Tosh and his comedy, but I'm not his target demographic. I don't spend a great deal of time thinking about his existence or brand of humor because I don't need to. He is an unapologetic misogynist but many people find him funny so there must be *something* there. However funny he may be, though, his humor is utterly lacking in grace. He does not possess the transformative power of his betters, so when he tries to be edgy and transgressive, it tends to fall flat.

During one episode of his television show on Comedy Central, *Tosh.0*, Tosh encouraged his audience to film themselves touching women softly on their stomachs. I am not quite sure how this encroachment on personal space and ignorance of appropriate boundaries constitutes humor, but it takes all kinds. I'm also a woman, and we are, from what I hear, not funny. Nonetheless, the incident gave me pause, particularly when his ardent fans actually began filming themselves touching women softly on their stomachs and posting the videos to YouTube. Somehow, these fans thought this behavior was acceptable because the comic they admired told them so. You'd be amazed what people are willing to do when they are given permission, either implicitly or explicitly.

Given Tosh's general history of immature, frattish humor, I wasn't surprised when he made inappropriate statements about rape humor during a set at the Laugh Factory. Rape jokes are part of his shtick. During that set, a young woman in the audience yelled, "Actually, rape jokes are never funny." Tosh maturely responded, "Wouldn't it be funny if that girl got raped by like five guys right now? Like right now? What if a bunch of guys just raped her . . ."

What if, indeed. There's no better follow-up for a rape joke than a gang rape joke because if rape is funny, gang rape is funnier.

Rape humor is designed to remind women that they are still

not quite equal. Just as their bodies and reproductive freedom are open to legislation and public discourse, so are their other issues. When women respond negatively to misogynistic or rape humor, they are "sensitive" and branded as "feminist," a word that has, as of late, become a catchall term for "woman who does not tolerate bullshit."

Perhaps rape jokes are funny, but I cannot fathom how. Humor is subjective, but is it *that* subjective? I don't have it in me to find rape jokes funny or to tolerate them in any way. It's too close a topic. Rape is many things—humiliating, degrading, physically and emotionally painful, exhausting, irritating, and sometimes, it is even banal. It is rarely funny for most women. There are not enough years in this lifetime to create the kind of distance where I could laugh and say, "That one time when I was gang-raped was totally hilarious, a real laugh riot."

Somewhere along the line we started misinterpreting the First Amendment and this idea of the freedom of speech the amendment grants us. We are free to speak as we choose without fear of prosecution or persecution, but we are not free to speak as we choose without consequence.

The woman who called Tosh out on his comments walked out of the club, and a friend posted about it on Tumblr. The Internet picked up her story. Tosh has since offered a small act of contrition qualified by his assertion that his comments were shared out of context; he was heckled. He clearly doesn't think he has done anything wrong. His half-assed apology is the kind where he is merely sorry someone has taken offense rather than taking responsibility for his actions. He will never think it is wrong to joke about rape. Like I said—it takes all kinds.

Many comedians are very proud of themselves for saying the things others are supposedly *afraid* to say. They are at the forefront of this culture of entitlement where we get to do anything, think anything, and say anything.

Those who refrain from using humor to comment on the "awful things in the world" don't abstain because they are afraid. Maybe, just maybe, they have common sense; they have conscience. Sometimes, saying what others are afraid or unwilling to say is just being an asshole. We are all free to be assholes, but we are not free to do so without consequence.

What Tosh calls heckling, I'd call taking a stand. All too often, when we see injustices, both great and small, we think, *That's terrible,* but we do nothing. We say nothing. We let other people fight their own battles. We remain silent because silence is easier.

Qui tacet consentire videtur is Latin for "Silence gives consent." When we say nothing, when we do nothing, we are consenting to these trespasses against us.

When that woman stood up and said, "No, rape is not funny," she did not consent to participating in a culture that encourages lax attitudes toward sexual violence and the concerns of women. Rape humor is what encourages a man to feel comfortable tweeting to Daniel Tosh, "the only ppl who are mad at you are the feminist bitches who never get laid and hope they get raped so they can get laid," which is one of the idiotic, Pavlovian responses a certain kind of *person* has when women have the nerve to suggest that they don't find sexual violence amusing. In that man's universe, women who get properly laid are totally fine with rape humor. A satisfied vagina is a balm in Gilead.

We know the appalling statistics. We know sexual violence is embedded within our culture so deeply that there exists a website, Hollaback, where women regularly report street harassment. Sexual violence is so problematic that there is a Sexual Assault Awareness Month, and there are countless organizations whose sole function is to support victims of sexual violence. We live in a society where the phrase "rape culture" exists because the culture itself exists. This climate is staggering. Either you recognize that or you don't. Rape humor is not "just jokes" or "stand-up."

Humor about sexual violence suggests permissiveness—not for people who would never commit such acts but for the people who have whatever weakness allows them to do terrible things unto others. If any number of young men were willing to film themselves touching women lightly on their stomachs, how many were encouraged to ignore a woman's no because Daniel Tosh finds rape amusing? What are the consequences if the answer is even one?

What surprises me, what really troubles me, is this: only one person stood up and had the strength of conviction to say, "Enough."

Dear Young Ladies Who Love Chris Brown So Much They Would Let Him Beat Them

Do you know what you're saying? Do you really?

You may think you're joking. I want to believe you're joking, because *haha, a man putting his hands on you is so funny* in the reality from where you are communicating. Clearly, we have different definitions of funny, but perhaps you truly do find it amusing to joke about domestic violence. I am not here to judge you.

I am afraid you're not joking. I'm afraid you are quite serious.

You are saying you are willing to be abused; you are willing to sacrifice your dignity.

For what?

You are impressed by some combination of a young man's music, charisma, dancing ability, and/or good looks. That is understandable. Everybody's got his or her something. However. You are also saying that suffering Chris Brown's abuse would be a fair exchange for his attention, however fleeting you must realize that attention would be. When you look past the image, a celebrity is merely a person you know nothing about. You are willing to be abused for the mirage of fame in the desert of your life.

For people who enjoy BDSM, there's this thing called consent, which should always exist in human interactions, but which is exceedingly important when you entrust your body and mind to someone else in such ways. You can say, "I want you to hurt me," or "I want you to humiliate me," or "I want you to dominate me," and someone else will do so. But, and this is important, when you say, in some form or fashion, *stop*, the pain or humiliation or domination stops, no questions asked. That is a powerful, perfect moment. There is nothing better than knowing the suffering can stop; than knowing you must endure but if you no longer wish to do so, you don't have to because it is safe to withdraw your consent. There is nothing better than knowing you have some control in a situation that feels so far beyond your control.

When you tell a man like Chris Brown, at least the man he has shown himself to be, to stop, he won't. With abuse there is no stopping. There is no consent. You will never have any control. You will never know how good it feels to endure by your choice because that choice does not belong to you and never will. Do you see that distinction?

I don't know Chris Brown. I have never met him and probably never will. I know his music. Sometimes, it's catchy. Mostly, to my ears, it's contrived and overproduced. I've seen him dance—he can work with choreography. He is reasonably attractive. I don't really get it, to be honest, but I don't need to get it. You likely wouldn't understand whom I find attractive, either. What I do understand is that Chris Brown means something to you, that he arouses you physically or emotionally. He arouses you to such an extent you are willing to do whatever it takes to be within his incandescent sphere for even a little while.

Did you read the police report from the infamous incident where Chris Brown beat his then girlfriend Rihanna? The details are disturbing and graphic and leave the distinct impression that what took place on that night in 2009 was perhaps not an isolated incident. If you were to "get with" Chris Brown there's a good chance you would regret it, because time and again he has shown he cannot control his rage. He would hardly be concerned with you at all. This is the man he has shown himself to be.

I am sorry our culture has treated women so poorly for so long that suffering abuse to receive celebrity attention seems like a fair and reasonable trade. We have failed you, utterly.

We failed you when Chris Brown received a slap on the wrist for his crime and was subsequently allowed to perform at the 2012 Grammys not once but twice. We failed you when he was awarded Best R&B Album at that same ceremony. This is not to say he has no right to move on from his crime, but he has demonstrated not one ounce of contrition. Instead, he has flagrantly reveled in his bad-boy persona and taunted the public at every turn. He's young and troubled, but that's an explanation for his behavior, not an excuse.

We failed you when Charlie Sheen was allowed and eagerly encouraged to continue to star in movies and have a hit television show that basically printed him money after he shot Kelly Preston "accidentally," and he allegedly hit a UCLA student in the head when she wouldn't have sex with him, and he threatened to kill his ex-wife Denise Richards, and he held a knife to his ex-wife Brooke Mueller's throat. We failed you when Roman Polanski received an Oscar even though he was accussed of committing a crime so terrible he hasn't been able to return to the United States for more than thirty years. We failed you when Sean Penn fought violently with Madonna and continued a successful, critically acclaimed career and also received an Oscar.

We fail you every single time a (famous) man treats a woman badly, without legal, professional, or personal consequence.

Over and over again we tell you it is acceptable for men—famous, infamous, or not at all famous—to abuse women. We look the other way. We make excuses. We reward these men for their bad behavior. We tell you that, as a young woman, you have little value or place in this society. Clearly we have sent these messages with such alarming regularity and consistency we have encouraged you to willingly run toward something violent and terrible with your eyes and arms wide open.

I am sorry.

I'm not shocked by your willingness to suffer without the right to consent. We are all susceptible to the charisma of people who behave badly, myself included. I am painfully reminded of how bad a feminist I am when I consider someone like Richard Pryor. He was a comic genius. I am always floored by how he tackled the complexities of race with his humor. Pryor was also flagrantly abusive toward the women he loved. His brilliance cannot be overlooked. That's what I tell myself, but then I imagine all the hurt he caused and how rarely that hurt is discussed. That may be the saddest thing of all.

Blurred Lines, Indeed

In his single "Blurred Lines," Robin Thicke sings soulfully about giving a good girl what she *really* wants—buck-wild sex—even if she can't come out and admit it. It's a catchy enough song. Some might even call it the anthem of Summer 2013. But "Blurred Lines" is also a song that revisits the age-old belief that sometimes when a woman says no she really means yes.

Critics have been vocal about the sexual violence undertones in the song, and they're not wrong. Robin just knows you want it, girl. He just does, so shut up and let him give it to you. Scores of men and women are, apparently, on board. "Blurred Lines" is Thicke's most popular song to date. In his single "Give It 2 U," Thicke doubles down on his bad-boy phase with lyrics that tell a woman what he has for her, including a reference to his endowment. In the wake of the criticism, Thicke is fairly unapologetic, saying, "Women and their bodies are beautiful. Men are always gonna want to follow them around." I guess that's that. Men want what they want.

As much as it pains me to admit, I like these songs. They make

me want to dance. I want to sing along. They are delightful pop
confections. But. I enjoy the songs the way I have to enjoy most
music—I have to forget I am a sentient being. I have to lighten up.

Take Kanye West's *Yeezus*. The album is compelling and ambitious, with sounds that are aggressive if not hostile. When *Yeezus*
was released, I listened to the album on repeat. I wanted to love
Yeezus, but I can't because of lyrics like "You see it's leaders and
it's followers / But I'd rather be a dick than a swallower," from
the song "New Slaves." Kanye's disdain for women overwhelms
nearly every track—but then there's a song like "Blood on the
Leaves" that is so outstanding you can't possibly dismiss the
album entirely. We are constantly faced by this uncomfortable
balance between brilliance and bad behavior.

This is just music, right? These artists are merely expressing
themselves.

As a writer, I recognize the necessity of creative freedom. I
have finally heard a couple of funny rape jokes—Ever Mainard's
joke about the fear instilled in women and the assumption of
the inevitability of rape and Wanda Sykes's joke about wanting a
detachable vagina to better avoid rape while out and about. I still
hate rape jokes, but I hate censorship more. I hate that I have to
choose.

Ken Hoinsky is a pickup artist who ran a successful Kickstarter
fund-raising campaign for his book *Above the Game*, where he
doles out his wisdom to help men who might be shy or awkward
around the ladies. When a critical mass of people became aware
of Hoinsky's project, there was outcry because some of Hoinsky's
advice—well, it's questionable. It blurs lines. Still Kickstarter
didn't cancel the project. Later, the company apologized. Moving
forward, it promised not to allow the creators of seduction guides
to use the Kickstarter platform. Additionally, Kickstarter made a
significant financial contribution to RAINN. Hoinsky will publish his book and join a small legion of pickup artists who treat

women as conquests rather than human beings, who believe that when a woman says no, she's really saying maybe.

Men want what they want.

So much of our culture caters to giving men what they want. A high school student invites model Kate Upton to attend his prom, and he's congratulated for his audacity. A male fan at a Beyoncé concert reaches up to the stage to slap her ass because her ass is there, her ass is magnificent, and he wants to feel it. The science fiction fandom community is often embroiled in heated discussions, across the Internet, about the ongoing problem of sexual harassment at conventions—countless women are telling all manner of stories about how, without their consent, they are groped, ogled, lured into hotel rooms under false pretenses, physically lifted off the ground, and more.

But men want what they want. We should all lighten up.

It's hard not to feel humorless, as a woman and a feminist, to recognize misogyny in so many forms, some great and some small, and know you're not imagining things. It's hard to be told to *lighten up* because if you lighten up any more, you're going to float the fuck away. The problem is not that one of these things is happening; it's that they are all happening, concurrently and constantly.

These are just songs. They are just jokes. It's just a hug. They're just breasts. Smile, you're beautiful. Can't a man pay you a compliment? In truth, this is all a symptom of a much more virulent cultural sickness—one where women exist to satisfy the whims of men, one where a woman's worth is consistently diminished or entirely ignored.

Or I could put it this way. Let's say this is simply the world we live in. If there is a spectrum of misogyny with pop culture on one end and the disrespect for women's boundaries in the middle, on the other end we have our nation's lawmakers, who implicitly encourage this entire spectrum to thrive.

In 2013, state legislators in Texas, Ohio, and North Carolina, among others, trampled all over reproductive freedom—trying to limit when a woman can have an abortion and where abortions can be provided as well as redefining what a fetus is.

A culture that treats women as objects, that gleefully supports entertainment that is more often demeaning toward women than it is not, that encourages the erosion of a woman's autonomy and personal space, is the same culture that elects state lawmakers who work tirelessly to enact restrictive abortion legislation. Or is it that state lawmakers who work tirelessly to enact restrictive abortion legislation encourage their constituents to treat women as objects? Perhaps this is trickle-down misogyny—which came first, the chicken or the egg?

On June 30, 2013, in the Room for Debate section, the *New York Times* asked, "Would support for abortion rights grow if more women discussed their abortions?" When I first saw the question, I bristled. Women shouldn't have to sacrifice their personal histories to enlighten those who are probably uninterested in enlightenment. At some point, the greater good isn't enough of a justification for such sacrifice.

Here's a woman's story. Who she is doesn't matter. She could be any woman—a friend, a sister, a mother, an aunt. Say she becomes pregnant. Say the pregnancy is unplanned but she's financially and emotionally stable enough that she and her boyfriend decide, *Let's do this.* Say she's pro-choice but from the moment she realizes she's pregnant, it feels like she's carrying a baby. Still, she is staunchly pro-choice, always will be. Say if she didn't think she and her boyfriend could give the baby a good life, she would have an abortion. Say she's in the kitchen during her twenty-seventh week when she falls to her knees because there is a terrible cramping in her abdomen. Say she starts bleeding and it won't stop. Say she and her boyfriend rush to the hospital. Say she loses consciousness. Say when she wakes up, the baby is gone because it came down to her life or the baby's. Say she spends years feeling like the wrong choice was made. This is a story about reproductive freedom. This is a story about a woman's life and the value of her life. Choices were made. Choices were taken away. Say this woman lived in a state where certain choices were sacrificed in favor of the sanctity of life. Say she died, and so much for sanctity. Who would tell her story then?

And what if she doesn't want to tell her story? What if it's too personal, too painful? What do these confessions really do? Some people will be moved, but those are rarely the same people who support legislation to erode reproductive freedom. Immovable people will not be moved by testimony. Her story becomes an emotional spectacle, something for people to consider, briefly, before moving on to the next sad story. There is no shortage of sad stories when it comes to women and their reproductive lives.

Robin Thicke sings about what he knows a woman wants. Fine. Daniel Tosh encourages his fans to touch women lightly on the stomach and film themselves doing so. Fine. Ken Hoinsky believes persistence is a virtue. Fine. Texas governor Rick Perry says, of Senator Wendy Davis, "She was the daughter of a single woman. She was a teenage mother herself. She managed to eventually graduate from Harvard Law School and serve in the Texas Senate. It's just unfortunate that she hasn't learned from her own example that every life must be given a chance to realize its full potential and that every life matters." Fine. In Ohio, any woman seeking an abortion must get an ultrasound. If she has complications from an abortion, she must go to a private rather than public hospital. The state legislators pushing the various initiatives across the country are just looking out for women. Fine, fine, fine. Men want to protect women—unless, of course, they want to grab those women's asses.

Lighten up. Men want what they want. Sometimes they make their desires plain with music to which I can't help but sing along. Blurred lines, indeed.

The Trouble with Prince Charming, or He Who Trespassed Against Us

We all know the common fairy tale. There's a man and a woman—needless to say, we rarely see stories about a woman and a woman or a man and a man—who must overcome some obstacle to reach happily ever after. There is always a happily-ever-after.

I enjoy fairy tales because I need to believe, despite my cynicism, that there is a happy ending for everyone, especially me. The older I get, though, the more I realize how fairy tales demand a great deal from the woman. The man in most fairy tales, Prince Charming in all his iterations, really isn't that interesting. In most fairy tales, he is blandly attractive and rarely seems to demonstrate much personality, taste, or intelligence. We're supposed to believe this is totally fine because he is Prince Charming. His charm is supposedly enough.

The Disney versions of fairy tales, the ones with which we are probably most familiar, don't offer much in the way of Prince Charming. In *The Little Mermaid*, Prince Eric has a great woman right in front of him but is so obsessed with this pretty voice he once heard he can't appreciate what he has. In *Snow White*, the prince doesn't even find Snow White until she is comatose, and he is so lacking in imagination he simply falls in love with her seemingly lifeless body. In *Beauty and the Beast*, Belle is given away by her father to the Beast himself, and then must endure the attentions of a man who essentially views her as chattel. Only through sacrificing herself, and loving a beast of a man, can she finally learn that he is, in fact, a handsome prince.

The thing about fairy tales is that the princess finds her prince, but there's usually a price to pay. A compromise is required for happily ever after. The woman in the fairy tale is generally the one who pays the price. This seems to be the nature of sacrifice.

Consider the Twilight series. The four books are about vampires and werewolves and the sweeping love story between Bella, a young girl, and Edward, an old vampire. Really, though, the Twilight series is a new kind of fairy tale. Is there anything particularly compelling about Edward Cullen? He sparkles. He's theoretically attractive but seems to have only one interest: loving Bella and controlling every decision she makes. We're supposed to believe his obsessive control and devotion are somehow appealing. We're supposed to believe he is Prince Charming, albeit flawed because he needs to drink blood to survive. Accepting Edward's controlling obsession and vampirism is the compromise required of Bella. Eventually, becoming a vampire, becoming undead, is the price Bella must pay for her happily-ever-after. We're supposed to believe she's fine with that because Bella is the one who advocates so fiercely for Edward to turn her into a vampire. We're supposed to believe Edward is worth that sacrifice.

Fifty Shades of Grey, Fifty Shades Darker, and *Fifty Shades Freed,* by E. L. James, together compose a modern fairy tale with a dark erotic twist. The trilogy began as fan fiction—fiction written by fans of an original series without actually being a part of it— inspired by Twilight. While grounded in the fairy tale tradition and rising out of fan fiction, Fifty Shades is also the first series that could be categorized as erotica *and* that has been embraced by the mainstream—if you forget, of course, Anne Rice's Sleeping Beauty trilogy.

Fan fiction and erotica are not new, but there is something about the Fifty Shades trilogy that has piqued the popular imagination. The books are erotic, amusing in their absurdity, and disturbing in their cultural implications about just how much trouble Prince Charming can be.

In *Fifty Shades of Grey*, a bright, young college student, Anastasia Steele, is forced to take the place of her student reporter best friend, Kate, who has fallen ill. Anastasia, or Ana, travels to Seattle to interview Christian Grey, a handsome, reclusive, and enigmatic billionaire, for the student paper. During their initial meeting, Ana stammers her way through an uncomfortable interview, distracted by Christian's extraordinary good looks. Of course. He encourages Ana to work for him. They banter. True love is born, but there is a catch. There has to be a catch, an obstacle. This is the way of fairy tales.

Over three books, Ana and Christian try to have a relationship, but they are impeded by Christian's abiding interest in BDSM (or at least E. L. James's fantasy version of BDSM), his unwillingness to engage in a "normal" relationship, and Ana's desire for a "normal" relationship. There is all kinds of drama, and with each book, that drama becomes increasingly absurd but strangely addictive. A crazy former submissive! An older former lover and mistress who earns the nickname Mrs. Robinson! A sexually harassing boss with a chip on his shoulder! Family drama! Helicopter crashes! Arson! Oh my!

When she meets Christian, Ana is, conveniently, a twenty-one-year-old virgin who has never even masturbated. Of course. Christian gets to show Ana the ropes, so to speak, in a very dramatic scene where he grabs her by the wrist and leads her to his bedroom to properly deflower her. The kinkiness can wait, but her vagina cannot. As he sweeps Ana off her feet, Christian says, "We're going to rectify the situation right now," which is surely what every woman wants to hear when she has sex for the first time. In a never-ending scene, Christian makes their first love-making encounter all about Ana. He makes her come by stimulating her nipples. They fool around some more, and finally, Christian can no longer control himself. He takes off his boxers and tears open a condom wrapper while Ana stares at his enormous cock, bewildered because she is so innocent and pure. Of course. Christian says, "Don't worry . . . You expand too." You haven't lived until you've read such prose. Before long, Christian "rips through" Ana's virginity, they both come, and her virginity situation is, indeed, rectified, pleasantly for all involved.

The books quickly devolve into passionate(ish) sex scenes interrupted by arguments about their different desires—Christian's recalcitrance toward normalcy, and the ridiculous drama, both within the relationship and beyond.

Whenever women do something in significant numbers, the media immediately becomes frenzied as they try to understand this new mystery of womanhood. If that *something* involves female desire (as if female desire is entirely uniform), the frenzy takes on a sharper pitch. Nearly every major publication has offered at least one "think piece" about the Fifty Shades series. The books have been labeled with the condescending term "mommy porn" because the trilogy has found a great deal of success among a certain demographic. Once that happens, we have to call it a trend, and then we need to write trend pieces that exhaustively analyze something that probably isn't very worthy of analysis. Is it really newsworthy that a number of women have *finally* found something that turns them on, or is the response to Fifty Shades a depressing commentary on the state of modern desire?

A great deal of the conversation about these books focuses on the erotic elements—there is so much explicit, highly implausible sex to be found in Fifty Shades, and it always ends in the most amazing orgasms ever. Ana and Christian have sex on an airplane and in an elevator and in a car. They have sex in several different beds and they have sex in Christian's playroom, which Ana calls the Red Room of Pain—a dungeon so outlandishly equipped that, when she first sees it, Ana thinks, "It feels like I've time-traveled back to the sixteenth century and the Spanish inquisition." Inside, she finds deep burgundy walls, a large wooden cross, an iron grid hanging from the ceiling, lots of ropes and chains and paddles and whips and crops and other toys, as if real BDSM is manifested solely in the extravagant display of toys.

This analogy might help illustrate the difference between BDSM in the real world and BDSM in the world of E. L. James— Fifty Shades : BDSM :: McDonald's : Food.

I understand why these books are so popular, beyond the underlying fairy tale. There are hot moments. Chances are you will be turned on by *something* in these books. The trilogy tries valiantly to make the reader believe female pleasure is the most important part of a sexual experience despite Christian Grey's dominant proclivities. In nearly all the sex scenes, Christian is meticulous about pleasuring Ana. He lavishes her body with all manner of sexual attention. The books are generous in detailing lady orgasms that make it clear Christian Grey is the best lover ever. It's a nice little fantasy.

When you look deeper, though, which is challenging in a trilogy with the depth of a murky wading pool, these books are really about Ana trying to change/save Christian from his demons—she is the virginal good girl who can lead the dark bad boy to salvation, as if, historically, trying to change a man has ever worked out well. At one point during their courtship, Ana thinks, "This man, whom I once thought of as a romantic hero, a brave shining white knight—or the dark knight as he said. He's not a hero; he's a man with serious, deep emotional flaws, and he's dragging me into the dark. Can I not guide him into the light?" I wanted to take Ana aside and say, "Girl, you cannot lead this man into the light. Let that dream go."

After all the trials this couple faces, and after all the *hot* sex, we're supposed to think this trilogy is about a young woman and her happily-ever-after. It's not. Ana's sexual awakening is a convenient vehicle for the awakening of Christian's humanity. Fifty Shades is about a man finding peace and happiness because he finally finds a woman willing to tolerate his bullshit for long enough.

Fifty Shades is engaging in that simplistic, formulaic manner of romance novels or fairy tales, but the books are terribly written in really delightful ways. I embraced the absurdity with open arms and laughed and laughed.

Ana has no gag reflex, which is so very convenient. On those rare occasions she goes down on Christian, Ana has no problem orally accommodating Christian's girth. She even swallows, so she's obviously a keeper.

Christian is one of those chatty lovers who, throughout all

three books, spends a great deal of time narrating what he is doing, wants to do, and/or will do to Ana, adding at least an extra ten thousand words to each book.

In one of the books, Ana asks for a glass of "white Pinot Grigio." Whenever I reconsider that phrase, I die laughing because it is the laziest mistake possible. There is product placement by Audi—Christian drives an Audi, gives his favorite submissives Audis, and gives Ana, over the course of their relationship, two Audis. His generosity truly knows no bounds. Christian gives Ana expensive clothes, La Perla lingerie, a MacBook, an iPad, a BlackBerry, expensive rare books, a honeymoon on a yacht, and on and on. If you have a materialistic fantasy, this book will curb that edge.

Swaths of the story are told via reproduced e-mail exchanges. That is, we literally see the e-mails Ana and Christian exchange, with all the annoying banter you might expect from a couple falling in love and much more. These e-mails, alone, are worth the price of admission.

In the first book, when Christian is trying to introduce Ana to his *lifestyle*, James reproduces Christian's Dominant/submissive contract three or four times, as if we couldn't get the gist the first time. The contract is clearly something James found hanging around the Internet. It dictates all manner of supposedly submissive behaviors including: personal grooming, sleep hygiene, wardrobe, diet, comportment, and sexual activity. An exhaustive amount of the first book is given over to Ana and Christian negotiating this contract, what they each will or won't do, only Ana never signs the contract so mostly this is a device to repeatedly show us how different the lovers are.

Ana says or thinks "Jeez" more times than I can count. There are so many repetitive tics, this trilogy would be ideal for a drinking game where the aim is to destroy someone's liver. Drink every time Ana thinks "Jeez." Drink every time Ana bites her lower lip, which, by the way, makes Christian want to ravish her. Drink every time the palm of Christian's hand twitches because he wants to spank Ana. Drink every time Ana thinks of Christian as "enigmatic" or "mercurial." Drink every time Ana reflects on his extraordinary good looks. Drink every time Ana gets possessive of Christian because every single human woman in the world eyes him lustily and becomes instantly tongue-tied. Drink every time the narrative continuity goes wildly off track. The game goes on and on.

To hold all this nonsense together, Ana has two little friends— her subconscious and her inner goddess, each personified. These ladies glare at Ana. They peer at her over their glasses. They twirl and swoon and sigh and grin and nod and otherwise reflect Ana's state of mind. For example, toward the end of the first book, Christian and Ana are about to get freaky and there's this gift: "My subconscious is frantically fanning herself, and my inner goddess is swaying and writhing to some primal carnal rhythm. She's so ready."

Like Ana's inner goddess, I was so ready for these books, and that's an uncomfortable realization, that I can take pleasure in something so terrible. Like most people, I am a mass of contradictions.

There are times when Fifty Shades is amusing because the writing is terrible and fun, and then there are times when the book is terrible and infuriating in its irresponsibility.

As Prince Charming, Christian fits the bill. He is ridiculously wealthy and handsome but utterly lacking in imagination. E. L. James decides to complicate her Prince Charming. She gives the reader a little something more than the average dullard we generally have to yearn for in fairy tales: Christian has a tormented past. His mother is a crackhead, you see, which he casually discloses after a night of kinky passion. Ana is falling asleep next to him, and he says, "The woman who brought me into this world was a crack whore, Anastasia. Go to sleep." He seems to expect his confession will satisfy Ana's curiosity, but eventually he begins to disclose his *dark* past—abuse by his mother's boyfriends, neglect, hunger. There's a lot of trauma there and he wears it openly. As you might expect, Christian's past shapes his present in significant ways and provides a great deal of the incessant drama throughout the books. Forgive my indelicacy, but Christian Grey is a man who loves to run the fuck and he's not afraid to show it. His need to be a Dominant rises out of his need for control.

In the second book we learn Christian Grey enjoys dominating women, always beautiful brunettes, because they remind him of his mother. He's working on it with his therapist, Dr. Flynn, who makes the occasional appearance in ways that contradict the tenets of modern psychotherapy. There are any number of reasons why people engage in BDSM, but for James to so flagrantly pathologize the BDSM lifestyle as strictly a way for fucked-up people to work out their emotional issues is beyond the pale. It is not an accurate portrayal of the community. It sends a wrong and unfair message about kink.

The Fifty Shades books have also opened the door for pundits, including Ellen DeGeneres, to treat the BDSM lifestyle with derision, mockery, and outright ignorance. Whips and chains are so very funny, or they are freaky and weird. For those who don't understand different expressions of sexuality, humor seems to be the easiest coping mechanism—unless, of course, you are critic Katie Roiphe, who concludes that the popularity of Fifty Shades merely proves that independent women today secretly yearn to be dominated by men but are afraid to admit their submissive desires. Roiphe takes her typical anti-feminist stance by supporting her argument with an odd range of vaguely related texts. Take *Secretary* and *The Story of O* and a few other cultural artifacts, *et voilà*: irrefutable proof that women want to surrender sexually. At no time does Roiphe actually speak to submissive women about their desires. At no time does she try to understand the complexity of submissive sexual desire, instead making a tenuous connection between a popular, highly fictional series of books and the state of modern female sexuality.

Very little of the conversation about Fifty Shades has included people who actually participate in the BDSM lifestyle and can speak intelligently and ethically on the subject, even though these people exist and are easy to find. Instead, people who know not of what they speak have made wild, lazy, insulting, or inaccurate conjectures about BDSM all because a writer who is not terribly familiar with the lifestyle (she did a lot of online research, don't you know) thought kink would be a nice hook to hang her Twilight fan fiction on.

My amusement with the Fifty Shades series only goes so far. The books are, essentially, a detailed primer for how to successfully engage in a controlling, abusive relationship. The trilogy represents the darkest kind of fairy tale, one where controlling, obsessive, and borderline abusive tendencies are made to seem intensely desirable by offering the reader big heaping spoonfuls of sweet, sweet sex sugar to make the medicine go down.

We can certainly credit the source material. Twilight offers similar instruction. Edward goes to absurd lengths to control Bella, all in the name of *love*. In Fifty Shades, there are no limits to Christian's need to control Ana's life, her decisions, and their relationship. Even before they date, he conducts a background check. He tracks her movements via her cell phone in a way that is never quite explained but that we're supposed to go along with because he is wealthy and stalking people electronically is simply what wealthy people do. He tries to control when and how much

Ana eats, the kind of alcohol she drinks, how she behaves around him, whom she allows in her life, how she travels, and we're supposed to believe this is all fine because he has *issues*, because he *loves her*.

In addition to the highly restrictive contract Christian wants Ana to sign, he also makes all his submissives sign a nondisclosure agreement limiting what Ana is even legally allowed to share with her friends and loved ones about her life with Christian. Ana inexplicably signs this agreement because, as she tells Christian, she wouldn't have said anything anyway. She's a good girl. That's a common tactic of abusers—isolating their victims—but we're supposed to think the way Christian isolates Ana in luxury is romantic. A prison is still a prison even when the sheets are 1200 thread count, but the premise, in my weaker moments, is seductive enough to make that prison seem tolerable.

In the first book, Ana decides to visit her mother in Georgia. Christian offers to travel with Ana, but she refuses because she, understandably, needs a little time and space to clear her head so she can decide if the BDSM lifestyle is one she can handle. Christian has to have *some* control over the situation so he upgrades her to first class. We're supposed to think this is romantic, but mostly it's creepy because he has gone to the trouble of figuring out her itinerary and changing it without consulting her. Then he simply flies down to Georgia to join Ana because he cannot bear to be apart from her. He's a man who knows what he wants; his needs are the only needs that matter.

As the story proceeds, Christian is jealous when Ana is merely in the presence of another man. He gets angry or pouts when she won't pay enough attention to him. During a visit to his family's home, Ana defies Christian in some obscure way so he drags her off to the boathouse to punish her. Her first instinct is to whisper, "Please don't hit me." This fear of being hit will come up more than once throughout the trilogy. He hires a security detail for her after one of his "crazy" (read: "heartbroken") former submissives has a mental breakdown after her boyfriend dies, but mostly it's an opportunity for him to control the boundaries of Ana's world in every possible way. When Ana gets a job, Christian buys the company where she works to "protect" her. In the third book, on their honeymoon, Ana decides to sunbathe topless at a nude beach. Christian, of course, does not appreciate his woman revealing herself to the world. She's not his submissive, but by God, she is his wife. He makes a scene. Later, they are making love in their hotel room and he leaves hickeys all over her breasts so not only can she no longer go topless, she cannot even wear a bikini top for the duration of their honeymoon. He literally marks his territory like a sixteen-year-old boy.

Christian Grey uses sex as a weapon. He takes real pleasure in fucking her into submission when he cannot otherwise will her into submission. Nearly every sexual encounter between the young couple ends with Ana drowsy and unable to move, her limbs heavy and satiated with pleasure. In a consensual BDSM relationship this dynamic would be fine, welcome even, but the overarching premise of the trilogy is that Ana doesn't want a BDSM relationship, at least not the kind Christian wants. She certainly enjoys their kinky sexual relationship, but she consistently clarifies her overall disinterest in serving as Christian's submissive. Their relationship is beyond refractory; Ana is, like Bella in Twilight, the vanquished, the undead, and Christian Grey is the proud vanquisher.

After each instance of abusive, controlling behavior, Ana gets righteously indignant but never for long. Time and again, she chooses to sacrifice what she really wants for the opportunity to be loved by her half-assed Prince Charming. We're supposed to believe Ana is independent because she "defies" Christian by having very reasonable expectations and boundaries. He willfully ignores these boundaries, though, and she allows him to. She forgives all his trespasses.

The trilogy also relies heavily on the trope of the imperiled woman—in each book, Ana faces some kind of danger, either innocuous or quite serious, that reminds us she is a woman, and therefore in need of rescue by her Prince Charming. After each crisis, Christian clutches Ana desperately and says he doesn't know what he would do if anything happened to her. If you look up the word "codependent" in the dictionary, this couple's picture will be featured prominently.

I'm all for reading for pleasure. I'm a fan of dirty books and kink. I am down with female submission. By the end of *Fifty Shades Freed*, however, where Ana acknowledges that Christian is as controlling as ever even though they have found a happily-ever-after, his pattern of abusive, petty, and at times childish behavior is exhausting and far too familiar. This Prince Charming has lost all his charm.

When considering the overwhelming popularity of this trilogy, we cannot simply dismiss the flaws because the books are fun and the sex is hot. The damaging tone has too broad a reach. That tone reinforces pervasive cultural messages women are already swallowing about what they should tolerate in romantic relationships, about what they should tolerate to be loved by their Prince Charming.

Fifty Shades is a fairy tale. There's a man and a woman, and an obstacle that eventually they are able to overcome. There is a happily-ever-after, but the price exacted is terribly high. It is frightening to consider how many women might be willing to pay that price.

[RACE & ENTERTAINMENT]

The Solace of Preparing Fried Foods and Other Quaint Remembrances from 1960s Mississippi: Thoughts on *The Help*

When my brothers and I have a particularly frustrating day with white people, we'll call one another and say, "Today is a *Rosewood* day." Nothing more needs to be said. *Rosewood* is set in 1923 and tells the story of Rosewood, a deeply segregated, primarily black town in Florida. A married white woman in nearby Sumner is beaten by her lover. With no other way to explain the marks on her body to her husband, she cries rape, and when the townsmen ask her who has done this terrible thing, the white woman, predictably, shrieks, "It was a nigger."

The white men proceed to lose their minds, surrender to a mob mentality, and create a lot of havoc, lynching an innocent black man and tormenting the townsfolk of Rosewood. The angry mob destroys nearly every home and other structure in the town. There are some heartbreaking subplots, but mostly the story hinges on a little white lie, so to speak. It's all very distressing, and the injustice of what happened in Rosewood is, at times, unbearable because it is based on a true story. The first time I saw *Rosewood,* I turned to my friend and said, "I don't want to see a white person for three days." She said, "That's not fair," but she was white so that was to be expected. Fortunately, it was a Friday, so I locked myself in my apartment and by Monday I was mostly ready to reengage with the world.

If *Rosewood* demands a three-day window of voluntary segregation, *The Help* demands three weeks, maybe longer.

Watching historical movies about the black experience (or white interpretations of the black experience) have become nearly impossible for the same reason I hope I never read another slave narrative. It's too much. It's too painful. Too frustrating and infuriating. The history is too recent and too close. I watch movies like *Rosewood* or *The Help* and realize that if I had been born to different parents, at a different time, I too could have been picking cotton or raising a white woman's babies for less than minimum wage or enduring any number of intolerable circumstances far beyond my control. More than that, though, I am troubled by how little has changed. I am troubled by how complacently we are willing to consume these often revisionist stories of this country's complex and painful racial history. History is important, but sometimes the past renders me hopeless and helpless.

When I first saw the trailer for *The Help*, I was not familiar with the book. The moment I saw the first maid's uniform grace the screen, I knew I was going to be upset. By the end of the trailer, which contained all the familiar, reductive elements of a movie about the segregated South, I had worked myself into a nice, frothy rage. In the following months, I continued to see the trailer, only now it was plastered all over the Internet and on television, and the reprinted tie-in book version was heavily hyped, even climbing back to the top of the Amazon bestseller list because this is one of those books nearly everyone seems to love. After seeing the movie, I borrowed the book from a friend, read it, and raged more.

The Help is billed as inspirational, charming, and heartwarming. That's all true if your heart is warmed by narrow, condescending, mostly racist depictions of black people in 1960s Mississippi; overly sympathetic depictions of the white women who employed *the help*; the excessive, inaccurate use of dialect; and the glaring omissions with regards to the stirring civil rights movement in which, as Martha Southgate points out in *Entertainment Weekly*, "white people were the help": "the architects, visionaries, prime movers, and most of the on-the-ground laborers of the civil rights movement were African-American." *The Help*, I have decided, is science fiction, creating an alternate universe.

Hollywood has long been enamored with the magical negro—the insertion of a black character into a narrative who bestows upon the protagonist the wisdom he or she needs to move forward in some way—or, as Matthew Hughey defines the phenomenon in a 2009 article in *Social Problems*,

> *The [magical negro] has become a stock character that often appears as a lower class, uneducated black person who possesses supernatural*

or magical powers. These powers are used to save and transform di-
sheveled, uncultured, lost, or broken whites (almost exclusively white
men) into competent, successful, and content people within the con-
text of the American myth of redemption and salvation.

(See: *Ghost, The Legend of Bagger Vance, Unbreakable, Robin Hood: Prince of Thieves, The Secret Life of Bees, Sex and the City: The Movie, The Green Mile, Corrina, Corrina,* etc.)

In *The Help*, there are not one but twelve or thirteen magical negroes who use their mystical powers to make the world a better place by sharing their stories of servitude and helping Eugenia "Skeeter" Phelan grow out of her awkwardness and insecurity into a confident, racially aware, independent career woman. It's an embarrassment of riches for fans of the magical negro trope.

The theater was crowded for the screening of *The Help* I attended. Women came in groups of three or four or more, many of them clutching their well-worn copies of the book. As we waited for the movie to start, and a long wait it would be because the projector was malfunctioning (a sign perhaps), I listened to the women around me, certainly well meaning, many of them of the *Golden Girls* demographic, chattering about how much they loved the book and how excited they were and how long they had been waiting for this movie to open. I wondered if they were reminiscing about the *good old days*, then decided that was unfair of me. Still, they were quite enthusiastic. My fellow moviegoers applauded when the movie began, and they applauded when the movie ended. They applauded during inspiring moments and gasped or groaned or clucked their tongues during the uncomfortable or painful moments. Their animated response to the movie was not mild. My faith in humanity was tested. I was the only black person in the theater, though to be fair, that mostly speaks to where I live. As I walked to my car, I came to the bitter realization that *The Help* would make a whole lot of money and be really well received by many.

If you go to the theater without your brain (leave it in the glove compartment), *The Help* is a good movie. The production is competent. The cast is uniformly excellent and includes the immensely talented supporting cast of Cicely Tyson, Allison Janney, and Sissy Spacek. Both Viola Davis and Octavia Spencer received Oscar nominations because they do excellent work in the movie and Hollywood loves to reward black women for playing magical negroes. Spencer would go on to win, and deservedly, the Oscar for Best Supporting Actress. While I wondered how so many talented people signed on to this movie, the cast is not the problem here. As others have noted, *The Help* is endemic of a much bigger problem, one where even today, a prime role for a two-time Tony Award winner and one-time Oscar nominee like Viola Davis is that of a maid.

Davis, who is always sublime, brings intelligence, gravitas, and heart to the role of Aibileen Clark, an older maid who has just lost her only son to a mill accident and has worked her whole life as a maid and nanny, raising seventeen white children. When we meet her, Aibileen is mourning her son and working as the maid for Elizabeth Leefolt and her daughter, Mae Mobley, a chubby, homely girl who is often neglected by her mother. Aibileen's magical power is making young white children feel good about *theyselves*. Whenever Mae Mobley is feeling down, Aibileen chants, "You is kind. You is smart. You is important." She showers the child with love and affection even while having to listen to young white women discuss black people as a subhuman species, dealing with the indignity of using a bathroom outside of the main house, and coping with her grief. Magic, magic, magic. At the end of the movie, Aibileen offers her inspirational incantation to young Mae Mobley even after she is fired for an infraction she did not commit because that's what the magical negro does—she uses her magic for her white charge and rarely for herself.

Spencer is also formidable as Minny Jackson, the "sassy" maid (where "sassy" is code for "uppity"), who works, at the beginning of the movie, for the petty, vindictive, and socially powerful Hilly Holbrook (Bryce Dallas Howard), president of the Junior League. Hilly Holbrook's claim to fame is, among other cruelties, proposing an initiative ordering all white homes to provide separate bathrooms for the "colored" help. After Minny is fired from her job where she uses her negro magic to look after Hilly's elderly mother, she goes to work for Celia Foote. The women of the Junior League in Jackson ostracize Celia because she was pregnant when she married, is considered white trash, and has committed other petty social sins. Minny uses her mystical negritude to help Celia cope with several miscarriages and learn how to cook, and at the end of the movie, the narrative leads you to believe that Celia indirectly empowers Minny to leave her abusive husband, as if a woman of Minny's strength and character couldn't do that on her own. Then Celia cooks a whole spread for Minny and allows the help to sit at her dining room table just like white folk, aww shucks. Minny asks, "I'm not losing my job?," and Celia's husband says, "You have a job here for the rest of your life." Minny, of course, beams gratefully because a lifetime of servitude to a white family, doing backbreaking work for terrible pay, is like winning the lottery and the best a black woman could hope for in the alternate science fiction universe of *The Help.*

Emma Stone plays Skeeter, who has just returned to Jackson after graduating from Ole Miss. She gets a job as an advice columnist for the local paper, but she has bigger aspirations and a whole lot of gumption. We know this because she sasses her mother and doesn't make finding a man her first priority. Her first priority is to give grown black women a voice. Being back in Jackson forces Skeeter to confront many of the social norms she has taken for granted for most of her life. While her friends baldly treat "the help" terribly, Skeeter sits silently, rarely protests, but often frowns. Her frown lets us know that racism is very, very bad and that good southern girls should be nice to their mammies.

Skeeter gets the bright idea to tell the stories of the maids who spend their lives cleaning white people's houses, raising white people's babies. Stone is charming and believable even if the character she plays is willfully ignorant. The charm, though, grates because it is fairly obscene to imagine that this wet-behind-the-ears lass would somehow guide the magical negroes to salvation through the spiritual cleansing of occupational confession. When Aibileen reminds Skeeter they shouldn't be seen together, Skeeter briefly educates herself on Jim Crow laws and then ignores whatever she learned, imposing herself on Aibileen's bewildering goodwill, urging her to share her story about what it's *really like* to be a maid in Jackson, Mississippi, as if the truth were not plainly obvious. At the end of *The Help*, Skeeter offers to turn down her dream job in New York City so she can stay and "protect" Aibileen and Minny. We're supposed to see this as a heartwarming gesture, but it only brings the movie's overall condescension into bitter relief.

The Help is, in the absence of thinking, a good movie, but it is also an unfairly emotionally manipulative movie. There are any number of times during the interminable two hours and seventeen minutes of running time when I felt like my soul would shrivel up and die. I was devastated by all of it. Everyone around me cried openly throughout most of the movie. My eyes were not dry. I am certain we were often crying for different reasons. Every transgression, injustice, and tragedy was exploited so that by the end of the movie it was like the director had ripped into my chest, torn my heart out, and jumped up and down on it until it became a flattened piece of worn-out muscle—cardiac jerky, if you will.

The movie is emotionally manipulative but in a highly controlled way. *The Help* provides us with a deeply sanitized view of the segregated South in the early 1960s. There are many unpalatable moments, but they are tempered by a great deal of easy humor and contrived, touching emotional moments. The movie gives the impression that life was difficult in Mississippi in the 1960s for women, white and black, but still somewhat bearable because that's just how things were.

The implausibilities in the science fiction universe of *The Help* are many and wild. Certainly, that happens in most movies, especially these days. What makes these implausibilities offensive in *The Help* is that most of us know better. We know our history. There is not enough height in the atmosphere for us to suspend our disbelief.

If you do bring your brain to *The Help*, the movie is worse than you might imagine. Seeing *The Help* through a critical lens is excruciating. At one point, while teaching Celia Foote to make fried chicken, Minny says, "Frying chicken tend to make me feel better about life." That a line about the solace found in the preparation of fried foods made it into a book *and* movie produced in this decade says a great deal about where we are in acting right about race. We are nowhere. That line was one of many that made me cringe, cry, roll my eyes, or hide my face in my hands. To say I was uncomfortable is an understatement.

Little things also grate. The overexaggerated dialect spoken by the maids evokes cowed black folk shuffling through their miserable lives, singing negro spirituals. In Aibileen's home, for example, there are pictures of her recently deceased son and a portrait of white Jesus. After Medgar Evers is shot and JFK attends his funeral, the camera pans to the wall where a picture of JFK joins the other two, not, say, a picture of Medgar Evers himself or another civil rights leader. In another subplot, of which there are many, Skeeter's childhood nanny, Constantine (Cicely Tyson), is so devastated after being fired by the white family for whom she worked for more than twenty-seven years, she dies of a broken heart. The gross implication is that her will to live came from wiping the asses and scrubbing the toilets of white folks. This white wish fulfillment makes the movie rather frustrating.

Men, black and white, are largely absent from the movie. White men are apparently absolved from any responsibility for race relations in 1960s Mississippi. The movie is devoid of any mention of the realities of the sexual misconduct, assault, and harassment black women faced working for white men. We see nary an unwelcome ass grab. I don't think lynching was brought up once. We don't know how Aibileen came to have a son, so we're left to assume, because she is magical, that her child's conception was immaculate. Minny's husband, whom we never see, is abusive. We hear her being abused during a phone call, and toward the end of the movie, we see Minny's bruised face, but we never see Leroy, the man who has committed these acts of violence. There is also the bizarre subtext that the woman with sass is the one who has to be kept in line through brutality. As in most popular portrayals, black men are dealt with in depressing, reductive ways when they are addressed at all. This movie shamelessly indulges in the myth of the absent black man. The actual consequences of black men consorting with a young white girl are glossed over as merely inconvenient instead of mortal.

The white women are portrayed as domestically tyrannical while living highly constrained lives as desperate southern housewives, so we can sympathize with *their* plight.

Race is regularly handled ineffectually in movies and fiction. I have become accustomed to this reality. And yet. I have struggled with writing about *The Help* because there is something more to my anger and frustration.

At first I thought I resented the fact that a deeply flawed book has sold more than three million copies, spent more than a hundred weeks on the bestseller list, and is a major motion picture. But books I don't like do well all the time. I don't lose sleep over it. I also cannot deny that the book and movie have their moments. There were times when I laughed or was moved, though certainly, those instances were few and far between.

I think of myself as progressive and open-minded, but I have biases, and in reading and watching *The Help*, I have become painfully aware of just how biased I can be. My real problem is that *The Help* is written by a white woman. The screenplay is written by a white man. The movie is directed by that same white man. I know it's wrong but I think, *How dare they?*

Writing difference is complicated. There is ample evidence that it is quite difficult to get difference *right*, to avoid cultural appropriation, reinscribing stereotypes, revising or minimizing history, or demeaning and trivializing difference or otherness. As writers we are always asking ourselves, *How do I get it right?* That question becomes even more critical when we try to get race right, when we try to find authentic ways of imagining and re-imagining the lives of people with different cultural backgrounds and experiences. Writing difference requires a delicate balance, and I don't know how we strike that balance.

I write across race, gender, and sexuality all the time. I would never want to be told I can't write a story where the protagonist is a white man or a Latina lesbian or anyone who doesn't resemble me. The joy of fiction is that, in the right hands, anything is possible. I firmly believe our responsibility as writers is to challenge ourselves to write beyond what we know. When it comes to white writers working through racial difference, though, I am conflicted and far less tolerant than I should be. If I take nothing else from the book and movie in question, it's that I know I have work to do.

I don't expect writers to always get difference right, but I do expect writers to make a credible effort. *The Help* demonstrates that some writers shouldn't try to write across race and difference. Kathryn Stockett tries to write black women, but she doesn't try hard enough. Her depictions of race are almost fetishistic unless they are downright insulting. At one point in the book, Aibileen compares her skin color to that of a cockroach, you know, the most hated insect you can think of. Aibileen says, staring at a cockroach, "He big, inch, inch an a half. He black. Blacker than me." That's simply bad writing, but it's an even worse way of writing difference. If white writers can't do better than to compare a cockroach to black skin, perhaps they should leave the writing of difference in more capable hands. In *The Help*, Stockett doesn't write black women. She caricatures black women, finding pieces of truth and genuine experience and distorting them to repulsive effect. She makes a very strong case for writers strictly writing what they know, not what they think they know but actually know nothing about.

Surviving *Django*

I was as tense about seeing *Django Unchained* as I was seeing *The Help*. It doesn't help that so much of the black experience, particularly in movies, is mediated through the vision of white writers and directors (as if they are the most qualified to speak to black history) who then want to be congratulated for their efforts, no matter how mediocre those efforts might be. This mediation, its constancy and impoverished quality, gets old.

As expected, I was the only black person in the audience during the screening I attended of *Django Unchained*. When the movie opens, five male slaves are being herded, on foot, wearing little to protect them from the elements. Their backs bear the evidence of their torment—thick braids of scar reaching from their shoulders down to their lower backs. Most movies about slavery reveal the camera's (director's) predilection for depicting the broken bodies of slaves as if only through such visual evidence can a viewer truly understand the horrors of human bondage.

It is night when these shivering, suffering slaves and their overseers run into Dr. King Schultz (Christoph Waltz), a dentist he calls himself. He talks real fancy as he explains that he's looking for a slave named Django (Jamie Foxx) who, Schultz hopes, can identify the Brittle Brothers he is looking for. Schultz is charming and suave in the ways of the European, showing up the American slave dealers as the ignorant men they are. It's easy to laugh during these early moments, despite the men, practically naked and bound together by shackles, shivering in the frigid night cold. It's a relief to laugh because then we can forget that just beyond the verbal sparring there is a deeply uncomfortable history waiting to be told.

After a negotiation, of sorts, Schultz buys Django and frees the other slaves, who dispatch the remaining slave dealer before heading, well, who knows where. This story isn't about them. Schultz and Django head to a Texas town where everyone stares, agog, at a black man on a horse. The unlikely pair soon install themselves in a saloon, the owner having run to get the sheriff because slaves are as unwelcome in drinking establishments as they are on horses, and thus begins the first of several plots throughout the movie. There is action and humor and an anemic love story. There is no shortage of killing, with elaborate blood spurts arcing through the air, accompanied by the moist hollow sounds of bullets landing in human flesh. At the end there is, we are lead to believe, a happy ending, and through it all we're supposed to believe that what writer-director Quentin Tarantino has created is art.

From the beginning, the audience around me laughed, quite heartily. What was particularly disconcerting is how they were laughing at the wrong times. Some of the laughter was nervous tittering during the first instances of the N-word being bandied among characters. As the word's usage became ubiquitous, that laughter grew heartier while there was silence during the movie's subtler and far funnier moments, like when Django explains to Calvin Candie (Leonardo DiCaprio) that Django's business partner, King Schultz, offered to pay for a runaway slave because he was not used to Americans. When the movie's dark humor focused on people who looked like them, the audience was silent. I became paranoid—were the people around me gleeful because they could enjoy hearing the word being used without consequence? Were they, like moviegoers during *The Help*, longing for a different time?

But there might be a better way to start this conversation. Any offense I take with *Django Unchained* is not academic or born of political correctness. Art can and should take liberties and interpret human experiences in different ways, even if those interpretations make us uncomfortable. My offense is personal—entirely human and rising from the uncomfortable reality that I could have been a slave. There's no denying I would have made a terrible slave, either in the big house or in the fields, which means slavery would have been extra unpleasant for me. I can't debate the artistic merits of *Django Unchained* because the palms of my hands are burning with the desire to slap Tarantino in the face until my arms grow tired.

Or I could start by saying that "offense" isn't even the word to best describe how I felt while watching *Django Unchained*, which I have now seen twice. "Offense" is far too mild. Most movies these days offend me with their very mediocrity. *Django Unchained* disappoints, irritates, and at times angers and inflames.

It's also impossible to discuss *Django Unchained* without discussing the N-word, used so ubiquitously in the movie. Tarantino seemingly believes the N-word to be a new conjunction—a part of speech that connects two words, phrases, clauses, or sentences together. To be fair, I hate the N-word and avoid using it because the N-word has always been a pejorative, a word designed to remind black people of their place, a word to reinforce a perception of inferiority. I have no interest in using the word to describe myself or any person of color, under any circumstance. There is no reclamation to be had.

There are 110 instances of the N-word in nearly three hours, something Tarantino seems to believe is historically accurate and therefore justified. Had Tarantino used historical accuracy as a guide in every aspect of *Django Unchained*, one might take his weak explanation seriously, but this is a movie that also includes, among other oddities, a moment with a slave merrily enjoying herself on a tree swing on a plantation run by a man named Big Daddy while nearby, another slave is about to be beaten. When Tarantino suggests he is trying to achieve verisimilitude by infusing his script with the N-word, I cannot help but feel he is being disingenuous or, at the very least, rather selective about how and where he chooses to honor historical accuracy.

Certainly, the N-word is part of our history as much as it is part of our present. The first documented instance of the word dates back to the 1600s, and it has since appeared in nearly every aspect of American life, from legal documents to entertainment to our vernacular. American presidents and Supreme Court justices and average citizens have used the word with equal comfort. As Randall Kennedy notes in *Nigger: The Strange Career of a Troublesome Word*, "A complete list of prominent whites who have referred at some point or other to blacks demeaningly as niggers would be lengthy indeed. It would include such otherwise disparate figures as Richard Nixon and Flannery O'Connor." The N-word is certainly not a word that has, as many suggest, been kept alive solely by hip-hop and rap artists. White people have been keeping the word alive and well too. Any movie about slavery or black history could reasonably include the word a few times just to remind us of how terrible we all used to be, to remind us of the work we have yet to do. And still, the televised version of *Roots* manages to depict the realities of slavery without the N-word and the miniseries is nearly ten hours long.

I knew from the start I wasn't this movie's target audience. Racism and slavery aren't terribly amusing to me unless Dave Chappelle is running the show. In truth, I am exhausted by slavery—thinking about it, talking about it, reading about it, and seeing movies about it. Each time I hear of a new book or movie that takes up slavery in some way, I feel, mostly, dread. What more could possibly be said on the topic?

But *Django Unchained* isn't even really a movie about slavery. *Django Unchained* is a spaghetti western set during the 1800s. Slavery is a convenient, easily exploited backdrop. As with *Inglourious Basterds* using World War II, Tarantino once again managed to find a traumatic cultural experience of a marginalized people that has little to do with his own history, and used that cultural experience to exercise his hubris for making farcically violent, vaguely funny movies that set to right historical wrongs from a very limited, privileged position.

Like most westerns, like most movies for that matter, *Django Unchained* concerns the whims of men. The movie is at times brilliant but mostly infuriating. It is a good movie in that masturbatory way most Tarantino films are good. The man knows his craft and clearly loves movies and loves to make movies where he shows us all just how much he loves movies. Hollywood, for whatever reason, is more than happy to indulge Tarantino's self-referential homage to those filmic genres with which he is so intensely enamored.

Still, I found myself enjoying certain parts of the movie. Strange as it may seem, the movie's sound design is impeccable. I needed something to focus on so I wouldn't lose my temper, so I paid real close attention to those sound effects. Fine work is done there.

The acting is solid, as is the direction and set design. The script is particularly strong, and certainly worthy of critical respect and the Oscar nomination it received. There are a few particularly intelligent bits of dialogue, like when Django and Dr. King Schultz go to a plantation owned by Big Daddy (Don Johnson), who has to instruct a slave, Betina, about how to treat Django as a free man. She says, "You want I should treat him like white folks?" That, of course, flusters Big Daddy, who says no, of course not, and Betina, rightly confused, says, "Well then I don't know what you mean."

This is how Tarantino works—he tries to make you forget his many offenses by lulling you into complacency with his competence and flashes of brilliance. He tries to make the viewer believe that if the art is good enough, the message can be overlooked. I tried to overlook the message, but Tarantino never let me. Each time I tried to settle into the movie and enjoy myself, he made another indulgent, obnoxious choice that did little more than reveal what I can only assume is Tarantino's serious problem with race.

Christoph Waltz was, as he always is, a revelation. His character, as a European struggling to understand American culture, reveals the absurdity of slavery and gives the movie at least one white person who isn't wholly hateful. But he is still complicit in slavery, using the system to his advantage in the early going. Schultz tells Django he will only free him after they successfully capture the Brittles. Schultz finds slavery abhorrent unless it suits his purposes, which is, I imagine, the dilemma many white people found themselves in during the slavery era. Django isn't given the autonomy to decide for himself if he wants to help Schultz or not, and we're still supposed to go along with this. We're still supposed to root for Schultz not because he is the best person. Rather, he is the least evil.

I suppose that's the point Tarantino is trying to make, that in the 1800s, everyone was complicit in the institution of slavery, but he does a half-assed job of getting that point across. And then there is his hero, Django. Foxx does a fine job as Django, but his character is largely one-dimensional, which is a shame because his character provides a rich opportunity to explore what finding freedom might look like. Instead, Django mumbles a few moderately amusing lines about killing white people. When he gets to choose his own outfit (thanks, Massa), he picks a bright blue fop of a suit that makes the audience laugh at the simple negro rather than with him. Then, toward the end of the movie, he is somehow self-actualized and has regained his dignity, just like that.

Django really has one goal in the movie: to find and free his beloved wife, Broomhilda (Kerry Washington), who was also sold at a slave auction. Some reviews have suggested that *Django Unchained* is a love story, but that is simplistic, wishful thinking. Broomhilda is, like most of the people of color in this movie, rather incidental. She has barely any screen time and speaks very few lines. At various points, we see Django imagining Broomhilda in the distance, smiling at him with her eyes. We learn she speaks German, which delights Schultz because, really, what are the odds?

Tarantino spends an inordinate amount of time gleefully depicting the suffering of the movie's rarely seen or heard heroine, Broomhilda, as she is branded, flogged, punished in a hot box, and humiliated during a dinner by being forced to reveal her scars to dinner guests. Mostly, she looks pretty or tormented or prettily tormented as the situation demands. We hardly get to see a loving moment between Django and Broomhilda, even though their story is *supposed* to be the movie's centerpiece.

One thing we know about slavery is that in order to survive, some black people did what they had to do and sometimes that meant becoming a part of the slavery system so that said system wouldn't break them all the way down. Samuel L. Jackson, who frequently appears in Tarantino movies, makes a deeply disturbing turn as Stephen, an irascible right hand to Calvin Candie— one part butler, one part household overseer, one part world's crankiest hype man to his master. We're supposed to hate Ste-

phen because he's about as bad as the white people. Jackson
plays the role so convincingly that we do, indeed, come to hate
Stephen. There's no acknowledgment, however, of why Stephen
might have become so cruel. There's no acknowledgment that
surrender was his only choice or that we should feel as sympathetic toward Stephen as we do toward Django or Broomhilda,
or any of the other enslaved people in the movie.

What struck me most was how *Django Unchained* is a white
man's slavery revenge fantasy, one where white people figure
heavily and where black people are, largely, incidental. Tarantino's arrogance, as always, is impressive. Django is allowed to
regain his dignity because he is freed by a white man. He re-
unites with his wife, again, with the help of a white man. *Django
Unchained* isn't about a black man reclaiming his freedom. It's
about a white man working through his own racial demons and
white guilt.

There is no collective slavery revenge fantasy among black
people, but I am certain, if there were one, it would not be about
white people, not at all. My slavery revenge fantasy would probably involve being able to read and write without fear of punishment or persecution coupled with a long vacation in Paris. It
would involve the reclamation of dignity on my own terms and
not with the "generous" assistance of benevolent white people
who were equally complicit in the ills of slavery.

I could also start by saying that in Haiti, January 1 not only ushers
in a new year; it is also the day Haitians recognize as Independence Day. On that same day in 1804, Jean-Jacques Dessalines
declared Haiti a free nation, the first of its kind in Latin America,
ending a thirteen-year slave rebellion. Since then, Haiti has been
a troubled country but her people have been free, or as free as
anyone can be while trying to overcome the complex legacy of

slavery. As a first-generation American of Haitian descent, I was raised with stories of how my ancestors fought for freedom, and how no matter what burdens we may suffer as a Haitian people, we know we set ourselves free. I am Haitian, but I was raised here in the United States. You cannot know my heritage just by looking at me. I'm black in America. Like many people who share my skin color, slavery is this terrible, looming thing that is part of an inescapable distant past. Instead of offering me some new insights on this troubling reality, *Django Unchained* simply served as a reminder that the more things change, the more they stay the same.

Beyond the Struggle Narrative

Hattie McDaniel, the first black person to win an Oscar, did so for her role in *Gone with the Wind* as Mammy in 1939. McDaniel was a formidable actress, but for better or worse, her career was dominated by roles as maids because, in that time, domestic servitude was the only way popular culture could conceive of black women. In 2012, Octavia Spencer won an Oscar for playing a maid, Minny Jackson, in the popular but deeply problematic *The Help*, which received four Oscar nominations. While there's a lot of shallow rhetoric about post-racial America, when it comes to the Oscars, Hollywood has very specific notions about how it wants to see black people on the silver screen. There are certainly exceptions, but all too often, critical acclaim for black films is built upon the altar of black suffering or subjugation.

In 2013, we saw quite the cinematic parade of black suffering and subjugation. In the excellent *Fruitvale Station*, writer-director Ryan Coogler deftly tells the story of the last day of Oscar Grant's life before Grant was murdered by a BART officer on New Year's Day 2009. *Lee Daniels' The Butler* chronicles the life of Cecil Gaines, a black butler in the White House for thirty-four years. Through the story of Gaines's life, we also learn the story of black America, the challenges of desegregation, and how with dignity one man persevered. The pinnacle of black suffering, though, comes by way of *12 Years a Slave*. Since the movie's debut on the festival circuit, it has enjoyed massive critical acclaim. It's the movie everyone *must see*, the definitive accounting of America's brutal legacy of slavery.

Such rhetoric is always curious because slavery has been well accounted since the early 1800s. What more could possibly be said about slavery? Who has labored under the impression that slavery is anything but an abject horror? *12 Years a Slave* offers a relatively original conceit—the true story of Solomon Northup, a free black man who was kidnapped and sold into slavery for twelve years. As Michelle Dean notes for Flavorwire, "If on no other grounds, *12 Years a Slave* is remarkable because it is the only film to date that is based on a slave's own account of his experience." The movie is also the first major studio-backed slavery film helmed by a black director. These milestones are not insignificant. Despite the source material and the director, however, *12 Years a Slave* does not offer new insight into the slave narrative. There is little to justify this movie's existence beyond the filmmaker's desire to tell this particular story.

I chose not to read many reviews before seeing *12 Years a Slave*. I wanted as unadulterated a viewing experience as possible. I confess: I was not impressed and I do not understand the effusive acclaim. The movie was brutal, almost mind-numbingly so. Nothing was spared in portraying the harsh realities of human enslavement—the loss of dignity, the physical, sexual, and emotional violence. The reality depicted is so harsh I cannot help but wonder if people find the movie excellent because of the sheer relentlessness. I cried, more than once, but I was not moved. I was simply broken, the way anyone would be broken by witnessing such atrocities.

12 Years a Slave is a good enough movie—certainly worth seeing if you're unclear about slavery and its legacy. The actors acquit themselves formidably. Director Steve McQueen makes some lovely artistic choices, but at times those artistic choices are jarring and out of place—extended, poetic shots of plantation beauty, overindulgent cinematic pauses that make no sense. The movie drags on at times, the boredom only interrupted by yet another unbearable violence.

Black women's suffering is used to tell a man's story. Though Northup is, himself, the victim of senseless brutality, it is more often the women who suffer and Northup who becomes more miserable by being forced to bear witness. It is his suffering that is painted as more profound. Yes, this is his story, but great swaths of the movie focus on everyone but him.

Early on Eliza, played by the immensely talented Adepero Oduye, has been separated from her children—an alarmingly regular occurrence during the slave era. Eliza is so overcome with grief she can hardly bear it. She spends most of her time sobbing, inconsolable. Solomon questions her grief sharply and offers some pabulum about wanting to survive. Before long, Eliza is sold off because no one wants to share in her pain or be forced to see it. Solomon is seemingly unmoved by this turn of events, which begs the question, which comes up often, of why the subplot has been included.

In the second half of the movie, Solomon is sold to Edwin Epps (Michael Fassbender), who is renowned for his ability to break slaves. Epps is insane and unrepentant. He has a predator's fondness for Patsey (Lupita Nyong'o), whom he reveres and abuses in equal measure. Ultimately, Patsey's suffering is the most devastating in a movie where nearly everyone suffers. So profound is her misery that Patsey begs Solomon to kill her so that her suffering might end. He declines, which is as cruel as it is understandable.

It should be noted that *12 Years a Slave* does a remarkable job of revealing the ways in which white women were complicit in slavery. Sarah Paulson is absolutely chilling as Epps's wife, Mistress Epps. Epps acts like a jealous lover whenever Patsey is not within his reach and does not bother hiding his feelings from his wife. Mistress Epps resents Patsey for the place the woman holds in her husband's heart and misses no opportunity to direct cruelty toward Patsey.

Most movies about slavery have a fetish for depicting the mortification of black flesh, and *12 Years a Slave* is no different. There are a number of scenes where slaves are whipped for one infraction or another. When Solomon is first captured, he is "taught his place" with a beating. Slaves are punished for not picking enough cotton. The most harrowing scene is one where Patsey is punished for going to the neighboring plantation for a bar of soap with which to clean herself. Epps is so angry and sick with jealousy, he finally brings himself to whip Patsey, but then he can't do it. He hands the whip to Solomon, who is reluctant to take part in this brutality but well aware he has no choice. Solomon does his best to mete out his master's punishment, but in the end, Epps is not satisfied. He takes the whip from Solomon and uses it on Patsey himself. By the end of the scene, she is barely conscious, her back rent open and bloody. The scene is visceral, as it should be, but it also feels gratuitous because the scene is not designed to amplify Patsey's plight. The scene is designed to amplify Solomon's plight, as if he is the more tragic figure in this situation.

I do not want to diminish the suffering of anyone during the slave era. Men and women were subjected to unspeakable atrocities. Solomon Northup's story is particularly troubling because it shows how vulnerable all black people were, free or not. What I resent in *12 Years a Slave* is how the suffering of women is used to further a man's narrative. There is, for example, a rape scene that carries little narrative relevance. Patsey lies, inert, beneath Epps. It's a repulsive scene, so in that regard, McQueen has done his job, but it doesn't seem essential to the movie because the primary story is not Patsey's. It's a gratuitous, unnecessary reminder that yes, women were raped during the slave era.

Ultimately, Solomon Northup is freed because he has finally gotten word to his family in New York that he is alive. The moment, like much of the movie, is strangely muted. We're clearly supposed to feel something, but it's hard to know quite what to do with that emotion. Before Solomon leaves the Epps plantation, Patsey runs into his arms, and they embrace. We know nothing of what happens to Patsey, beyond what we might imagine, because she has already done the necessary work of staying on the sidelines while Solomon is dispatched unto freedom once more.

My reaction to *12 Years a Slave* is born, largely, of exhaustion. I am worn out by slavery and struggle narratives. I am worn out by broken black bodies and the broken black spirit somehow persevering in the face of overwhelming and impossible circumstance. There seems to be so little room at the Hollywood table for black movies that to earn a seat, black movies have to fit a very specific narrative. Movies like *Love & Basketball* or *The Best Man* and *The Best Man Holiday* are perhaps not Oscar material, but they are certainly movies that also capture the black experience, and somehow, they are often overlooked in conversations about serious movies. Filmmakers take note and keep giving Hollywood exactly what it wants. Hollywood showers these struggle narratives with the highly coveted critical acclaim. It's a vicious cycle.

There is no one way to tell the story of slavery or to chronicle the black experience. It is not that slavery and struggle narratives shouldn't be shared but that these narratives are not enough anymore. Audiences are ready for more from black film—more narrative complexity, more black experiences being represented in contemporary film, more artistic experimentation, more black screenwriters and directors allowed to use their creative talents beyond the struggle narrative. We're ready for more of everything but the same, singular stories we've seen for so long.

Not everyone is ready for this change, however. *12 Years a Slave* received nine Oscar nominations and won the 2013 Oscars for Best Performance by an Actress in a Supporting Role, Best Writing—Adapted Screenplay, and Best Picture.

The Morality of
Tyler Perry

Tyler Perry loves to tell a good morality tale. Whether his movies or stage plays are offering up what goes for humor in Perry's universe by way of Perry in drag as Madea, or chronicling a wealthy man learning how to be true to himself and others, or following tight-knit friends as they weather the trials of marriage, there is always a lesson to be learned, one supported by fidelity, fortitude, faith, and a touch of fire and brimstone. Tyler Perry would have us believe that his conception of God is in everything.

He has been writing plays and films since he was twenty-two. Perry's start was modest, staging his first play at a community theater, and less than a decade later, his plays were a popular mainstay on the chitlin' circuit. In 2005, he wrote and produced his first movie, *Diary of a Mad Black Woman*. Since then, Perry has been a box office success, his films grossing more than a half billion dollars.

Perry's rise is noteworthy for many reasons, not the least of which is that he understands real power in Hollywood lies in the complete ownership of creative work. Perry writes, directs, produces, and often stars in his movies. He has several television projects in production and a lucrative distribution deal with Lionsgate films. He owns and runs Tyler Perry Studios, the rare black-owned production studio in the United States. He has collaborated with kingmaker Oprah Winfrey and counts among his coterie of friends any number of influential and "important" people. In many ways, Tyler Perry seems unstoppable, and to see a black man achieve this kind of success in a notoriously exclusive and predominantly white industry is laudable. I cannot bring myself to say more than that, though some might call Perry's success inspiring.

The problem is that Tyler Perry is building his success on the backs of black women and the working class, by using them, all too often, to teach his lessons, to make his points, or to make them the butts of his jokes. In many of Perry's movies, women are not to be trusted. Women are regularly punished in these movies, whether by abuse, addiction, or adultery. While there are "good" women in his films, there are so many bad women—women who are unfulfilled by their lives and/or marriages and are then punished when they try to find fulfillment. An unspoken message, all too often, is "You should be grateful for what you've got."

Temptation features a fairly talented cast including Jurnee Smollett-Bell, Lance Gross, Vanessa Williams, Brandy Norwood, and, perhaps most oddly, Kim Kardashian, who is exactly as terrible in this movie as you would expect. There were high hopes for this film, born of the optimism that finally, after years of writing, directing, and producing plays, screenplays, and television scripts, Perry might finally move beyond the mediocrity so much of his work is mired in.

Certainly, *Temptation* is one of the most polished of Perry's films, but that is not saying much. The movie is still hampered by uneven acting, strange directorial choices (e.g., Vanessa Williams's "French" accent), a weak screenplay, and some rather sloppy editing. At one point Lance Gross, as Brice, hoarsely shouts "JUDITH," over and over. During the screening I attended, every single person began laughing, loudly. It was not meant to be a humorous moment.

It is saying something that these are the least of *Temptation*'s worries.

When the movie opens, a marriage counselor chooses to ignore professional standards and tells a client contemplating infidelity about her own "sister": Judith fell in love with her husband, Brice, when they were mere children, married very young, and ended up in Washington, DC. She works as a counselor for a high-end dating service while Brice is a pharmacist for a small drugstore. They have a modest apartment and a modest but good relationship.

We're supposed to believe Judith is dissatisfied, though her dissatisfaction is never really expressed save for when Judith is dismayed by things like her husband forgetting her birthday for the second year in a row or when she balks at Brice suggesting it will be ten or fifteen years before she can start her own counseling practice.

Enter Harley, a handsome billionaire in talks to partner with Janice, Judith's boss. This is the flimsiest of pretenses, and Perry never bothers to make this plot even a little plausible. Judith and Harley's attraction is palpable, and thus begins a seduction that Judith rebuffs for quite some time because she is married and a "good girl." The seduction includes innuendo, flowers, and meaningful staring. This is a morality play, after all.

Eventually, Harley flies Judith to New Orleans for "business" on his private jet, always the gateway to sin, and they enjoy the city, oblivious to her marital obligations. On the return flight, despite Judith openly saying no to Harley's sexual advances and fighting him off, the couple engages in what looks a lot like rape but is thinly disguised as sex. This is the beginning of Judith's end. This is the climax of Perry's morality tale. Woman, thou art fallen.

By the end of *Temptation*, Judith has been punished and severely. She descends into a so-called hell on earth, dressing provocatively, drinking too much, quitting her job, and disrespecting her mother, her marriage, and herself. She is violently beaten by Harley, only to be rescued by Brice—the good man, the steady man. Most egregiously, Judith contracts HIV and ends up single, a broken woman, limping to church while Brice lives happily ever after with a beautiful new wife and young son. He is, of course, still his ex-wife's pharmacist.

There are so many appalling elements to how this sordid morality tale plays out. There are so many appalling messages about sexuality, consent, the ways men and women interact, ambition, happiness, and HIV.

As with most of Perry's movies, good black men who are content with their stations are the moral compasses by which we should all set our true north. Perry would have you believe the road to hell is paved with personal and professional happiness. Ambition is dangerous and not to be trusted, especially in a woman.

Perry has a finely honed obsession with fetishizing the working class, which, in and of itself, is not a problem and could almost be admired. It's that his motives are disingenuous. It's that Perry denigrates one thing in order to elevate another instead of suggesting that there is pride to be had in being working class but that aspiring toward anything more isn't inherently evil. That the wealthy are regularly demonized in Perry films is quite the irony given the enormous wealth Perry has amassed from a largely working-class audience.

Time and again Perry's movies follow a pathological formula

where truth, salvation, and humility will be found by returning to working-class roots. In *Diary of a Mad Black Woman*, a wealthy lawyer, Charles, throws Helen, his wife of eighteen years, out on the street. She learns to stand on her own, with the help of her working-class family. She slowly falls in love with Orlando, a working-class man. Because Perry loves to punish his characters to make a point, Charles is shot in the back by an angry client and only has Helen to turn to because his mistress has abandoned him. Through Helen's kindness and the goodness of God, Charles learns to walk again, and though he wants to reconcile with his wife, she divorces him and runs to Orlando. The working-class man triumphs over all.

In *The Family That Preys*, ambitious Andrea desperately wants more out of life than she has with her construction worker husband. She has an affair with her wealthy boss, William, enjoying all the trappings of both her own success and her infidelity. There are lots of machinations involving a family business and the like. In the end, Andrea ends up poor, alone with her son in an apartment while her now ex-husband thrives. Yet again, the working-class hero rises.

Good Deeds, one of Perry's more recent films, follows wealthy Wesley Deeds, who has always done what is right and expected of him. When he meets Lindsey, a down-on-her-luck single mother who cleans his building, he begins to realize he wants more out of life. Instead of relying on the "magical negro" trope seen in many movies (see *The Help*), Perry uses the "magical sassy maid" trope to his advantage. To round things out, Wesley's wealthy mother is kind of evil and his wealthy brother is a resentful alcoholic, but Wesley is saved from the perils of wealth by quitting his job so he can go find himself, accompanied by Lindsey and her daughter of course, in Africa.

Perry is not only intensely concerned with class. Sexuality should be chaste and contained if you are a woman. Trying new sexual moves with your husband is unbecoming, but if you are a man, you should take whatever it is you want from a woman. Perry would have you believe a just punishment for infidelity and human frailty is HIV. He is gleefully trading on ignorance because he is a small man with a limited imagination.

Part of the pleasure of the movies is stepping away from reality. One of Perry's most significant problems, however, is how he completely reconstructs reality to suit his purposes in ways that are utterly lacking in artistic merit.

Many of the choices he makes in *Temptation* are blatantly contradicted by factual reality. People are marrying later than ever before, so we have to suspend our disbelief as Perry constructs this fairy tale that Judith and Brice would meet as young children, stay in love, marry as teenagers, and go on to complete both undergraduate and graduate educations. In a study of first marriages as part of the 2006–2010 National Survey of Family Growth, researchers found that the median age for a first marriage is 25.8 for women and 28.3 for men. Black women had the lowest probability of being in a first marriage by the age of 25. Women with a bachelor's degree were also less likely to be in a first marriage by the age of 25. But let's suspend our disbelief just enough to imagine this young couple married and happily so.

Perry has also set *Temptation* in a world where divorce is the exception rather than the rule. The reality is that marriages end and often. The statistics for marital longevity are not on Judith and Brice's side, so the idea that Judith is a sinner among sinners for wanting more from her marriage or wanting out of her marriage is absurd.

Then there is this matter of so callously dealing with HIV as if we are still in the 1980s, full of profound ignorance about the disease. Perry shamelessly exploits HIV for the sake of his very narrow and subjective morality when HIV disproportionately affects black women who make up so much of his core audience. The disservice he does to this audience is hard to stomach.

According to the Centers for Disease Control, the rate of new HIV infections is twenty times higher for black women than white women. An estimated 1 in 32 black/African American women will be diagnosed with HIV infection in her lifetime, compared with 1 in 106 Hispanic/Latino women and 1 in 526 white women. These are staggering statistics. Dealing with HIV prevention, treatment, and the stigma surrounding HIV are important issues for the black community, issues deserving of both critical and creative attention. That attention should be handled ethically and with human decency—concepts with which Tyler Perry seems to have no familiarity. His oeuvre has given me little confidence that Perry can handle any part of the human experience.

Of course, also according to the Centers for Disease Control, HIV prevalence rates are inversely related to annual household income in urban poverty areas. The likelihood of a woman in Judith and Brice's demographic contracting HIV is not very. Statistics show that the more educated people are and the more money they make, the less likely they are to contract HIV. As he so often does, Tyler Perry wants to have it every which way but right, and a high cost is being exacted so this man can get exactly what he wants.

I attended a press screening of *Peeples* with a predominantly black crowd. It was the first time I'd seen a Tyler Perry production with his target audience. An hour before the screening, the line snaked all the way out the theater and into the auxiliary parking lot—I'd guess more than a hundred people were turned away (and they were none too pleased, so eager were they to get a sneak peek at Perry's latest project). Those who did get in were vocally appreciative throughout.

However troubling Perry's messages, however poorly written, directed, and produced his movies might be, he gives black people a chance to see some version of themselves on the big and small screens. For better or worse, he is the oasis in a cultural desert of black entertainment.

Peeples was written and directed by a black woman, Tina Gordon Chism, who also wrote the winning *Drumline*, which starred Nick Cannon and Zoe Saldana. *Peeples* has an even better cast, including Craig Robinson, Kerry Washington, David Alan Grier, S. Epatha Merkerson, Diahann Carroll, and Melvin Van Peebles. Robinson plays Wade Walker, an affable man who surprises his live-in lawyer girlfriend, Grace Peeples (Washington), at her family compound in Sag Harbor, only to learn her family doesn't even know he exists. Hijinks ensue as a family normally hell-bent on keeping up appearances and pleasing the patriarch—Grace's father, federal judge Virgil Peeples (Grier)—learns to be more honest with one another about who they each really are.

Peeples is a pretty good movie, even if we've all seen it before. (It's basically *Meet the Parents*.) It is not a great movie, mind you; like many of Perry's own movies, the talented cast is forced into roles that are written without much substance. But they make the very best of the material and keep us entertained from beginning to end. Chism's direction is assured. Though she hasn't written great characters, Chism does make sly jokes that audiences familiar with black culture are sure to enjoy, shrewdly sending up black fraternities, for instance.

I had hoped that *Peeples* would help push Tyler Perry to become an incubator of black talent. The movie made me want to see more from Chism, as both a screenwriter and director. And I still hope this is a beginning of a vibrant career for her—and that Perry provides similar opportunities for other talented black artists.

Sadly, *Peeples* bombed. I had high hopes for this movie, not because it was good but because it was certainly as good as any other movie being released these days. In its opening week, the movie made only $4.6 million while appearing in more than two thousand theaters. The second week was even worse, with the movie bringing in only $2.1 million. Early May 2013 was, perhaps, a bad time for a movie like *Peeples* to be released, what with all the early summer blockbusters like *Iron Man 3*, *The Great Gatsby*, and *Star Trek Into Darkness* being released around the same time. Still, the movie should have done better. At the very least, it should have gotten a boost as counterprogramming to the explosive 3-D and CGI-enhanced pomposity of summer movies. Audiences were not swayed by the imprimatur of "Tyler Perry Presents." This box office failure implies that moviegoers wanted the high drama and heavy-handed messages Perry normally offers his audience, or they wanted the caricature of Madea to make them laugh.

All of this got me thinking again about what, exactly, Perry is up to—and why he's so popular. I have to consider the possibility that Tyler Perry movies are successful because of their moralism and their sneering at women, not in spite of them. It's a bitter pill to swallow. He knows his audience and gives them exactly what they want, and what they have come to expect. When Perry doesn't give his audience what they want—caricatures of black men and women and broad moral messages—well, the box office doesn't lie.

This is more complex an issue, though, than most critical discourse about Perry implies. Yes, Tyler Perry is a deeply problematic figure in entertainment, for so many reasons. But. He also gives his audience some of what they so very much need. As Todd Gilchrist notes for Movies.com, "he uncovers, and highlights, real, honest moments of human interaction, in a way that almost no other filmmaker is doing today." Maybe I continue watching Perry's films because I too see a glimmer of these "real, honest moments." Or I am stubbornly clinging to the hope that someday, he might live up to his potential and his responsibility to create good art for black people, however unreasonable that responsibility might be. I am eager to see more diverse experiences represented in modern entertainment. It is bittersweet that something is better than nothing, even if the something we have is hardly anything at all.

The Last Day of a
Young Black Man

Three hours before the advance screening of *Fruitvale Station* I attended in Chicago, a line of eager fans stretched through the Cineplex. Many were dressed up, hair done right, faces beat— that is, their makeup was applied impeccably. Writer and director Ryan Coogler and stars Octavia Spencer and Michael B. Jordan were on hand for a talk-back after the screening. The Reverend Jesse Jackson introduced the actors and the drama, which won the 2013 Grand Jury Prize at Sundance, referring to the movie's subject matter as "Trayvon Martin in real time" and leading a vigorous call-and-response.

Contemporary black film is not nearly as robust as it should be. When movies by a promising black writer-director like Coogler's *Fruitvale Station* premiere, black audiences wonder if finally they might enjoy a movie that is well written, acted, directed, and produced. Of course, this is the holy grail of all cinema, but it seems particularly unreachable in much of what black cinema has to offer. Broadly speaking, if contemporary black cinema were divided into categories, we'd have raunchy comedies like *Soul Plane*, the feel-good family films frequented by Eddie Murphy and Ice Cube, the awareness-raising films that tackle major race-related issues, and, of course, the work of Tyler Perry. Most black movies, for better or worse, carry a burden of expectation, having to be everything to everyone because we have so little to choose from.

Suffice it to say, a movie about a notorious incident of police brutality like *Fruitvale Station* enters an already fraught conversation. On New Year's Day in 2009, Bay Area Rapid Transit (BART) police officer Johannes Mehserle, working at the BART station in Oakland's heavily Latino Fruitvale district, shot Oscar Grant, a young black man returning to Oakland after celebrating with friends in San Francisco, in the back. Earlier that night, BART police had responded to reports of a fight by removing Grant and several of his friends from the train. Accounts of what happened next differ, but matters escalated quickly.

Bystanders took a number of videos and images of the incident, and soon these artifacts of Grant's death went viral. Oakland residents held a vigil and rioted, releasing a long-simmering rage over the plight of young black men in the city. Protests, some violent, would continue for more than a year. Four years later, digital traces of Grant's death linger across the Internet, continuing to bear witness.

Fruitvale Station begins with Oscar (Michael B. Jordan) and his girlfriend, Sophina (Melonie Diaz), talking about their New Year's resolutions. Then the film jumps to 2:15 a.m. in the nearly empty station. Oscar and a group of his friends are seated on the ground. Officers surround them, both the young men and the police shouting. The footage, from a cell phone, is shaky and grainy, but there is no ambiguity about what is taking place.

The rest of the movie chronicles the events leading up to that moment. Oscar is shown as a charming young man with a troubled past who is finally on the right path. After two stints in prison for drug dealing, he is working to reconnect with Sophina. He dotingly cares for his daughter, Tatiana, and strives to be a good son to his mother, Wanda (Octavia Spencer). A movie about limited options for young inner-city black men, *Fruitvale* also explores the multiple identities many of these men must adopt. Oscar is a master of code-switching—the man he is with his mother is different from the man he is with his girlfriend and child, with his friends, or in prison. As director Coogler, who is from the Bay Area, notes, "Oftentimes you've got to be different people just to stay alive."

When Oscar picks Tatiana up from day care, they race back to the car, their bodies so full of joy it's like they're trying to outrun the feeling. Actor Michael B. Jordan, best known as Wallace, the sixteen-year-old dealer from *The Wire*, and Vince, the high school quarterback from *Friday Night Lights*, expresses that joy from his face to the kick of his heels. In scenes with Diaz, Jordan brings out the raw appeal of a young man in his prime—slow drawls, sexy smiles, toned body. He also expresses openness and vulnerability when Oscar confesses to Sophina that he has lost his job and when, in prison, he begs his mother not to leave him alone.

As Wanda, Octavia Spencer is the movie's moral center. She embodies nurturing, tough love, and the small ways a mother never lets go. She chides Oscar for driving and talking on his cell phone, urging him to take the train home so he doesn't drink and drive. In a powerful flashback, Wanda visits Oscar in prison. He's in his uniform, thrilled to see a familiar face. Wanda is loving but weary, trying to hang on to what normalcy she can. During her visit, Oscar gets drawn into a verbal altercation with another inmate, revealing the aggressive, defiant man he can be when pushed. Wanda tries to calm him. But it's too much, how he has to straddle two worlds, and when he sits back down, his body is coiled with frustration. Wanda tells Oscar she won't be coming back to see him. Spencer's handling of the moment, with quiet control and resolve and no hysterics, is heartbreaking.

There are moments of levity, like when Oscar has to buy a birthday card on behalf of his sister. Despite the sister's express instructions not to, he gets a card with white people on the front. Such moments not only humanize Oscar, they allow the audience to laugh, to exhale. We need that.

Director Coogler had only the length of a movie—ninety minutes, in this case—to give us a sense of who Oscar Grant was, someone to mourn when the end came. He conducted extensive research on Grant's whereabouts on that final day and overcame the family's apprehension to work closely with them. In a prophetic scene, Oscar comforts a bleeding dog hit by a car, whispering kind words so the animal won't die alone. When Oscar is at the grocery store buying crab for his mother, a young woman at the butcher counter wants to fry fish but is unsure how. Oscar gets his grandma Bonnie on the phone to school her. On the streets of San Francisco after midnight, surrounded by revelers, Oscar and his friends convince a store owner closing shop to let their girlfriends, and the pregnant wife of a couple they don't know, use the restroom. The men enjoy the camaraderie of strangers, and we see Oscar plan for a future he will not be part of.

At times, Coogler's choices verge on the sentimental, if not manipulative. His investment in Grant's story is palpable. There are indulgent directorial choices, like the superimposing of text messages and phone numbers on the screen when Oscar is using his cell phone. It is a testament to the movie's excellence that the flaws are in the details.

Fruitvale Station could have been an angry movie, but Coogler has crafted an intimate, at times exuberant, portrait. This was a deliberate choice, costar Octavia Spencer said during the question-and-answer session after the screening: "Anger without action leads to riots. I didn't know if that was the best emotion to associate with this film." Still, it is hard to consider what made the movie possible without surrendering to some amount of rage.

As Coogler notes, "Grant's murder came at a time where people in Oakland were optimistic about race." In one night, that optimism was taken away. Oakland, the eighth-largest city in California, is a particularly difficult place for young black men. According to a June 2011 report from the Oakland Unified School District's Office of African American Male Achievement, "In Oakland, African American male students have the worst outcomes of any demographic group, despite improvements in some areas in recent years."

The world beyond the school system provides little statistical solace. According to the NAACP, nearly 1 million of the 2.3 million Americans in prison are African American. Further racial disparities persist in the length of sentencing and the effect of incarceration after release. These institutional biases make it difficult to envision how young black men can succeed. Or as Oscar seems to say in the movie, feeling defeated by a series of failures, *I'm tired. Thought I could start over fresh but shit ain't working out.*

Year after year, we discuss these statistics and the impossibility of them. Year after year, we tell the same stories, using these statistics, to show how *shit ain't working out.* Accurately conceiving of what young black men face when we talk about them as numbers, though, is difficult. Some statistics loom so pervasively they have become myths. For example, a commonly recited "fact" is that more black men end up in jail than attend college. Ivory A. Toldson, a professor at Howard University, refutes this statement, noting in a series on black education for *The Root* that "today there are approximately 600,000 more black men in college than in jail, and the best research evidence suggests that the line was never true to begin with." Behind the statistics for black men in Oakland and across the United States are men who are being failed by society. These statistics, when offered without any kind of reflection, do little to advance the conversation, and when they go unquestioned, as Toldson suggests, they distort the conversation.

It is in this context that *Fruitvale Station* works compellingly to treat Oscar Grant as a man. Forced to decide whether to sell drugs to support his family, Oscar makes what we hope is the right choice, throwing a large quantity of marijuana into the bay. He tries to get his job back at a local grocer after being fired. Not only are his options drastically limited, his learning curve is steep. There is little room for error. For some young black men, there is no room for error at all.

Depicting this reality was Coogler's primary aim because, he says, "we struggle with a mass loss of life [in the Bay Area], and the root of these issues is a demonization of young black men." Contemporary black cinema will not end the demonization of young black men, but a movie like *Fruitvale Station* offers us a necessary insight into the consequences.

When black movies fail at the box office, too often it becomes a race to see who will first say, "This is why we can't have nice things." Take the case of *Red Tails*, produced by George Lucas and directed by Anthony Hemingway, which only earned a bit less than $50 million domestically.

In interviews at the time of the film's release, Lucas, having put his own money behind the project to ensure it would receive a wide launch, essentially insisted the moviegoing public bore a responsibility to see the movie. In an interview with *USA Today*, Lucas said, "I realize that by accident I've now put the black film community at risk [with *Red Tails*, whose $58 million budget far exceeds typical all-black productions]. I'm saying, if this doesn't work, there's a good chance you'll stay where you are for quite a while. It'll be harder for you guys to break out of that [lower-budget] mold." Self-important and grandiose as his statement is, Lucas also gets at a frustrating truth. Each time a black movie is made, it has to succeed or risk fallout for the movies that follow. *Fruitvale Station*, though, bodes well for both the commercial viability and the artistic promise of black film. Early box office returns were excellent. In its opening weekend, *Fruitvale Station* grossed $377,285 with a $53,898 per screen average, and the movie went on to gross more than $16 million domestically during its theatrical run. The quality of the movie itself offers the hope that a broader range of quality black movies might be made and that we will see black people portrayed in more nuanced ways.

Movies matter. But still, there is this painful reality. Each time Oscar says good-bye to his girlfriend or family in *Fruitvale Station*, he adds, "I love you." Coogler remarked that many young men in the inner city do this because "every time we leave the house, we know we might not make it back." Such is an uncanny burden. There is also this. Oscar Grant was twenty-two years old when he was murdered. Johannes Mehserle, after serving just one year of a two-year sentence, was released from prison on June 13, 2011.

When Less Is More

The Internet tells me I'm supposed to love the television series *Orange Is the New Black*. The show is reasonably well written, there's an "interesting" premise, and the cast is diverse. You can't blink without someone celebrating the show's diversity. *Orange Is the New Black* is very, very diverse. Did you know?

I should love *Orange Is the New Black* for the same reason I should (but do not) love *Red Tails* or *The Butler* or *42*. Here is popular culture about people who look like me. That's all I should need, right? Time and again, people of color are supposed to be grateful for scraps from the table. There's this strange implication that we should enjoy certain movies or television shows simply because they exist.

The critical response has been overwhelmingly positive. Emily Nussbaum, the *New Yorker*'s television critic wrote, "Smart, salty, and outrageous, the series falls squarely in the tradition of graphic adult cable drama; were you pitching it poolside in Beverly Hills, you might call it the love child of 'Oz' and 'The L Word.'" The description is perfect—there's grit and heartache balanced by charm and the soapy, outrageous goodness of melodrama. *Orange Is the New Black* also has impressive staying power in the cultural conversation, particularly given that the show streams exclusively on Netflix, a subscriber service.

By the way, did you know this show is remarkably diverse?

I put off watching *Orange Is the New Black* because I read the memoir, which was good, and watching the show didn't feel necessary. I never felt a need to move from one episode to the next, and toward the end, getting through the season became a chore.

There are, undoubtedly, merits. I've enjoyed getting to know some of the characters. Sexuality is addressed in interesting, often nuanced ways, at least for the imprisoned white women. There is an amazing Nicholson Baker reference that made word nerds around the world rejoice. How the women build community and seek connection offers a compelling observation about what people need to survive.

Laverne Cox is unequivocally outstanding as Sophia Burset, a transgender woman with a wife and son. This detail is exactly what makes *Orange Is the New Black* as good as it is infuriating. Burset's story is original and refreshing. Cox and Tanya Wright, who plays Burset's wife, Crystal, create beautifully acted scenes that are intimate, bittersweet, and honest. Their story line is the one thing on this show that is genuinely unlike anything else on television, the one element that lives up to the hype.

It is frustrating that *Orange Is the New Black* is not nearly as good as the rapturous reception suggests. Creator Jenji Kohan can't commit to excellence or mediocrity. Instead, she dances along the razor-sharp line between the two.

So many opportunities for the show to be truly original and smart are missed by wide margins. There's a Haitian character, Miss Claudette, quite the rarity, but her accent is inconsistent, bizarre, and bears no resemblance to a Haitian accent. She doesn't even seem like a Haitian woman. Perhaps, on this point, I am biased because I am Haitian American. Another inmate, Crazy Eyes, is more caricature than character. She is fixated on Piper. Her infatuation is supposed to be funny because crazy people are, I guess, hilarious. To be fair, her character is more fully developed as the season unfolds, but the early going is rough. In one scene, Crazy Eyes pisses just outside of Piper's bunk, the whites of her crazy eyes shining in the dark. I laughed along because Crazy Eyes is entertaining and the talented Uzo Aduba makes the most of the role. The pleasure, though, is guilt-ridden because I'm too aware of how cavalierly dignity is sacrificed for pleasure's sake.

Through no fault of actor Taylor Schilling, Piper, the central character, is the least interesting, primarily because *Orange Is the New Black* is a lovingly crafted monument to White Girl Problems. Certainly, Piper suffers as she comes to terms with the reality of her incarceration. There are deeply affecting scenes illustrating her plight. She has a wry sensibility that translates well. And still, we cannot ignore how the show's diverse characters are planets orbiting Piper's sun. The women of color don't have the privilege of inhabiting their own solar systems. This is what we consider diversity these days.

Orange Is the New Black is based on Piper Kerman's memoir. The source material concerns a privileged white woman serving a prison sentence. This show cannot be anything but what it is, and that's fine. Unfortunately, we will never see a similar show about a woman of color as a stranger in a strange land, bewildered by incarceration. We will never see someone dare to write against the dominant narrative about women of color and incarceration.

There is also the grating sense that we should congratulate Kohan for making a good choice, a long overdue choice, instead of an easy choice. We should be *grateful* diverse actors finally have more opportunity to practice their craft, despite the fact that *Orange Is the New Black* is diverse in the shallowest, most tokenistic ways. In *The Nation*, Aura Bogado notes,

> *With very little exception, I saw wildly racist tropes: black women who, aside from fanaticizing about fried chicken, are called monkeys and Crazy Eyes; a Boricua mother who connives with her daughter for the sexual attentions of a white prison guard; an Asian woman who never speaks; and a crazy Latina who tucks away in a bathroom stall to photograph her vagina . . .*

This is the famine from which we must imagine feast.

I'm tired of feeling like I should be grateful when popular culture deigns to acknowledge the experiences of people who are not white, middle class or wealthy, and heterosexual. I'm tired of the extremes.

So few movies or shows fall between those extremes, but thankfully the ones that do—*The Game, Grey's Anatomy* and *Scandal, Love & Basketball, The Best Man, Jumping the Broom, Peeples*, and the like—are good, not always great, but well within reach. We need more. We need pop culture that demonstrates not only the ways people are different but also the ways we are very much alike.

In her review, Nussbaum also says the show is "smarter and subtler about the entire range of female-female dynamics than almost anything on TV." She's right. The bar is so low for portrayals of people out of the mainstream that "smarter and subtler" seems like so much more than it actually is. Why are we still talking about *Orange Is the New Black*? The conversation is a measure of how much we are forced to settle or, perhaps, how much we're willing to settle.

[POLITICS, GENDER & RACE]

The Politics of Respectability

When a black person behaves in a way that doesn't fit the dominant cultural ideal of how a black person should be, there is all kinds of trouble. The authenticity of his or her blackness is immediately called into question. We should be black but not too black, neither too ratchet nor too bougie. There are all manner of unspoken rules of how a black person should think and act and behave, and the rules are ever changing.

We hold all people to unspoken rules about who and how they should be, how they should think, and what they should say. We say we hate stereotypes but take issue when people deviate from those stereotypes. Men don't cry. Feminists don't shave their legs. Southerners are racist. Everyone is, by virtue of being human, some kind of rule breaker, and my goodness, do we hate when the rules are broken.

Black people often seem to be held to a particularly unreasonable standard. Prominent figures have a troubling habit of coming forward with maxims about how black people should be and behave. One such person is Bill Cosby. In an op-ed for the *New York Post*, Cosby identified apathy as one of the black community's biggest problems. If we just care enough about ourselves and our communities, we will reach a hallowed place where we will no longer suffer the effects of racism. Most of Cosby's commentary on race, in recent years, might be summarized as such: if we act right, we will finally be good enough for white people to love us.

CNN anchor Don Lemon offered five suggestions for the black community to overcome racism: black people should stop using the N-word, black people should respect their communities by not littering, black people should stay in school, black people should have fewer children out of wedlock, and, most inexplicably, young black men should pull their pants up. Lemon also offered anecdotal evidence that he rarely sees people litter in white communities. He then played on the assumption of homophobia, explaining, with regard to sagging pants, that "in fact, it comes from prison. When they take away belts from prisoners so they can't make a weapon. And then it evolved into which role each prisoner would have during male-on-male prison sex." Implicit in Lemon's argument was that the white, heterosexual man is the cultural ideal toward which we should all aspire—curious thinking from Lemon.

Cosby, Lemon, and others who espouse similar ideas are, I would like to believe, coming from a good place. Their suggestions are, on one level, reasonable, mostly grounded in common sense, but these leaders traffic in respectability politics—the idea that if black (or other marginalized) people simply behave in "culturally approved" ways, if we mimic the dominant culture, it will be more difficult to suffer the effects of racism. Respectability politics completely overlook institutional racism and the ways in which the education system, the social welfare system, and the justice system only reinforce many of the problems the black community faces.

We are having an ongoing and critical conversation about race in America. The question on many minds, the question that is certainly on my mind, is how do we prevent racial injustices from happening? How do we protect young black children? How do we overcome so many of the institutional barriers that exacerbate racism and poverty?

It's a nice idea that we could simply follow a prescribed set of rules and make the world a better place for all. It's a nice idea that racism is a finite problem for which there is a finite solution, and that respectability, perhaps, could have saved all the people who have lost their lives to the effects of racism.

But we don't live in that world and it's dangerous to suggest that the targets of oppression are wholly responsible for ending that oppression. Respectability politics suggest that there's a way for us to all be model (read: like white) citizens. We can always be better, but will we ever be ideal? Do we even want to be ideal, or is there a way for us to become more comfortably human?

Take, for example, someone like Don Lemon. He is a black man, raised by a single mother, and now he is a successful news anchor for a major news network. His outlook seems driven by the notion that if he can make it, anyone can. This is the ethos espoused by people who believe in respectability politics. Because they have achieved success, because they have transcended, in some way, the effects of racism or other forms of discrimination, all people should be able to do the same.

In truth, they have climbed a ladder and shattered a glass ceiling but are seemingly uninterested in extending that ladder as far as it needs to reach so that others may climb. They are uninterested in providing a detailed blueprint for how they achieved their success. They are unwilling to consider that until the institutional problems are solved, no blueprint for success can possibly exist. For real progress to be made, leaders like Lemon and Cosby need to at least acknowledge reality.

Respectability politics are not the answer to ending racism. Racism doesn't care about respectability, wealth, education, or status. Oprah Winfrey, one of the wealthiest people in the world and certainly the wealthiest black woman in the world, openly discusses the racism she continues to encounter in her daily life. In July 2013, while in Zurich to attend Tina Turner's wedding, Winfrey was informed by a store clerk at the Trois Pommes boutique that the purse she was interested in was too expensive for her. We don't need to cry for Oprah, prevented from buying an obscenely overpriced purse, but we can recognize the incident as one more reminder that racism is so pervasive and pernicious that we will never be respectable enough to outrun racism, not here in the United States, not anywhere in the world.

We must stop pointing to the exceptions—these bright shining stars who transcend circumstance. We must look to how we can best support the least among us, not spend all our time blindly revering and trying to mimic the greatest without demanding systemic change.

In July 2013, President Obama made a historic speech about race. His remarks were, by far, the most explicit remarks the president has made on the subject. In addition to sharing his own experiences with racism, he offered suggestions about how we might improve race relations in the United States—ending racial profiling, reexamining state and local laws that might contribute to tragedies like Trayvon Martin's murder, and finding more effective ways to support black boys. These suggestions are a bit vague (and black girls seem to be forgotten, as if they too don't need support), but at least Obama's ideas place the responsibility for change on all of us. We are, after all, supposed to be one nation indivisible. Only if we act as such, might we begin to truly effect change.

When Twitter Does What Journalism Cannot

On Tuesday, June 25, 2013, Texas state senator Wendy Davis stood for nearly thirteen hours without food or drink, without rest, without leaning, without the ability to use the restroom, to filibuster Senate Bill 5 (SB5), a legislative measure that would have closed thirty-seven of the forty-two abortion clinics in Texas, the largest state in the contiguous United States. Interested people from around the country, nay, the world, were able to watch this filibuster, and the political maneuverings of those who tried to stop it, via a live stream on YouTube—one watched, at times, by more than 180,000 people.

The filibuster was a gripping spectacle that kept me rapt for hours. On Twitter, people were able to offer support, however symbolic, for Senator Davis's efforts. There was a sense of community. For some levity, I couldn't help but remark on Senator Davis's flawless hair, several hours into her ferocious stand.

Near midnight, after some intense and partisan efforts to

derail Senator Davis's efforts, the impassioned crowd in the gallery began shouting and cheering, letting the senator know she did not stand alone. It was a sound of women fighting for their reproductive freedom in the only way they could—with their voices. I will never forget that sound. It awoke something in me I hadn't realized had gone dormant.

And why were so many of us watching this amazing set of events happen on a YouTube stream? Because none of the major news networks, not one, carried or covered the last hours of the filibuster. The gap between old and new media yawned ever wider.

That, however, is not where this story begins.

The reason I knew anything about what was going on in Texas was thanks to the efforts and boundless energy of Jessica W. Luther (@scATX), a Texas activist who shared information about SB5 for weeks. I don't know her personally but we became connected online. I'll be honest—at first, I was completely clueless about what was happening in Texas. At times, I thought, *I do not have the energy to care about this.*

Luther was so committed, though, and so full of passion and good information, that I started to care. I started to pay attention. I read the articles and commentaries she shared and began to understand what was at stake not just for women in Texas but for all American women. I was reminded that change sometimes does begin with one person who raises her voice.

And there I was, watching a YouTube live feed of a state senate filibuster, something I never thought I would do.

Social media is a curious thing. On the one hand, it offers an endless parade of ephemera from the daily lives of friends, family, and strangers—discussions of a fondness for yogurt, a picture of a barista's decoration in latte foam, descriptions of excellent meals, pictures of pets and small children or maybe an abandoned easy chair on a crowded street corner. There's all manner of self-promotion and relentless affirmation. There are knee-jerk, ill-informed reactions to, well, everything. The abundance of triviality is as hypnotic as it is repulsive.

But there are times when social media is anything but trivial. During Hurricane Sandy, social media allowed public officials along the eastern corridor to disseminate information about available resources and evacuation routes, and provide updates on the storm. Social media allowed community members to offer information and assistance and human connection through small, grassroots networks. Certainly, there were flies in the ointment as people of questionable moral stability spread rumors and began, with astonishing speed, to develop fraudulent schemes, but for the most part, social media was used to accomplish some good.

I cannot think of a significant event in recent memory I did not first learn about via Twitter—the midnight shootings in Aurora, Colorado; the massacre at Sandy Hook Elementary; the uprisings across the Middle East during the Arab Spring; the activities of the Occupy movement; the results of the 2012 presidential election; the shooting of Trayvon Martin and ensuing debacle; the fertilizer plant explosion in West, Texas; the bombings at the Boston Marathon.

When these major news stories are breaking, there's always a significant difference between what's being shared via social media and what major news outlets are covering. That difference becomes more pronounced and more pathetic with each passing day.

Good journalism takes time that social media, which advances at a breathtaking pace, rarely affords. Good journalists need to verify information before they can report it. They need this time because, in the best of all worlds, we're supposed to trust that they are offering us accurate, unbiased information. But even after they've applied the necessary rigor to their profession, journalists from major news outlets still seem like they can't keep up—or, perhaps, it's that they won't keep up. Somehow, though,

smaller journalism outlets manage to get the work done. The feed
of Wendy Davis's filibuster was made possible because the *Texas
Tribune*, a nonprofit news organization in Texas, was there from
the start.

On Tuesday, June 25, Senator Wendy Davis stood and fought
for reproductive freedom in her state, and the networks were
largely silent. MSNBC offered some coverage earlier in the evening, but during the last few hours, the news networks—the
twenty-four-hour news networks created for this very purpose—
were silent. They reported inaccurate information when they
bothered to report at all. The next morning, CNN anchor Chris
Cuomo referred to the efforts of Davis and the Texas men and
women who held vigil with her as "odd politics at work," and
before that suggested, "Why not spend the time trying to compromise and figure out the bill in the first place?," as if reproductive
freedom is simply a matter of compromise. He was incompetent,
a frustrating combination of dismissiveness and negligence.

When journalism is working effectively, and it often is, I appreciate having journalists explain what I might not understand
or know enough about. An Internet connection does not make
me, or anyone, an expert on culturally significant events. Smart
journalistic perspective would have been useful to many people
while Senator Davis spoke. Instead of being able to turn to news,
though, people were on Twitter and elsewhere across the Internet, researching parliamentary procedures of the Texas legislature, sharing the most significant moments of the night, and
holding the Texas Republican senators accountable when they
tried to break their own rules even though they were in plain
sight. Average people with Internet connections did the work we
used to trust major journalism outlets to do.

Smart journalistic perspective was useful earlier on June 25,
when the Supreme Court, in an appalling 5–4 decision, struck
down Section 4 of the Voting Rights Act, essentially disenfran-

chising a significant number of Americans—voters of color, rural voters, elderly voters, and impoverished voters. It was useful to see what people were thinking about that decision across social networks, but it was even more useful to read and watch well-considered reporting about a topic I don't know much about. It was more useful to be informed than to assume the responsibility of having to inform.

That same Supreme Court overturned the Defense of Marriage Act and dismissed California's Proposition 8 appeal, offering one step forward after innumerable steps back. Again, social networks were active, mostly with jubilation (or not, depending on whom you consort with). The Twitter discussions about DOMA also provided a useful reminder that the institution of marriage can and should be critiqued as we move forward with marriage equality. There were discussions about the implications for gay and lesbian couples in binational marriages and the financial benefits the wedding industry will reap from this decision. Social networking broadened the conversation.

The news networks covered these decisions on marriage equality fairly robustly. Around the same time, they also covered George Zimmerman's trial for the murder of Trayvon Martin, the ongoing intrigue involving Edward Snowden and revelations about the NSA, and Paula Deen's damage control. There is no shortage of news, and there never has been. We live in a big, messy world.

Social networks are more than just infinite repositories for trivial, snap judgments; they are more than merely convenient outlets for mindless joy and outrage. They offer more than the common ground and the solace we may find during culturally significant moments. Social networks also provide us with something of a flawed but necessary conscience, a constant reminder that commitment, compassion, and advocacy neither can nor ever should be finite.

We cannot lose sight of what happened on June 25 because we are so consumed by what happened next, nor can we lose sight of what happens today in favor of what tomorrow will bring. Traditional journalism can give us the grounding and context we dearly need, while social networks remind us that we do have today, that we can be mindful of the past and future while taking some time to appreciate the present.

The Alienable
Rights of Women

Reproductive freedom is on my mind. How could it not be? I'm a woman of reproductive age, and depending on where I live, my reproductive choices are limited.

Often, when I read the news, I have to make sure I am not, in fact, reading *The Onion*. We continue to have national and state debates about abortion, birth control, and reproductive freedom, and men, mostly, are directing that debate. That is the stuff of satire.

The politicians and their ilk who are hell-bent on reintroducing reproductive freedom as a "campaign issue" have short memories. Of course they have short memories. They only care about what is politically convenient or expedient.

Women do not have short memories. We cannot afford that luxury as our choices dwindle.

Politicians and their ilk forget that women, and to a certain extent men, have always done what they needed to do to protect female bodies from unwanted pregnancy. During ancient times, women used jellies, gums, and plants both for contraception and to abort unwanted pregnancies. These practices continued even into the 1300s, when Europe needed to repopulate and started to hunt "witches" and midwives who shared their valuable knowledge about these contraceptive methods.

Whenever governments wanted to achieve some end, often involving population growth, they restricted access to birth control and/or criminalized birth control unless, of course, the population growth concerned the poor, in which case, contraception was enthusiastically promoted. Historically, society has only wanted the "right kind of people" to have a right to life. We shouldn't forget that fact.

Here's the thing about history—it repeats itself over and over and over. The witch hunts, and the demonization of contraception and abortion and the women who provided these services from the fourteenth and fifteenth centuries, are happening all over again. This time, though, the witch hunt is a cynical ploy to distract the populace from some of the truly pressing issues our society is facing: the devastated economy and a Wall Street culture that remains unchecked even after the damage it has done, the raging class inequalities and widening gap between those who have and those who have not, the looming student loan and consumer debt crises, the fractured racial climate, the lack of full civil rights for gay, lesbian, and transgender people, a health care system too many people don't have access to, wars without cease, impending global threats, and on and on and on.

Rather than solve the real problems the United States is facing, some politicians, mostly conservative, have decided to try to solve the "female problem" by creating a smoke screen, reintroducing abortion and, more inexplicably, birth control into a national debate.

Women have been forced underground for contraception and

pregnancy termination before, and we will go underground again if we have to. We will risk our lives if these politicians, who so flagrantly demean women, force us to do so.

Thank goodness women do not have short memories.

Pregnancy is at once a private and public experience. Pregnancy is private because it is so very personal. It happens within the body. In a perfect world, pregnancy would be an intimate experience shared by a woman and her partner alone, but for various reasons that is not possible.

Pregnancy is an experience that invites public intervention and forces the female body into the public discourse. In many ways, pregnancy is the least private experience of a woman's life.

Public intervention can be fairly mild, more annoying than anything else—people wanting to touch your swollen belly, offering unsolicited advice about how to raise a child, inquiring as to due dates or the gender of the not-yet-child as if strangers have a right to this information simply because you are pregnant. Once your pregnancy starts to show, you cannot avoid being part of this discourse whether you want to or not.

Public intervention can be necessary because pregnant women must, generally, seek appropriate medical care. You cannot simply hide in a cave and hope for the best, however tempting that alternative may be. Pregnancy is many things, including complicated and, at times, fraught. Medical intervention, if you're lucky enough to have health insurance or otherwise afford such care, helps to ensure the pregnancy proceeds the way it should. It allows your fetus to be tested for abnormalities. It allows the mother's health to be monitored for the number of conditions that can arise from a pregnancy. If things go wrong in a pregnancy, and they can go horribly, horribly wrong, medical intervention can save the life of the mother and, if you're lucky, the life of the fetus. Public intervention is also necessary when a woman delivers her child, whether by the hands of a doctor, midwife, or doula.

It is only after a baby is born that a woman might finally have some privacy.

And then there's the manner in which the legislature, in too many states, intervenes in pregnancy, time and again, particularly when a woman chooses to exercise her right to terminate. This choice increasingly feels heretical, or at least that is how it is framed by the loudest voices carrying on this conversation.

Since 1973, women in the United States have had the right to choose to terminate a pregnancy. Women have had the right to choose not to be forced into unwanted motherhood. Since 1973, that right has been contested in many different ways, and during election years, the contesting of reproductive freedom flares hotly.

Things have gotten complicated, in too many states, for women who want to exercise their right to choose. Legislatures across the United States have worked very hard to shape and control the abortion experience in bizarre, insensitive ways that intervene on a personal, should-be-private experience in very public, painful ways.

In recent years, several states have introduced and/or passed legislation mandating that women receive ultrasounds before they receive an abortion. Seven states now require this procedure.

States like Virginia tried to pass a bill requiring women seeking an abortion to receive a medically unnecessary transvaginal ultrasound, but that bill failed. The Virginia legislature subsequently passed a bill requiring a regular ultrasound, in a bit of bait-and-switch lawmaking. This bill also requires that, whether or not a woman chooses to see the ultrasound or listen to the fetal heartbeat, the information about her choice be entered into her medical record with or without her consent.

The conversation about transvaginal ultrasounds has been particularly heated, with some pro-choice advocates suggesting this procedure is akin to state-mandated rape. That is an irresponsible tack at best. Rape is rape. This procedure—and legislation requiring this procedure—is something else entirely, although, I can assure you, a transvaginal ultrasound is not a pleasant procedure, primarily because there is very little that is pleasant about being half naked, in front of strangers, while being probed by a hard plastic object, at least within a medical context. A transvaginal ultrasound is a medical procedure that sometimes must be done, but we cannot even have a reasonable conversation about the procedure and its lack of medical necessity for women who want an abortion because the procedure is carelessly being thrown into the abortion conversation as yet another distraction tactic.

Restrictive abortion legislation, in whatever form it takes, is a rather transparent ploy. If these politicians can't prevent women from having abortions, they are certainly going to punish them. They are going to punish these women severely, cruelly, unusually for daring to make choices about motherhood, their bodies, and their futures.

In the race to see who can punish women the most for daring to make these choices, Texas has outdone itself, going so far as to require women to receive multiple sonograms, to be told about all the services available to encourage them to remain pregnant, and, most diabolically, to listen to the doctor narrate the sonogram.

This legislation designed to control reproductive freedom is so craven as to make you question humanity. It is repulsive. Our legal system, which by virtue of the Eighth Amendment demands that no criminal punishment be cruel and unusual, affords more human rights to criminals than such legislation affords women. Just ask Carolyn Jones, who suffered through this macabre ordeal in Texas when she and her husband decided to terminate her second pregnancy because their child would have been born into a lifetime of suffering and medical care. Her story is nearly unbearable to hear, which speaks to the magnitude of grief she must have experienced.

Pennsylvania governor Tom Corbett supported legislation that will require women to get an ultrasound before an abortion. He suggested women simply close their eyes during the ultrasound. They will, apparently, let anyone run for office these days, including men who believe that not witnessing something will make it easier to endure.

Georgia State representative Terry England suggested—in support of HB 954, which would ban abortion in that state after twenty weeks—that women should carry stillborn fetuses to term because cows and pigs do it too. Then he tried to backtrack and say that's not what he meant. Women and animals are not much different for this man or for most of the men who are trying to control the conversation and legislation regarding reproductive freedom.

Thirty-five states require women to receive counseling before an abortion to varying degrees of specificity. In twenty-six states women must also be offered or given written material. The restrictions go on and on. If you think you're free from these restrictions, think again. In 2011, 55 percent of all women of reproductive age in the United States lived in states hostile to abortion rights and reproductive freedom.

Waiting periods, counseling, ultrasounds, transvaginal ultrasounds, sonogram storytelling—all of these legislative moves are invasive, insulting, and condescending because they are deeply misguided attempts to pressure women into changing their minds, to pressure women into not terminating their pregnancies, as if women are so easily swayed that such petty and cruel stall tactics will work. These politicians do not understand that once a woman has made up her mind about terminating a pregnancy, very little will sway her. It is not a decision taken lightly, and if a woman does take the decision lightly, that is her right. A woman should always have the right to choose what she does with her body. It is frustrating that this needs to be said, repeatedly. On the scale of relevance, public approval or disapproval of a woman's choices should not merit measure.

And what of medical doctors who take an oath to serve the best interests of their patients? What responsibility do they bear in this? If medical practitioners banded together and refused to participate in some of these restrictions, would that make any difference?

This debate is a smoke screen, but it is a very deliberate and dangerous smoke screen. It is dangerous because this current debate shows us that reproductive freedom is negotiable. Reproductive freedom is a *talking point*. Reproductive freedom is a *campaign issue*. Reproductive freedom can be repealed or restricted. Reproductive freedom is not an inalienable right even though it should be.

The United States as we know it was founded on the principle of inalienable rights, the idea that some rights are so sacrosanct not even a government can take them away. Of course, this country's founding fathers were only thinking of wealthy white men when they codified this principle, but still, it's a nice idea, that there are some freedoms that cannot be taken away.

What this debate shows us is that even in this day and age, the rights of women are not inalienable. Our rights can be and are, with alarming regularity, stripped away.

I struggle to accept that my body is a legislative matter. The truth of this fact makes it difficult for me to breathe. I don't feel like I have inalienable rights.

I don't feel free. I don't feel like my body is my own.

There is no freedom in any circumstance where the body is legislated, none at all. In her article "Legislating the Female Body: Reproductive Technology and the Reconstructed Woman," Isabel Karpin argues, "In the process of regulating the female body, the law legislates its shape, lineaments, and its boundaries." Too many politicians and cultural moralists are trying to define the shape and boundaries of the female body when women should be defining these things for ourselves. We should have that freedom, and that freedom should be sacrosanct.

Then, of course, there is the problem of those women who want to, perhaps, avoid the pregnancy question altogether by availing themselves of birth control with the privacy and dignity and affordability that should also be inalienable.

Or, according to some, whores.

Margaret Sanger would be horrified to see how, nearly a century after she opened the first birth control clinic, we're essentially fighting the same fight. The woman was by no means perfect, but she forever altered the course of reproductive freedom. It is a shame to see what is happening to her legacy because we are now seemingly forced to argue that birth control should be affordable and freely available and there are people who disagree.

In the early 1900s, Sanger and others were fighting for reproductive freedom because they knew a woman's quality of life could only be enhanced by unfettered access to contraception. Sanger knew women were performing abortions on themselves or receiving back-alley abortions that put their lives at risk or rendered them infertile. She wanted to change something. Sanger and other birth control pioneers fought this good fight because they knew what women have always known, what women have never allowed themselves to forget: more often than not, the burden of having and rearing children falls primarily on the backs of women. Certainly, in my lifetime, men have assumed a more equal role in parenting, but women are the only ones who can get pregnant and women then have to survive the pregnancy, which is not always as easy as it seems. Birth control allows women to choose when they assume that responsibility. The majority of women have used at least one contraceptive method in their lifetime, so this is clearly a choice women do not want to lose.

We are having inexplicable conversations about birth control, conversations where women must justify why they are taking birth control, conversations where a congressional hearing on birth control includes no women because the men in power are well aware that women don't need to be included in the conversation. We don't have inalienable rights the way men do.

In 2012, Arizona introduced legislation that would allow an employer to fire a woman for using birth control. Mitt Romney, a supposedly viable presidential candidate that same year, declared he would do away with Planned Parenthood, the majority of whose work is to provide affordable health care for women.

A mediocre, morally bankrupt radio personality like Rush Limbaugh publicly shamed a young woman, Sandra Fluke, for having the nerve to advocate for subsidized birth control because birth control can be so expensive. He called her a slut and a prostitute.

More troubling than this oddly timed debate about birth control is the vehemence with which women need to *justify* or explain why they take birth control—health reasons, to regulate periods, you know, as if there's anything wrong with taking birth control simply because you want to have sex without that sex resulting in pregnancy. In certain circles, birth control is being framed as whore medicine. We are now dealing with a bizarre new morality where a woman cannot simply say, in one way or another, "I'm on the pill because I like dick." It's extremely regressive for women to feel like they need to make it seem like they are using birth control for reasons other than what birth control was originally designed for: to control birth.

When progress is made, such as the Affordable Care Act requiring private health insurance companies to cover preventative services and birth control without a copay, said progress is hampered by the government shutdown in October 2013 because Republicans tried to include a one-year delay for the act in their budget proposal. Time and again, we see how women's bodies are negotiable.

I cannot help but think of the Greek play *Lysistrata*.

What often goes unspoken in this conversation is how debates about birth control and reproductive freedom continually force the female body into being a legislative matter because men refuse to assume their fair share of responsibility for birth control. Men refuse to allow their bodies to become a legislative matter because they have that inalienable right. The drug industry has no real motivation to develop a reversible method of male birth control because forcing this burden on women is so damn profitable. According to Shannon Pettypiece, reporting for Bloomberg, Americans spent $5 billion on birth control in 2011. There are exceptions, bright shining exceptions, but most men don't seem to *want* the responsibility for birth control. Why would they? They see what the responsibility continues to cost women, publicly and privately.

Birth control is a pain in the ass. It's a medical marvel, but it is also an imperfect marvel. Most of the time, women have to put something into their bodies that alters their bodies' natural functions just so they can have a sexual life and prevent unwanted pregnancies. Birth control can be expensive. Birth control can wreak havoc on your hormones, your state of mind, and your physical well-being because, depending on the method, there are side effects and the side effects can be ridiculous. If you're on the pill, you have to remember to take it, or else. If you use an IUD, you have to worry about it growing into your body and becoming a permanent part of you. Okay, that worry is mine. There's no sexy way to insert a diaphragm in the heat of the moment. Condoms break. Pulling out is only believable in high school. Sometimes, birth control doesn't work; I know lots of pill babies. We use birth control because, however much it might be a pain in the ass, it is infinitely better than the alternative.

If I told you my birth control method of choice, which I kind of swear by, you'd look at me like I was slightly insane. Suffice it to say, I will take a pill every day when men have that same option. We should all be in this together, right? One of my favorite moments is when a guy, at that certain point in a relationship, says something desperately hopeful like, "Are you on the pill?" I simply say, "No, are you?"

I have regularly thought, with shocking clarity, *I want to start an underground birth control network.* Of course, I also think, *That's crazy. These smoke screens are just that. Things are going to be fine.* Later, I realized, the belief, however fleeting, that women might need to go underground for reproductive freedom is not as crazy as the current climate. I was, in my way, quite serious about creating some kind of underground network to ensure that a woman's right to safely maintain her reproductive health is, in some way, forever inalienable. I want to feel useful. I want to feel empowered.

When I started imagining this underground network, I had a feeling, in my gut, that women, and the men who love (having sex with) us, are going to need to prepare for the worst. The worst, where reproductive freedom is concerned, is probably not behind us. The worst is all around us, breathing down our necks, in relentless pursuit. Either these politicians are serious or they're trying to misdirect national conversations. Either alternative continues to expose the fragility of women's rights.

An underground railroad worked once before. It could work again. We could stockpile various methods of birth control and information about where women might go for safe, ethical reproductive health care in every state—contraception, abortion, education, all of it. We could create a network of reproductive health care providers and abortionists who would treat women humanely because the government does not and we could make sure that every woman who needed to make a choice had all the help she needed.

I spend hours thinking about this underground network and what it would take to make sure women don't ever have to revert to a time when they put themselves at serious risk to terminate a pregnancy. It could be fictionalized as a trilogy and made into a major motion picture starring Jennifer Lawrence.

It surprises me, though it shouldn't, how short the memories of these politicians are. They forget the brutal lengths women have gone to in order to terminate pregnancies when abortion was illegal or when abortion is unaffordable. Women have thrown themselves down stairs and otherwise tried to physically harm themselves to force a miscarriage. Dr. Waldo Fielding noted in the *New York Times*, "Almost any implement you can imagine had been and was used to start an abortion—darning needles, crochet hooks, cut-glass salt shakers, soda bottles, sometimes intact, sometimes with the top broken off." Women have tried to use soap and bleach, catheters, natural remedies. Women have historically resorted to any means necessary. Women will do this again if we are backed into that terrible corner. This is the responsibility our society has forced on women for hundreds of years.

It is a small miracle women do not have short memories about our rights that have always, shamefully, been alienable.

Holding Out for a Hero

There's a great deal about our culture that is aspirational—from how we educate ourselves, to the cars we drive, to where we work and live and socialize. We want to be the best. We want the best of everything. All too often, we are aware of the gaping distance between who we are and whom we aspire to be and we desperately try to close that distance. And then there are superheroes, mythical characters embodying ideals we may not be able to achieve for ourselves. Superheroes are strong, ennobled, and graceful in their suffering so we don't have to be. In *Superman on the Couch*, Danny Fingeroth writes, "A hero embodies what we believe is best in ourselves. A hero is a standard to aspire to as well as an individual to be admired." We crave the ability to look up, to look beyond ourselves and toward something greater.

We are so enamored with this idea of the heroic that we are always looking for ways to attribute heroism to everyday people so we might get just a bit closer to the best version of ourselves, so the distance between who we are and who we aspire to be might become narrower.

Heroism has become overly idealized, so ubiquitous that the idea of a hero is increasingly diluted. Athletes are heroic when they are victorious, when they persevere through injury or adversity. Our parents are heroes for raising us, for serving as good examples. Women are heroes for giving birth. People who survive disease or injury are heroes for overcoming human frailty. People who die from disease or injury are heroic for having endured until they could endure no longer. Journalists are heroes for seeking out the truth. Writers are heroes for bringing beauty into the world. Law enforcement officers are heroes for serving and protecting. As Franco and Zimbardo suggest in "The Banality of Heroism," "By conceiving of heroism as a universal attribute of human nature, not as a rare feature of the few 'heroic elect,' heroism becomes something that seems in the range of possibilities for every person, perhaps inspiring more of us to answer that call." Or maybe we have an excess of heroism because we have become so cynical that we no longer have the language or the ability to make sense of people who are merely human but can also rise to the occasion of greatness when called upon.

Heroism can be a burden. We even see this in the trials and tribulations of comic book superheroes. These heroes are often strong at the broken places. They suffer and suffer and suffer but still they rise. Still they serve the greater good. They sacrifice their bodies and hearts and minds because heroism, it would seem, means the complete denial of the self. Spider-Man agonizes over whether to be with the woman he loves and cannot forgive himself for the death of his uncle. Superman is reluctant to reveal his true identity to the woman he loves to keep her safe from danger. Every superhero has a sad story shaping his or her heroism.

Heroes also fight for justice. They stand up for those who cannot stand up for themselves. It's easy to understand why we might aspire toward heroism even as we are aware of our limitations. As I watched the George Zimmerman trial unfold in 2013, I also thought a great deal about justice and for whom justice is intended. Zimmerman was on trial for the murder of Trayvon Martin, an unarmed seventeen-year-old boy who was wearing a hoodie and walking around being black. Zimmerman was a neighborhood volunteer watchman in his gated community in Sanford, Florida. For whatever reason, he wanted to protect his community. Perhaps he was as susceptible as any of us are to aspiring toward heroism.

Nothing is ever simple. The Zimmerman case was about race—and when a high-profile case is about race, tension is inevitable. Very little about the conversation surrounding this case was rational. Zimmerman claims he shot Martin in self-defense, but Martin was unarmed, carrying a pack of Skittles and a bottle of iced tea. What, precisely, was Zimmerman defending himself from? This is one of the many questions for which we will never have answers. Some people, though, are trying. Fox News pundits hypothesized that yes, indeed, candy and a bottle of iced tea could become murder weapons.

What we do know is that a young black man is all too often suspected of criminality. Frankly, all black men are all too often suspected of criminality. In his beautiful essay for the *Sun*, "Some Thoughts on Mercy," Ross Gay writes,

> *Part of every black child's education includes learning how to deal with the police so he or she won't be locked up or hurt or even killed. Despite my advanced degrees and my light-brown skin, I've had police take me out of my vehicle, threaten to bring in the dogs, and summon another two or three cars. But I've never been thrown facedown in the street or physically brutalized by the cops, as some of my black friends have. I've never been taken away for a few hours or days on account of "mistaken identity."*

Throughout the essay Gay talks about how this education has shaped not only how he sees the world but also how he sees himself. No one is exempt. I don't believe, much, in statements like, "We are Trayvon Martin," but for black men, it is often true.

Zimmerman's lawyers worked, throughout the trial, to demonize Martin, to make him into the scary black man we should all fear, to make it seem like George Zimmerman had no choice and did the right thing. That strategy worked because Zimmerman was acquitted. Those lawyers played on the idea that a black man—or, in the case of Martin, a black boy—is someone to be feared, someone who is dangerous.

In theory, justice should be simple. Justice should be blind. You are innocent until proven guilty. You have the right to remain silent. You have the right to an attorney. You have the right to be judged by a jury of your peers. The principles on which our justice system was founded clearly outline how our judicial system should function.

Few things work in practice as well as they do in theory. Justice is anything but blind. All too often, the people who most need justice benefit the least. The statistics about who is incarcerated and how incarceration affects their future prospects are bleak.

I would like to believe in justice, but there are countless examples of how the justice system fails. In Georgia, Warren Hill, declared mentally retarded by four experts, was scheduled for execution on July 15, 2013. He was reprieved, though he remains on death row. Hill murdered his girlfriend, received a life sentence, and while in prison murdered another inmate, which led to the death sentence. Hill has committed a crime. He deserves to be punished. Will his death serve as justice for his victims?

Would justice in a courtroom, by way of a guilty verdict against George Zimmerman, really have been justice for the murder of Trayvon Martin? Would that measure of justice have comforted his parents and loved ones? "Justice" is, at times, a weak word.

We would like to believe that justice is about balancing a crime with a punishment, but it is never an equal transaction. For most victims of crimes, justice is merely palliative.

It would be just as easy to demonize George Zimmerman as it is to demonize young black men like Trayvon Martin. I hate what Zimmerman did. I hate how his trial unfolded. I hate the way his lawyers treated Rachel Jeantel, the young woman with whom Martin was speaking on the phone just before he died and a key witness for the prosecution. Jeantel did not bother hiding her disdain for Zimmerman's lawyer or the court proceedings, and he did not bother hiding his disdain for her. I hate what Zimmerman stands for and I hate that he was acquitted, but I also understand that he is a man who was raised in the same country as Paula Deen and he happened to have a gun. These things are connected.

Trayvon Martin is neither the first nor the last young black man who will be murdered because of the color of his skin. If there is such a thing as justice for a young man whose life was taken too soon, I hope justice comes from all of us learning from what happened. I hope we can rise to the occasion of greatness, where greatness is nothing more than trying to overcome our lesser selves by seeing a young man like Trayvon Martin for what he is: a young man, a boy without a cape, one who couldn't even walk home from the store unharmed, let alone fly.

A Tale of Two Profiles

There is no way to truly know whom we need to protect ourselves from. Dangerous people rarely look the way we expect. We were reminded of this in early 2013 when Dzhokhar Tsarnaev, who looks like the "boy next door," was identified as one of the two young men suspected in the terrorist bombings near the finish line of the Boston Marathon. Three people were killed and nearly three hundred others injured. This notoriety, I imagine, explains why Tsarnaev was featured on the cover of the August 1, 2013, issue of *Rolling Stone*.

The magazine was accused of exploiting tragedy, glorifying terrorism, and trying to make a martyr or a rock star out of Tsarnaev. But protests aside, the cover is provocative and pointed. It is a stark reminder that we can never truly know where danger lurks. It is also a reminder that we have certain cultural notions about who looks dangerous and who does not. These notions are amply reinforced by the article accompanying the cover, something few people seem to be talking about. The tone of Janet Reitman's reportage and the ongoing conversation about Tsarnaev as a "normal American teenager" are an interesting and troubling contrast to the way we talk about, say, Trayvon Martin, also a "normal American teenager," but not a criminal or terrorist. George Zimmerman killed Martin because Martin fit our cultural idea of what danger looks like. Zimmerman was acquitted for the very same reason.

Most striking in Reitman's extensive and well-reported article is how the people who knew Tsarnaev are still willing to see the man behind the monster. Tsarnaev is described by those who knew him in near reverential terms as "sweet" and "superchill" and "smooth as fuck" and "a golden person, really just a genuine good guy." While Tsarnaev's community acknowledges the terrible things the young man has done and mourn the tragedy of the bombings, they are unwilling to turn their backs on him.

The article also reveals how shocked Tsarnaev's friends and neighbors were to learn he and his brother were responsible for such a crime. They were shocked because we have a portrait, in our minds, of what danger and terror look like and it's not this golden boy on the cover of *Rolling Stone*. Time and again, the word "normal" comes up. He is described as "a beautiful, tousle-haired boy with a gentle demeanor, soulful brown eyes." He enjoyed what most teenagers seem to enjoy—popular television shows, sports, music, girls. He smoked "a copious amount of weed." He committed a monstrous act, but he retains his normalcy.

Reitman's article is breathless in its empathy for Tsarnaev. Not only does Reitman meticulously reveal how Tsarnaev went from boy next door to terrorist, she seems desperate to understand why. She is not alone in this. When danger has an unexpected face, we demand answers. Family friend Anna Nikeava discussed the Tsarnaev family's problems and concluded, "Poor Jahar was the silent survivor of all that dysfunction." Poor, poor Jahar. Reitman later notes that "though it seems as if Jahar had found a mission, his embrace of Islam also may have been driven by something more basic: a need to belong." The article seems ultimately to be asking, how can we not have some measure of empathy for a young man with so simple a desire to belong?

The empathy does not end with the reportage. There is also testimony from Wick Sloane, a community college professor who has taught many young immigrants like Tsarnaev. He says,

All of these kids are grateful to be in the United States. But it's the usual thing: Is this the land of opportunity or isn't it? When I look at what they've been through, and how they are screwed by federal policies from the moment they turn around, I don't understand why all of them aren't angrier. I'm actually kind of surprised it's taken so long for one of these kids to set off a bomb.

And there are even more of Tsarnaev's friends, who are still stunned. Friends from college who found a backpack with emptied fireworks fretted about what to do because "no one wanted Jahar to get in trouble." Even after all he has done, after all we know, Tsarnaev benefits from so much doubt from his friends, his community, and those who seek to understand him and the terrible things he has done.

This, it would seem, is yet another example of white privilege—to retain humanity in the face of inhumanity. For criminals who defy our understanding of danger, the cultural threshold for forgiveness is incredibly low.

When Trayvon Martin was murdered, certain people worked overtime to uncover his failings, even though he was the victim of the crime. Before his death, Martin had recently been suspended from school because drug residue was found in his backpack. There were other such infractions. This became evidence. He was a normal teenager but he was also a black teenager, so he was put on trial and he was indicted. With Tsarnaev, people continue to look for the good. The bounds of compassion for the "tousle-haired" young man know few limits. Trayvon Martin, meanwhile, should have walked home without "looking suspicious." He should have meekly submitted himself to Zimmerman's intentions instead of whatever took place on the fateful night of his murder. He should have been above reproach. As Syreeta McFadden noted, "Only in America can a dead black boy go on trial for his own murder."

Reitman's article is a solid piece of journalism. It reveals complex truths about the life of Dzhokhar Tsarnaev. Imagine, though, if *Rolling Stone* had dedicated more than eleven thousand words and the cover to Trayvon Martin to reveal the complex truth of his life and what he was like in the years and months and hours before his death. How did he deal with the burden of being the face of danger from the moment he was born? This is a question fewer people seem to be asking.

The way we see danger is, in large part, about racial profiling, a law enforcement practice that has been hotly debated for years because it implicitly connects race to criminality. Racial profiling is what emboldened an armed George Zimmerman to follow an unarmed young black man walking home, even after police told Zimmerman not to pursue Trayvon Martin. Zimmerman saw a young black man and believed he was looking into the face of danger. He hunted that danger down.

The New York City Police Department's "stop and frisk" program allows police to stop, question, and search anyone who raises a "reasonable" suspicion of danger or criminality. The majority of people who are stopped and frisked in New York are black or Latino because these demographics fit our cultural profile of danger. These are the supposed barbarians at the gate, not the boy with the "soulful brown eyes."

Though there are many objections to the "stop and frisk" program and other forms of racial profiling, these practices persist.

Former mayor Michael Bloomberg defiantly supported the program. On his radio program he said, "They just keep saying, 'Oh, it's a disproportionate percentage of a particular ethnic group.' That may be, but it's not a disproportionate percentage of those whom witnesses and victims describe as committing the murder. In that case, incidentally, I think we disproportionately stop whites too much and minorities too little."

In her book *The Color of Crime*, Katheryn Russell-Brown says, "Blacks are the repository for the American fear of crime," and also notes that

> for most of us, television's overpowering images of Black deviance—its regularity and frequency—are impossible to ignore. These negative images have been seared into our collective consciousness. It is no surprise that most Americans wrongly believe that Blacks are responsible for the majority of crime. No doubt, many of the suspects paraded across the nightly news are guilty criminals. The onslaught of criminal images of Black men, however, causes many of us to incorrectly conclude that most Black men are criminals. This is the myth of the criminalblackman.

Over the past year, countless black men have stepped forward to share their stories of how they have been forced into this myth. But very little has changed.

Racial profiling is nothing more than a delusion born of our belief that we can profile danger. We want to believe we can predict who will do the next terrible thing. We want to believe we can keep ourselves safe. It's good that Dzhokhar Tsarnaev is on the cover of *Rolling Stone*, tousled hair and all. We need a reminder that we must stop projecting our fears onto profiles built from stereotypes. We need a reminder that we will never truly know whom we need to fear.

The Racism We All Carry

In the Tony Award–winning Broadway musical *Avenue Q*, one of the most popular songs is "Everyone's a Little Bit Racist." The chorus ends, "Maybe it's a fact we all should face / Everyone makes judgments based on race." There's a lot of truth to the song's lyrics. Everyone holds certain judgments about others, and those judgments are often informed by race. We're human. We're flawed. Most people are simply at the mercy of centuries of cultural conditioning. Most people are a little bit racist, but they're not marching in Klan rallies or burning crosses or vandalizing mosques. The better among us try, to varying degrees of success, to overcome that cultural conditioning, or—as revelations about popular, butter-loving former Food Network host Paula Deen suggest—we don't.

Paula Deen, who lives in Savannah, Georgia, revels in southern culture, and her shows on Food Network, which aired for nearly fourteen years, paid decadent and unapologetic homage to all manner of southern cooking. She is a proud daughter of the South and, apparently, she carries the effects of the South's complex and fraught racial history.

A former employee, Lisa Jackson, sued Deen and her brother, Earl "Bubba" Hiers, for workplace harassment. A damning transcript of Deen's deposition found its way online, and in it, Deen reveals all manner of impolitic views on race. When asked if she used the N-word, Deen blithely replied, "Yes, of course," as if it was a silly question, as if everyone uses the N-word. She's probably right.

Deen goes on to explain that she used the word to describe a man who put a gun to her head during a holdup at the bank where she worked, as if this should justify the epithet. As Deen notes, she wasn't feeling "real favorable towards him." That's fair enough. No one would feel favorable toward a man holding a gun to her head, though one sin, however more grave, should not justify another. Two wrongs rarely make a right.

She also discussed the racist, anti-Semitic, and redneck jokes told in her kitchens and how her husband regularly uses the N-word. When asked about how she identifies people by race, she said, "I try to go with whatever the black race is wanting to call themselves at each given time. I try to go along with that and remember that." The entire transcript is as revealing as it is fascinating; it's a bit funny and a bit sad because Deen is so honest and her attitude is utterly unsurprising. I suppose I should be outraged but I'm not. I'm actually baffled by how much attention the story received, where everyone seemed shocked that an older white woman from the Deep South is racist and harbors a nostalgia for the antebellum era. Or, perhaps, my lack of surprise reveals my own biases. Though I know better, I have certain ideas about the South. Is this where I say, "I have southern friends"?

The Internet responded vigorously, as it tends to do, when news broke of Deen's racism or, as I've come to think of it, Deen's general outlook on life. The Twitter hashtag #paulasbestdishes instantly went viral and all the major news sites have breathlessly hashed and rehashed what little we actually know from the deposition transcript, some hearsay, and a whole lot of speculation.

The most interesting part of the deposition is the blitheness of Deen's responses and the complete lack of shame. Her attitude was one of a person who is surrounded by like-minded individuals, a person who has been so thoroughly culturally conditioned that she doesn't know any better and doesn't have enough of a sense of self-preservation to tell a few little white lies about her racial attitudes.

In truth, Deen does know better. She has, certainly, never said the N-word or made openly racist comments on air or in any of the countless media interviews she has done over the years. In the deposition she even acknowledges that she, her children, and her brother object to the N-word being used in "any cruel or mean behavior," as if there's a warm and friendly way for white people to use the word.

This entire debacle reveals how there are unspoken rules about racism. In her deposition, for whatever reason, Deen decided to break those rules or ignore them, or she believed she was rich and successful enough that the rules, frankly, no longer applied to her.

There is a complex matrix for when you can be racist and with whom. There are ways you behave in public and ways you behave in private. There are things you can say among friends, things you wouldn't dare say anywhere else, that you must keep to yourself in public.

Writer Teju Cole succinctly identified why so many people are, seemingly, agog about these Deen revelations when he tweeted, "The real reason Paula Deen's in the news is not because she's racist, but because she broke the unwritten rules about how to be racist." Most people are familiar with these rules. We suspect that everyone is, indeed, a little bit racist. It's often not a question of if someone will reveal his or her racism to whatever degree but, rather, when. Or maybe it's people of color who are familiar with these rules and willing to acknowledge they exist. Maybe it is people of color who wait, without bated breath, for that when.

My downstairs neighbors moved out. They were Korean, college students. I never met them but they seemed nice enough. They played loud music but it was never enough of a nuisance to complain. Who doesn't like to party? When I went to pay my rent at the beginning of the month after they left, my landlord's receptionist began detailing the extraordinary measures they were taking to air out the apartment because "you just wouldn't believe the smell." I nodded because I truly had no idea what to say, and then she leaned in to me and whispered, "You know how those people are."

This was one of those rare moments in which I got to see the rules of racism in action in a multiracial context. A white person felt comfortable confiding in me. In that moment, we were an us conspiring against a them. I couldn't think of anything snappy so I simply said, "I have no idea what you mean," and walked away. I wasn't interested in playing that game where we bond as we reveal our racist secret selves to each other. Later, I felt guilty I hadn't used that moment to educate this stranger about race-based generalizations. I wondered why she thought she could reveal that casual racism in mixed company. I wondered, as I often do about people, what she truly thinks about me.

Tragedy. Call.
Compassion. Response.

Every day, terrible things happen in the world. Every damn day too many people die or suffer for reasons that defy comprehension.

In Norway, in Oslo, in the city where the Nobel Peace Prize is awarded, on a Friday afternoon, a thirty-two-year-old man triggered a bomb at the government headquarters, killing eight people. On the small island of Utoya that same man killed sixty-nine people, most of them teenagers. Children hid behind rocks and fled into the water and pretended to be dead so they might have a chance to survive, to live a day beyond the unbearable day they were living. There is fear and there is fear. The scale of the tragedy is incomprehensible. The tragedy, like most tragedies, tests the limits of language. There is now a before and after. That's what the news tells us. There are pictures of the building, decimated, the architecture's broken skeleton revealed, the dust and debris, the wounded, the dead, the mourning, the mourned, candles melting, wilting flowers wrapped in clear plastic, handwritten signs trying to properly express the depths of a grief that, perhaps, cannot be expressed.

All too often, suffering exists in a realm beyond vocabulary so we navigate that realm awkwardly, fumbling for the right words, hoping we can somehow approximate an understanding of matters that should never have to be understood by anyone in any place in the world.

The man who committed these crimes has blond hair and blue eyes. These details are shared repeatedly in a litany of disbelief. Too many people expected the perpetrator of this crime to have brown skin and a Qur'an because we need to believe that there is only one brand of extremism. This is the world we now live in. We forget compassion. We pretend we are somehow different from those we otherwise condemn.

The man with blond hair and blue eyes has a Wikipedia page. A compendium of knowledge has been compiled about Anders Behring Breivik. We know his beliefs and his taste in music and what his parents do for a living. We know he has an exhaustive manifesto he worked on for nine years, some of which he took directly from the Unabomber. We have seen him posing with a big gun, wearing a wet suit. We have seen his face—his wide, open face, the youth in his features. We know he is extreme in his beliefs and that there must be hatred in his heart. We know he is crazy. He must hate. He must be crazy. We need to believe he is hateful and crazy because it is unfathomable to believe a man of sound mind and body could or would perpetrate such a crime.

"Crime" is a weak word, a weak, weak word. Those five letters cannot accurately convey what is, more accurately, an atrocity. Even that word does not suffice. The tragedy exceeds our vernacular in so many ways.

After this tragedy, the king of Norway said, "I remain convinced that the belief in freedom is stronger than fear. I remain convinced in the belief of an open Norwegian democracy and society. I remain convinced in the belief in our ability to live freely and safely in our own country." Tragedy. Call. Compassion. Response. He chose grace. He found a better vocabulary with which to respond amidst a suffering that defies vocabulary.

We all have the capacity to do hurtful things, but we differ from one another in terms of scale—how much we can hurt others, how far we will go to make a statement about our beliefs, how remorseful we might feel in the aftermath of committing a terrible act. Most of us, if we are lucky, will only commit petty hurtful acts, the kinds of hurt that can be forgiven. The man who committed this atrocity in Norway has a capacity to hurt few of us will ever understand. He turned himself in. He confessed to his crimes. He wants to explain himself. I don't know what that means, but it has to mean something. I wonder if he was scared before he took so many lives, before he created such unprecedented destruction. I wonder how he became the kind of man who could shoot children at point-blank range, who could be so careless with human lives. I wonder if he is sickened by what he did. I wonder how he feels, knowing he lives in a country where he will likely not be sentenced to life in prison; knowing that, even in the face of what he did, he will not be put to death. I wonder if he is grateful, if he is humbled, if he is staggered by the humanity of his people. Tragedy. Call. Humility. Response?

After the Norway tragedy, my on-again, off-again boyfriend called from many states away. He is politically conservative, though I'd like to think I've worn him down on certain matters. He asked, "Have you seen the news?" He asked, "Do you still believe the death penalty is wrong?" Tragedy. Call. Dial tone. Response.

We know much of what there is to know about Anders Behring Breivik. We know very little about his victims, who they were, what they wanted for their lives, how they loved and were loved, who they loved, how and by whom they will be mourned, what they felt in their last moments, if they suffered. We only know seventy-seven people were killed in one day by one man. Their killer is alive. There is a great deal of cruelty in this state of affairs.

I'm not a saint. I will not shed a tear for Anders Behring Breivik, but I do not wish him dead. I will try to think of him with the compassion he was unable to offer the seventy-seven people he murdered. I will likely fail in this. Still, I do not wish him dead. I do not believe his death is an appropriate punishment. I do not believe there is such a thing as an appropriate punishment for what that man did.

This is the modern age. When tragedies occur, we take to Twitter and Facebook and blogs to share our thoughts and feelings. We do this to know that maybe, just maybe, we are not alone in our confusion or grief or sorrow or to believe we have a voice in what happens in the world.

We take to these tools of the modern age, and there are those among us who, in the wake of tragedy, point fingers or proselytize or use humor as a means of distancing themselves from the emotional discomfort of knowing we are rarely as safe as we hope to be. We are rarely safe from knowing that every day terrible things happen everywhere. Tragedy. Call. Twitter. Response. Others use this time to take a political stance, to speculate as to why blond-haired, blue-eyed men aren't now being profiled in airports around the world. There is almost a certain glee in these kinds of statements. At a time like this, tragedy is used for political posturing. Righteousness gets in the way of what is right. Righteousness gets in the way of valid observations that might be better shared more carefully, more thoughtfully, under different circumstances. The tools of the modern age afford us many privileges, but they also cost us the privilege of time and space and distance to properly think through tragedy, to take a deep breath, to feel, to care. Tragedy. Call. Heart. Response. Tragedy. Call. Mind. Response.

There is a girl who was a woman, but really, she was a girl. She was a girl because she was only twenty-seven, had only lived a third of a life. She had a voice like fine whiskey and cigarettes, or at least what I imagine fine whiskey and cigarettes might sound like. She had a voice that made me think of dark, secret nightclubs where you need to know a guy to gain admittance, where musicians gather closely on a small stage and play their instruments for hours in a haze of sweat and cologne, booze and smoke, while a singer, this girl-woman singer, stands at the microphone, giving those gathered the exceptional gift of her voice.

The year her second album came out was the year of the Halloween dedicated to this girl-woman. Everywhere I looked, women and some men wore their hair (or a wig) long and black with a bouffant on top, and they lined their eyes blackly with that distinctive angle at the corner of each eye, and they drew tattoos on their bare arms and sang the chorus of her most popular song. *They tried to make me go to rehab.* Call. *I said, No, No, No.* Response. That's why we care. She was in our lives and our ears and our heads and our hair.

The girl-woman singer died in her flat, alone in bed. Too many people said, "It was to be expected," because we knew this girl who was a woman was really a girl. We knew she had problems, and she did not have the luxury the rest of us do to handle our problems privately, with dignity. She was a mess. So what? We are all stinking messes, every last one of us, or we once were messes and found our way out, or we are trying to find our way out of a mess, scratching, reaching. We knew she had demons that were bigger than her, demons she tried to fight or she didn't—we can't possibly know. Her struggles were documented and parodied, celebrated and ridiculed. Celebrity. Call. Gossip. Response. We have seen the pictures of this girl-woman in the street, barefoot, her midriff bare and swollen, her makeup smeared, her unforgettable hair stringy, pasted to her pale face, her body being carried from her home in a red body bag. There was no privacy for her, not even in death. That is a tragedy too.

I love her music and listen to it regularly. I always hoped she might survive herself, hoped she would give her adoring fans more of her voice, hoped she would give herself the blessing of a long life. I heard she died from my best friend, who sent me a text message, and we commiserated about what a shame it was for a girl-woman to die at the age of twenty-seven. It is a different kind of devastating to think about the life she will never know, about those gifts that come with more years of living. I do not wonder about the cause of her death. The how of her demise isn't my business. And yet. When I first heard of her death, I wondered if she died alone. I wondered if she was scared. There is fear and there is fear. Now, I wonder if she knew real happiness in her short life. I wonder if she felt loved or knew peace. She was someone's daughter. She was someone's sister. We know her father found out while he was on a plane. He did not have any kind of privacy to make sense of surviving his child. The death of a child is unbearable and suffocating. After Amy Winehouse's death, her parents had to try to cope with something the human heart is ill equipped to withstand. Tragedy. Call. Broken heart. Response.

I followed many conversations about what happened in Norway and the death of Amy Winehouse because they happened one after the next. Too many of those conversations tried to conflate the two events, tried to create some kind of hierarchy of tragedy, grief, call, response. There was so much judgment, so much interrogation of grief—how dare we mourn a singer, an entertainer, a girl-woman who struggled with addiction, as if the life of an addict is somehow less worthy a life, as if we are not entitled to mourn unless the tragedy happens to the right kind of people. How dare we mourn a singer when across an ocean seventy-seven people are dead? We are asked these questions as if we only have the capacity to mourn one tragedy at a time, as if we must measure the depth and reach of a tragedy before deciding how to respond, as if compassion and kindness are finite resources we must use sparingly. We cannot put these two tragedies on a chart and connect them with a straight line. We cannot understand these tragedies neatly.

Death is a tragedy whether it is the death of one girl-woman in London or seventy-seven men, women, and children in Norway. We know this, but perhaps it needs to be said over and over again so we do not forget.

I have never considered compassion a finite resource. I would not want to live in a world where such was the case.

Tragedy. Call. Great. Small. Compassion. Response. Compassion. Response.

[BACK TO ME]

Bad Feminist: Take One

My favorite definition of "feminist" is one offered by Su, an Australian woman who, when interviewed for Kathy Bail's 1996 anthology *DIY Feminism*, said feminists are "just women who don't want to be treated like shit." This definition is pointed and succinct, but I run into trouble when I try to expand that definition. I fall short as a feminist. I feel like I am not as committed as I need to be, that I am not living up to feminist ideals because of who and how I choose to be.

I feel this tension constantly. As Judith Butler writes in her 1988 essay "Performative Acts and Gender Constitution," "Performing one's gender wrong initiates a set of punishments both obvious and indirect, and performing it well provides the reassurance that there is an essentialism of gender identity after all." This tension—the idea that there is a right way to be a woman, a right way to be the most essential woman—is ongoing and pervasive.

We see this tension in socially dictated beauty standards—the right way to be a woman is to be thin, to wear makeup, to wear the right kind of clothes (not too slutty, not too prudish—show a little leg, ladies), and so on. Good women are charming, polite, and unobtrusive. Good women work but are content to earn 77 percent of what men earn or, depending on whom you ask, good women bear children and stay home to raise those children without complaint. Good women are modest, chaste, pious, submissive. Women who don't adhere to these standards are the fallen, the undesirable; they are bad women.

Butler's thesis could also apply to feminism. There is an essential feminism or, as I perceive this essentialism, the notion that there are right and wrong ways to be a feminist and that there are consequences for doing feminism wrong.

Essential feminism suggests anger, humorlessness, militancy, unwavering principles, and a prescribed set of rules for how to be a proper feminist woman, or at least a proper white, heterosexual feminist woman—hate pornography, unilaterally decry the objectification of women, don't cater to the male gaze, hate men, hate sex, focus on career, don't shave. I kid, mostly, with that last one. This is nowhere near an accurate description of feminism, but the movement has been warped by misperception for so long that even people who should know better have bought into this essential image of feminism.

Consider Elizabeth Wurtzel, who, in a June 2012 *Atlantic* article, says, "Real feminists earn a living, have money and means of their own." By Wurtzel's thinking, women who don't "earn a living, have money and means of their own," are fake feminists, undeserving of the label, a disappointment to the sisterhood. She takes the idea of essential feminism even further in a September 2012 *Harper's Bazaar* article, where she suggests that a good feminist works hard to be beautiful. She says, "Looking great is a matter of feminism. No liberated woman would misrepresent the cause by appearing less than hale and happy." It's too easy to dissect the error of such thinking. She is suggesting that a woman's worth is, in part, determined by her beauty, which is one of the very things feminism works against.

The most significant problem with essential feminism is how it doesn't allow for the complexities of human experience or individuality. There seems to be little room for multiple or discordant points of view. Essential feminism has, for example, led to the rise of the phrase "sex-positive feminism," which creates a clear distinction between feminists who are positive about sex and feminists who aren't—which, in turn, creates a self-fulfilling essentialist prophecy.

I sometimes cringe when I am referred to as a feminist, as if I should be ashamed of my feminism or as if the word "feminist" is an insult. The label is rarely offered in kindness. I am generally called a feminist when I have the nerve to suggest that the misogyny so deeply embedded in our culture is a real problem requiring relentless vigilance. The essay in this collection about Daniel Tosh and rape jokes originally appeared in *Salon*. I tried not to read the comments because they get vicious, but I couldn't help but note one commenter who told me I was an "angry blogger woman," which is simply another way of saying "angry feminist." All feminists are angry instead of, say, passionate.

A more direct reprimand came from a man I was dating during a heated discussion that wasn't quite an argument. He said, "Don't you raise your voice to me," which was strange because I had not raised my voice. I was stunned because no one had ever said such a thing to me. He expounded, at length, about how women should talk to men. When I dismantled his pseudo-theories, he said, "You're some kind of feminist, aren't you?" There was a tone to his accusation, making it clear that to be a feminist was undesirable. I was not being a good woman. I remained silent, stewing. I thought, *Isn't it obvious I am a feminist, albeit not a very good one?* I also realized I was being chastised for having a certain set of beliefs. The experience was disconcerting, at best.

I'm not the only outspoken woman who shies away from the feminist label, who fears the consequences of accepting the label.

In an August 2012 interview with *Salon*'s Andrew O'Hehir, actress Melissa Leo, known for playing groundbreaking female roles, said, "Well, I don't think of myself as a feminist at all. As soon as we start labeling and categorizing ourselves and others, that's going to shut down the world. I would never say that. Like, I just did that episode with Louis C.K." Leo is buying into a great many essential feminist myths with her comment. We are categorized and labeled from the moment we come into this world by gender, race, size, hair color, eye color, and so forth. The older we get, the more labels and categories we collect. If labeling and categorizing ourselves is going to shut the world down, it has been a long time coming. More disconcerting, though, is the assertion that a feminist wouldn't take a role on Louis C.K.'s sitcom, *Louie*, or that a feminist would be unable to find C.K.'s brand of humor amusing. For Leo, there are feminists and then there are women who defy categorization and are willing to embrace career opportunities.

Trailbreaking female leaders in the corporate world tend to reject the feminist label too. Marissa Mayer, who was appointed president and CEO of Yahoo! in July 2012, said in an interview,

I don't think that I would consider myself a feminist. I think that I certainly believe in equal rights, I believe that women are just as capable, if not more so in a lot of different dimensions, but I don't, I think, have sort of the militant drive and the sort of, the chip on the shoulder that sometimes comes with that. And I think it's too bad, but I do think that "feminism" has become in many ways a more negative

*word. You know, there are amazing opportunities all over the world
for women, and I think that there is more good that comes out of positive energy around that than comes out of negative energy.*

For Mayer, even though she is a pioneering woman, feminism is
associated with militancy and preconceived notions. Feminism is
negative, and despite the feminist strides she has made through
her career at Google and now Yahoo!, she'd prefer to eschew the
label for the sake of so-called positive energy.

Audre Lorde once stated, "I am a Black Feminist. I mean I recognize that my power as well as my primary oppressions come
as a result of my blackness as well as my womanness, and therefore my struggles on both of these fronts are inseparable." As a
woman of color, I find that some feminists don't seem terribly
concerned with the issues unique to women of color—the ongoing effects of racism and postcolonialism, the status of women in
the Third World, the fight against the trenchant archetypes black
women are forced into (angry black woman, mammy, Hottentot,
and the like).

White feminists often suggest that by believing there are issues
unique to women of color, an unnatural division occurs, imped-
ing solidarity, sisterhood. Other times, white feminists are simply
dismissive of these issues. In 2008, prominent blogger Amanda
Marcotte was accused of appropriating ideas for her article "Can
a Person Be Illegal?" from the blogger "brownfemipower," who
posted a speech she gave on the same subject a few days prior to
the publication of Marcotte's article. The question of where original thought ends and borrowed concepts begin was complicated
significantly in this case by the sense that a white person had yet
again taken the creative work of a person of color.

The feminist blogosphere engaged in an intense debate over

these issues, at times so acrimonious black feminists were labeled "radical black feminists," were accused of overreacting and, of course, "playing the race card."

Such willful ignorance, such willful disinterest in incorporating the issues and concerns of black women into the mainstream feminist project, makes me disinclined to own the feminist label until it embraces people like me. Is that my way of essentializing feminism, of suggesting there's a right kind of feminism or a more inclusive feminism? Perhaps. This is all murky for me, but a continued insensitivity, within feminist circles, on the matter of race is a serious problem.

There's also this. Lately, magazines have been telling me there's something wrong with feminism or women trying to achieve a work-life balance or just women in general. *The Atlantic* has led the way in these lamentations. In the aforementioned June 2012 article, Elizabeth Wurtzel, author of *Prozac Nation*, wrote a searing polemic about "1% wives" who are hurting feminism and the progress of women by choosing to stay at home rather than enter the workplace. Wurtzel begins the essay provocatively, stating,

> *When my mind gets stuck on everything that is wrong with feminism, it brings out the 19th century poet in me:* Let me count the ways. *Most of all, feminism is pretty much a nice girl who really, really wants so badly to be liked by everybody—ladies who lunch, men who hate women, all the morons who demand choice and don't understand responsibility—that it has become the easy lay of social movements.*

There are problems with feminism. Wurtzel says so, and she is vigorous in defending her position. Wurtzel knows the right way for feminism. In that article, Wurtzel goes on to state there is only one kind of equality, economic equality, and until women recognize that and enter the workforce en masse, feminists, and wealthy feminists in particular, will continue to fail. They will continue to be bad feminists, falling short of essential ideals of feminism. Wurtzel isn't wrong about the importance of economic equality, but she is wrong in assuming that with economic equality, the rest of feminism's concerns will somehow disappear.

In the July/August 2012 *Atlantic*, Anne-Marie Slaughter wrote more than twelve thousand words about the struggles of powerful, successful women to "have it all." Her article was interesting and thoughtful, for a certain kind of woman—a wealthy woman with a very successful career. She even parlayed the piece into a book deal. Slaughter was speaking to a small, elite group of women while ignoring the millions of women who don't have the privilege of, as Slaughter did, leaving high-powered positions at the State Department to spend more time with their sons. Many women who work do so because they have to. Working has little to do with having it all and much more to do with having food on the table.

Slaughter wrote,

> *I'd been the woman congratulating herself on her unswerving commitment to the feminist cause, chatting smugly with her dwindling number of college or law-school friends who had reached and maintained their place on the highest rungs of their profession. I'd been the one telling young women at my lectures that you* can *have it all and do it all, regardless of what field you are in.*

The thing is, I am not at all sure that feminism has ever suggested women can have it all. This notion of being able to have it all is always misattributed to feminism when really, it's human nature to want it all—to have cake and eat it too without necessarily focusing on how we can get there and how we can make "having it all" possible for a wider range of people and not just the lucky ones.

Alas, poor feminism. So much responsibility keeps getting piled on the shoulders of a movement whose primary purpose is to achieve equality, in all realms, between men and women. I keep reading these articles and getting angry and tired because they suggest there's no way for women to ever *get it right*. These articles make it seem like, as Butler suggests, there is, in fact, a right way to be a woman and a wrong way to be a woman. The standard for the right way to be a woman and/or a feminist appears to be ever changing and unachievable.

In the weeks leading up to the publication of Sheryl Sandberg's *Lean In*, critics had plenty to say about the Facebook chief operating officer's ideas about being a woman in the workplace—even though few had actually read the tome. Many of the resulting discussions bizarrely mischaracterized *Lean In*, tossing around misleading headlines, inaccurate facts, and unfair assumptions.

As it turns out, not even a fairly average entry into the world of corporate advice books is immune from double standards.

Sandberg intersperses personal anecdotes from her remarkable career (a vice presidency at Google, serving as the US Treasury's chief of staff during the Clinton administration) with observations, research, and pragmatic advice for how women can better achieve professional and personal success. She urges women to "lean in" to their careers and to be "ambitious in any pursuit." *Lean In* is competently written, blandly interesting, and it does repeat a great deal of familiar research—although it isn't particularly harmful to be reminded of the challenges women face as they try to get ahead.

Intentionally or not, much of the book is a stark reminder of the many obstacles women face in the workplace. I cannot deny that parts resonated, particularly in Sandberg's discussion about "impostor syndrome" and how women are less willing to take advantage of potential career opportunities unless they feel qualified.

But Sandberg is rigidly committed to the gender binary, and *Lean In* is exceedingly heteronormative. Professional women are largely defined in relation to professional men; *Lean In*'s loudest unspoken advice seems to dictate that women should embrace traditionally masculine qualities (self-confidence, risk taking, aggression, etc.). Occasionally, this advice backfires because it seems as if Sandberg is advocating, *If you want to succeed, be an asshole.* In addition, Sandberg generally assumes a woman will want to fulfill professional ambitions while also marrying a man and having children. Yes, she says, "Not all women want careers. Not all women want children. Not all women want both. I would never advocate that we should all have the same objectives." But she contradicts herself by placing every single parable within the context of heterosexual women who want a wildly successful career and a rounded-out nuclear family. Accepting that Sandberg is writing to a very specific audience, and has little to offer those who don't fall within that target demographic, makes enjoying the book a lot easier.

One of the main questions that has arisen in the wake of *Lean In*'s publication is whether Sandberg has a responsibility to women who don't fall within her target demographic. Like Slaughter, Sandberg is speaking to a rather narrow group of women. In the *New York Times*, Jodi Kantor writes, "Even [Sandberg's] advisers acknowledge the awkwardness of a woman with double Harvard degrees, dual stock riches (from Facebook and Google, where she also worked), a 9,000-square-foot house and a small army of household help urging less fortunate women to look inward and work harder."

At times, the inescapable evidence of Sandberg's fortune is grating. She casually discusses her mentor Larry Summers, working for the Treasury department, her doctor siblings, and her equally successful husband, David Goldberg. (As CEO of SurveyMonkey, Goldberg moved the company headquarters from Portland to the Bay Area so he could more fully commit to his family.) She gives the impression that her movement from one ideal situation to the next is easily replicable.

Sandberg's life is so absurd a fairy tale, I began to think of *Lean In* as a snow globe, where a lovely little tableau was being nicely preserved for my delectation and irritation. I would not be so bold as to suggest Sandberg has it all, but I need to believe she is pretty damn close to whatever "having it all" might look like. Common sense dictates that it is not realistic to assume anyone could achieve Sandberg's successes simply by "leaning in" and working harder—but that doesn't mean Sandberg has nothing to offer, or that *Lean In* should be summarily dismissed.

Cultural critics can get a bit precious and condescending about marginalized groups, and in the debate over *Lean In* "working-class women" have been lumped into a vaguely defined group of women who work too hard for too little money. But very little consideration has been given to these women as actual people who live in the world, and who maybe, just maybe, have ambitions too.

There has been, unsurprisingly, significant pushback against the notion that leaning in is a reasonable option for working-class women, who are already stretched woefully thin. Sandberg is not oblivious to her privilege, noting:

> *I am fully aware that most women are not focused on changing social norms for the next generation but simply trying to get through each day. Forty percent of employed mothers lack sick days and vacation leave, and about 50 percent of employed mothers are unable to take time off to care for a sick child. Only about half of women receive any pay during maternity leave. These policies can have severe consequences; families with no access to paid family leave often go into debt and can fall into poverty. Part-time jobs with fluctuating schedules offer little chance to plan and often stop short of the forty-hour week that provides basic benefits.*

It would have been useful if Sandberg offered realistic advice about career management for women who are dealing with such circumstances. It would also be useful if we had flying cars. Assuming Sandberg's advice is completely useless for working-class women is just as shortsighted as claiming her advice needs to be completely applicable to all women. And let's be frank: if Sandberg chose to offer career advice for working-class women, a group she clearly knows little about, she would have been just as harshly criticized for overstepping her bounds.

The critical response to *Lean In* is not entirely misplaced, but it is emblematic of the dangers of public womanhood. Public women, and feminists in particular, have to be everything to everyone; when they aren't, they are excoriated for their failure. In some ways, this is understandable. We have come far, but we have so much further to go. We need so very much, and we hope women with a significant platform might be everything we need—a desperately untenable position. As Elizabeth Spiers notes in *The Verge*,

> *When's the last time someone picked up a Jack Welch (or Warren Buffett, or even Donald Trump) bestseller and complained that it was unsympathetic to working class men who had to work multiple jobs to support their families? . . . And who reads a book by Jack Welch and defensively feels that they're being told that they have to adopt Jack Welch's lifestyle and professional choices or they are lesser human beings?*

Lean In cannot and should not be read as a definitive text, or a book offering universally applicable advice to all women, everywhere. Sandberg is confident and aggressive in her advice, but the reader is under no obligation to do everything she says. Perhaps we can consider *Lean In* for what it is—just one more reminder that the rules are always different for girls, no matter who they are and no matter what they do.

Bad Feminist: Take Two

I am failing as a woman. I am failing as a feminist. To freely accept the feminist label would not be fair to good feminists. If I am, indeed, a feminist, I am a rather bad one. I am a mess of contradictions. There are many ways in which I am doing feminism wrong, at least according to the way my perceptions of feminism have been warped by being a woman.

I want to be independent, but I want to be taken care of and have someone to come home to. I have a job I'm pretty good at. I am in charge of things. I am on committees. People respect me and take my counsel. I want to be strong and professional, but I resent how hard I have to work to be taken seriously, to receive a fraction of the consideration I might otherwise receive. Sometimes I feel an overwhelming need to cry at work, so I close my office door and lose it.

I want to be in charge and respected and in control, but I want to surrender, completely, in certain aspects of my life. Who wants to grow up?

When I drive to work, I listen to thuggish rap at a very loud volume even though the lyrics are degrading to women and offend me to my core. The classic Ying Yang Twins song "Salt Shaker"? It's amazing. "Bitch you gotta shake it till your camel starts to hurt."

Poetry.

(I am mortified by my music choices.)

I care what people think.

Pink is my favorite color. I used to say my favorite color was black to be *cool*, but it is pink—all shades of pink. If I have an accessory, it is probably pink. I read *Vogue*, and I'm not doing it ironically, though it might seem that way. I once live-tweeted the September issue. I demonstrate little outward evidence of this, but I have a very indulgent fantasy where I have a closet full of pretty shoes and purses and matching outfits. I love dresses. For years I pretended I hated them, but I don't. Maxi dresses are one of the finest clothing items to become popular in recent memory. I have opinions on maxi dresses! I shave my legs! Again, this mortifies me. If I take issue with the unrealistic standards of beauty women are held to, I shouldn't have a secret fondness for fashion and smooth calves, right?

I know nothing about cars. When I take my car to the mechanic, they are speaking a foreign language. A mechanic asks what's wrong with my car, and I stutter things like, "Well, there's a sound I try to drown out with my radio." The windshield wiper fluid for the rear window of my car no longer sprays the window. It just sprays the air. I don't know how to deal with this. It feels like an expensive problem. I still call my father with questions about cars and am not terribly interested in changing any of my car-related ignorance. I don't want to be good at cars. Good feminists, I assume, are independent enough to address vehicular crises on their own; they are independent enough to care.

Despite what people think based on my opinion writing, I very much like men. They're interesting to me, and I mostly wish they would be better about how they treat women so I wouldn't have to call them out so often. And still, I put up with nonsense from unsuitable men even though I *know better* and can do better. I love diamonds and the excess of weddings. I consider certain domestic tasks as gendered, mostly all in my favor as I don't care for chores—lawn care, bug killing, and trash removal, for example, are men's work.

Sometimes, a lot of the time honestly, I totally fake "it" because it's easier. I am a fan of orgasms, but they take time, and in many instances I don't want to spend that time. All too often I don't really like the guy enough to explain the calculus of my desire. Then I feel guilty because the sisterhood would not approve. I'm not even sure what the sisterhood is, but the idea of a sisterhood menaces me, quietly, reminding me of how bad a feminist I am. Good feminists don't fear the sisterhood because they know they are comporting themselves in sisterhood-approved ways.

I love babies, and I want to have one. I am willing to make certain compromises (not sacrifices) in order to do so—namely maternity leave and slowing down at work to spend more time with my child, writing less so I can be more present in my life. I worry about dying alone, unmarried and childless, because I spent so much time pursuing my career and accumulating degrees. This kind of thinking keeps me up at night, but I pretend it doesn't because I am supposed to be evolved. My success, such as it is, is supposed to be enough if I'm a good feminist. It is not enough. It is not even close.

Because I have so many deeply held opinions about gender equality, I feel a lot of pressure to live up to certain ideals. I am supposed to be a good feminist who is having it all, doing it all. Really, though, I'm a woman in her thirties struggling to accept herself and her credit score. For so long I told myself I was not this woman—utterly human and flawed. I worked overtime to be anything but this woman, and it was exhausting and unsustainable and even harder than simply embracing who I am.

Maybe I'm a bad feminist, but I am deeply committed to the issues important to the feminist movement. I have strong opinions about misogyny, institutional sexism that consistently places women at a disadvantage, the inequity in pay, the cult of beauty and thinness, the repeated attacks on reproductive freedom, violence against women, and on and on. I am as committed to fighting fiercely for equality as I am committed to disrupting the notion that there is an essential feminism.

I'm the kind of feminist who is appalled by the phrase "legitimate rape" and by political candidates such as Missouri's Todd Akin, who in an interview reaffirmed his commitment to opposing abortion, almost unilaterally. He said, "If it's a legitimate rape, the female body has ways to try to shut that whole thing down. But let's assume that maybe that didn't work or something: I think there should be some punishment, but the punishment ought to be of the rapist, and not attacking the child," drawing from pseudoscience and a lax cultural attitude toward rape.

Being a feminist, however, even a bad one, has also taught me that the need for feminism and advocacy also applies to seemingly less serious issues like a Top 40 song or a comedian's puerile humor. The existence of these lesser artifacts of our popular culture is made possible by the far graver issues we are facing. The ground has long been softened.

At some point, I got it into my head that a feminist was a certain kind of woman. I bought into grossly inaccurate myths about who feminists are—militant, perfect in their politics and person, man-hating, humorless. I bought into these myths even though, intellectually, I *know* better. I'm not proud of this. I don't want to buy into these myths anymore. I don't want to cavalierly disavow feminism like far too many other women have done.

Bad feminism seems like the only way I can both embrace myself as a feminist and be myself, and so I write. I chatter away on Twitter about everything that makes me angry and all the small things that bring me joy. I write blog posts about the meals I cook as I try to take better care of myself, and with each new entry, I realize that I'm undestroying myself after years of allowing myself to stay damaged. The more I write, the more I put myself out into the world as a bad feminist but, I hope, a good woman—I am being open about who I am and who I was and where I have faltered and who I would like to become.

No matter what issues I have with feminism, I am a feminist. I cannot and will not deny the importance and absolute necessity of feminism. Like most people, I'm full of contradictions, but I also don't want to be treated like shit for being a woman.

I am a bad feminist. I would rather be a bad feminist than no feminist at all.

Acknowledgments

Versions of these essays have appeared in *The Rumpus*, the *American Prospect*, *Virginia Quarterly Review*, *Ninth Letter*, *Frequencies*, *Bookslut*, *Jezebel*, *Iron Horse Literary Review*, the *Los Angeles Review*, *BuzzFeed*, and *Salon*. I am grateful to the editors of these publications for giving my work a home.

My agent, Maria Massie, is the greatest champion a writer can have. Cal Morgan and Maya Ziv are wonderful editors, and Cal, in particular, was so persistent in making a space for me at Harper. You know you've found the right people when your editor understands your love of *Beverly Hills 90210*. Maya and I are BFFs now. I also want to thank Mary Beth Constant for her witty, instructional care with my words. A great deal of this book was written to the sound track of *Law & Order: SVU*. I'm not sure what that says about me but I must give credit where credit is due. At *Salon*, Dave Daley and Anna North have been so welcoming of my work and made a lot of exciting opportunities possible. Isaac Fitzgerald and Julie Greicius edited my writing at *The Rumpus*, and I will always trust my writing in their intelligent, compassionate hands. Stephen Elliott was the first person to open the door to my nonfiction at *The Rumpus*, and it has been a pleasure working with him. Thanks also to Michelle Dean, Jami Attenberg, Cathy Chung, and Tracy Gonzalez. One of my brothers wants me to include a line from Bane in *Dark Knight Rises* in my acknowledgments, so, "You think darkness is your ally. You merely adopted the dark. I was born in it. Molded by it." I'm hoping my parents don't read this book, but they are beloved and have made all things possible. I am lucky.

About the Author

Roxane Gay's writing appears in *Best American Nonrequired Reading 2018, Best American Mystery Stories 2014, Best American Short Stories 2012, Best Sex Writing 2012, Harper's Bazaar, A Public Space, McSweeney's, Tin House, Oxford American, American Short Fiction, Virginia Quarterly Review*, and many others. She is a contributing opinion writer for the *New York Times* where she also writes the Work Friend column. She is the author of the books *Ayiti, An Untamed State*; the *New York Times* bestselling *Bad Feminist*; the nationally bestselling *Difficult Women*; and the *New York Times* bestselling *Hunger: A Memoir of My Body*. Selected nonfiction work of hers has been collected in *Opinions: A Decade of Arguments, Criticism, and Minding Other People's Business*. She is also the author of the Eisner Award–winning *World of Wakanda* for Marvel and the editor of *Best American Short Stories 2018*. She is at work on film and television projects, a book of writing advice called *How to Be Heard*, an essay collection about television and culture, and a young adult novel entitled *The Year I Learned Everything*. In 2018, she won a Guggenheim fellowship. She is also the Gloria Steinem Endowed Chair in Media, Culture and Feminist Studies at Rutgers University-New Brunswick.

"Gay has an ability to blend the personal and political in a way that feels simultaneously gentle and brutal.... For 1,400 or so words you look at a cultural moment through Gay's eyes and, by the end, you see the world differently."

—*The Guardian*

"*Hunger* is arresting and candid. At its best, it affords women, in particular, something so many other accounts deny them—the right to take up space they are entitled to, and to define what that means."

—*The Atlantic*

"The lauded social critic and provocateur curates a diverse and unvarnished collection of personal essays reckoning with the experiences and systemic dysfunction that produced #MeToo."

—*O, the Oprah Magazine*